Hazel Jane Raines
Pioneer Lady of Flight

Hazel in the Georgia Air Races and Show, 1940.

Hazel Jane Raines
Pioneer Lady of Flight

By Regina Trice Hawkins

MERCER UNIVERSITY PRESS
Macon, GA

ISBN 0-86554-532-4
MUP/H407

Hazel Jane Raines
Pioneer Lady of Flight
A Biography in Letters
by
Regina T. Hawkins

Mercer University Press
6316 Peake Road
Macon, Georgia 31210-3960

The paper used in this publication meets the minimum require-
ments of American National Standard for Information
Sciences—Permanence of Paper for Printed Library Materials,
ANSI Z39.48–1984.

Library of Congress Cataloging-in-Publication Data

CIP, unavailable at press time,
will appear in subsequent editions
and is available from the library of Congress

CONTENTS

Book I. England...As a Ferry Pilot

Book II. Avenger Field...As a Wasp

Book III. Brazil...As an Instructor

Book IV. United States Air Force...As a Desk Pilot

Dedicated to my husband, Jack,
and to my Aunt Hazel,
who has become a close friend of mine.

PREFACE

In editing the letters of my aunt Hazel, I have become acquainted with a remarkable member of the family. To have access to the letters, log books, and military manuals that chronicle Hazel's life away from home from 1942 until her death in 1956, has been an absorbing adventure. These forgotten possessions tell the story of a young girl whose passion for flying earned her a place in the Georgia Aviation Hall of Fame for her "contribution to aviation in peace and war as Georgia's Pioneer Lady of Flight."

Hazel Jane Raines was born in 1916 as the youngest of three daughters, Frankie, Martha, and Hazel, each separated in age by three years. Her early life in Macon, Georgia, was unexceptional. After graduating from Wesleyan Conservatory in 1936, Hazel accepted a dare and began learning to fly at Herbert Smart Airport near Macon. In 1938, she received her solo license and a private one in 1939. By 1940, Hazel had become the only woman in Georgia to earn a commercial license and was touring with the Georgia Air Races and Show. This was the same year that her father, Frank Raines, died of a stroke leaving her mother a widow at the age of fifty-five. As the only child living at home, Hazel's decision to leave must have been a difficult one. Her two older sisters were married with children, but Hazel's aspirations were not to be bound by a life in Macon. With a history of asthma and a heart condition, Hazel considered herself to have been made from "left-over parts." Perhaps these physical handicaps and a desire to prove herself drove her to take the necessary risks to achieve her goals.

The relationship between Hazel and her mother is a complicated one and not easy to pursue. It becomes obvious that Hazel was devoted to her mother and wanted approval, but at the same time was not willing to give into family demands and "settle down". The large volume of letters that were written for the most part to her mother, Mrs. Frank G. Raines, are letters of reassurance to ease the concern of a mother for her daughter. Events that surrounded Hazel during these years have been pieced together from newspaper articles and research. The letters speak for themselves. A limited number of comments and quotes have been added to explain certain situations. Hazel was a dutiful daughter in her correspondence, but she was determined to pursue her passion for flying that began with "barnstorming" in local air shows. Teaching in the Civilian Pilot Training Program, she logged enough flying hours to be chosen by Jacqueline Cochran as one of twenty-five American women to ferry planes in the Air Transport Auxiliary of the RAF. She flew in silence (no radio contact was allowed) through air corridors marked off by balloon barrages to deter the enemy, delivering airplanes from factories to RAF Squadrons. Hazel came home from England a local heroine, a title she deserved having pushed herself to the limit in wartime activities. In 1944, she joined the newly formed WASPs refusing to let health problems intimidate her. In this capacity, Hazel towed targets in a B-26 so that fledgling gunnery students could practice shooting. Working in the American West, Hazel became a test pilot "flying after repairs had been made to the aircraft and engines." After the WASPs were deactivated in 1944, Hazel instructed South American recruits for the Brazilian Air Ministry.

In 1950 during the Korean Crisis, Hazel was the first female reserve pilot called to active duty. In an article of the *LOWRY AIRMEN,* March 9, 1951, Hazel was featured as "Pert and pretty Lieutenant Raines, a former WASP, probably has logged more flying hours than any woman in the Air Force today and more than most of our Air Force pilots."

Hazel died of medical complications in 1956 at the age of forty. Her desire to write a book someday is expressed in letters to her mother and to her sister, Martha. The physical hardships that she endured to gain a place in the Aviation Hall of Fame are easier to document than the under-currents that surrounded female pilots in the 1940s. Hazel's decision to become a pilot took courage, and her letters span a period when women in aviation struggled to be accepted in our society. A final reflection upon my aunt Hazel is that she has become a close friend of mine and one who is worth remembering.

ACKNOWLEDGMENTS

I would first like to thank my parents, Frankie and Reginald Trice, and my sister, Fabia Trice Rogers, for believing in my ability to edit these letters. Special thanks to my grandmother, Mrs. Frank Raines, whose meticulous records, kept out of love and support, allowed me to chronicle Hazel's life. I am also grateful to my cousin, Hazel Jeaneane Briles, for her encouragement and enthusiasm about getting these letters published. Special praise goes to my husband, Jack, who has stood by me with endless enthusiasm for this project.

I would like to acknowledge Linda Bain, who brought me into the twentieth-century world of computers and held my hand when I baulked at learning a new way of communication.

Some close friends cheered me on; Judy Marriott was one of these.

And I have made some new friends; those who were a part of Hazel's life and shared their memories of her with me:

Mattie Lee Baxley, who befriended Hazel while she was training pilots in the Civilian Pilot Training Program in Cochran, Georgia.

Nancy Miller Stratford, who was also one of the twenty-two American women who flew with the Air Transport Auxiliary in England.

Peggie Parker Eccles, who flew with Hazel in the WASPs.

I have great respect for all the women who became pilots and had the courage to serve their country, whether in the A.T.A., the WASPs, or Foreign Service. This is their story. All had different experiences, but all of them were women of courage.

Book I.
ENGLAND...AS A FERRY PILOT
(SPRING OF 1942 TO SUMMER OF 1943)

Chapter 1

JACQUELINE COCHRAN RECRUITS HAZEL

The time is 1940 and and a young woman strolls through the crowd that surrounds the small airport. August is hot in Macon, Georgia, and she is wearing slacks, a short sleeved shirt, and brown leather boots.

Petite, with light brown hair, blue eyes, freckles and a confident grin that speaks of mischievousness; she, at twenty-four years old, is Georgia's only female commercial pilot, here to take part in the "World Premier of a Three Ring Air Circus". She is usually the only woman participate in these shows, and is recognized as one of the South's outstanding stunt pilots.

Hazel's association with air shows prompted numerous articles in Georgia newspapers. *The Cordele Dispatch,* (Cordele, Georgia, April 19, 1940) featured the following article about the All-States Air Show:

> One of the most thrilling acts of the show will be an acrobatic flying act by Miss Raines, holder of the highest license of any woman in the South. Hazel, who has been flying for the past four years, is known as one of the most daring pilots to perform acrobatic stunts. In her performance in Cordele Sunday, she will attempt to break her record of straight loops and spins. Hazel says, she will try to start looping the plane at about 5,000 feet and continue to loop it on down to 1,000 feet and start the plane in a mad spin, the ship being out of control, she will attempt to pull the ship out of the spin at 1,000 feet. Hazel will also compete against veteran pilots in the races on the program.

Hazel's first solo flight of any distance was recorded in the *Banner Herald,* (Athens, Georgia; October 22, 1940).

Macon Aviatrix Reaches Goal
By Circular Route

Hazel Raines, pretty Macon aviatrix, arrived in time tonight for a banquet preceding a gigantic air show here tomorrow, but she had the time of her life doing it.

Miss Raines hopped off from Macon shortly after 3 o'clock, flying alone for Athens. It was her first solo flight of any distance but she set her compass and headed for the classic city.

An extremely strong cross wind that threw several more experienced pilots off their course slightly blew Miss Raines to the north of Athens and started a series of the most thrilling experiences the young lady ever had.

"The first time I realized I was off course was when I came to a small town, dropped down to get my bearings, and saw a big sign reading 'Toccoa Tombstone Company.' I immediately turned south and it wasn't long until the motor of my plane went dead and there was nothing else to do except look for a place to land. There wasn't any emergency field, or at least I couldn't find one, but I did spot a fairly smooth wheat field and glided down on it for the landing. I landed okay and without damaging the ship, only to come face to face with a farmer, about ten kids and a double-barrel shotgun pointed at me. The farmer wanted to know what I was doing in his wheat field?

I said, 'well, my motor went dead and I had to make a forced landing.'

That seemed to satisfy him and he lowered his shotgun, agreed to hitch a mule to his buggy and carry me to Toccoa eight miles away. I got to Toccoa three minutes before the train pulled out to Gainesville, boarded it and after arriving in Gainesville, caught a taxi to Athens."

Hazel gradually began to venture further into the field of flying. In order to obtain her commercial license, she had to have 200 solo hours in the air; a feat she completed by delivering Taylor-crafts from the factory in Alliance, Ohio, to cities in the south. In a newspaper article of July 1940, Lt. L.J. Mercure, Civil Aeronautics Authority examiner, stated that Hazel's "flying is superior to that of the average licensed male pilot."

By the summer of 1941, Hazel had also received her instructor's rating and was one of six women in the United States who were employed as Civilian Pilot Training instructors.

The C.P.T. program was started in 1939 with $100,000 allotted by the United States President to train 300 private pilots in thirteen different colleges. This was so successful that 435 colleges and universities subscribed and contracted with small flying schools near the colleges. The program began to produce 3,000 pilots a month and the demand for flight instructors grew as many of them were needed in other defense activities. Teaching in Cochran, Georgia, Hazel was proud to announce that "out of my total of 17 students, eight have already been accepted in the Navy or Army Air Corps." (the *Atlanta Journal,* July 20, 1941).

By this time, Hazel was not only a member of the Macon Aero Club but the National Aeronautical Association and the 99's, a club composed of women pilots all over the United States. Hazel considered being a member of the "short snorters" also an honor. This was an unofficial organization among pilots in the United States. "The credential is a one dollar bill with the fledgling's name written upon it along with the member's signature who was the sponsor. If I am going anywhere, even out to the airport, I try to take it with me, for if I meet a fellow 'short snorter' and when asked can't show my badge of membership, then I have to come across with a dollar." (the *Atlanta Journal,* July 20, 1941.)

Nineteen forty-one was a turning point in Hazel's career. She left Cochran, Georgia, and joined the Thompson School of Aviation in Fort Lauderdale, Florida, to continue training pilots who were interested in joining the Air Force. As the only female instructor, Hazel was a novelty. One article in the *Fort Lauderdale Times* (August 11, 1941), read as follows:

LOCAL GIRL AIR INSTRUCTOR
DESIRES TO BE U.S. BOMBER
PILOT DESPITE MALE SNICKERS

She has a soft Georgian drawl- clear blue eyes, a love of aerobatics (acrobatics, loop-the loops, flying upside down) and a
powerful yen to pilot a Pan American clipper ship, or even a bombing plane— that's Hazel Raines, 25 year old flying instructor at Fort
Lauderdale airport. Hazel typifies the woman flyer of our day who
is interested in aviation as another woman is in making a career out
of being a fashion designer or in being a woman professor in some
great college.

To steer off masculine snickers at the idea of a woman flying a
bomber plane, a questionnaire direct from the war department was
received by Hazel the other day in which she was asked to tell of her
experience and qualifications and the accompanying letter hinted
that possibly if the U.S. does enter the war there will be a chance for
women flyers to do their part as English-women are doing at present."

By January of 1942, the C.P.T. program was in trouble due to the fact
that Congress did not pass on the proposed budget for the coming year, but
Hazel was making other plans in order to continue flying. She had completed
her application to join the English Ferry Pool Service. In a letter from the
Thompson School of Aviation, Hazel begins to prepare her mother for the
possibility. Her correspondence with her mother begins in January of 1942.

THOMPSON SCHOOL OF AVIATION
Government Approved Ground And Flight School
Fort Lauderdale Municipal Airport
Fort Lauderdale, Florida

Saturday Afternoon
January 31, 1942

Dearest Mother:

Just a note to let you know I am O.k. Haven't been doing so much
flying lately on account of awful windy weather. Also, we learned
today that we would not get any more C.P.T. so, I just don't know
what is going to happen. It seems they have discontinued C.P.T. on
the East and West coast on account of possible trouble on the coast
such as invasion or something like that. This war situation has really
hurt private flying and I just don't know how much longer I will be
here. In fact, I am very much down in the "dumps" over the situation.

I think I wrote you about getting my radio license and have now finished my training for my instrument rating but am going to discontinue that now that things look sorta black. Guess you saw in the paper about Jacqueline Cochran recruiting twenty-five women pilots for a year's service in England. Well, that is going to pay *only* 330.00 per month plus clothes or rather uniforms. Sounds sorta good and I don't know but if something doesn't break pretty soon I might investigate that further—that will be better than nothing at all to do. I have been told that they would be taken in immediately for instruction work in England. Well, don't worry about that but just thought I would tell you I was thinking about it, then too, I would get some very good experience over there if I did that.

How is the family? Hope everybody is well and o.k. now. I am feeling O.K. Well, write when you can and don't forget, I love you,

Hazel

In another letter, Hazel confirms her commitment to remain active in aviation, no matter what the job might be.

Saturday Morning
February 7, 1942

Dearest Mother:

Sure was glad to get your letter this morning, guess you think I am crazy cause I am up one day and down the next. Since I wrote you last I have been given some encouragement about my work. First of all I have been told that as long as he is in business I will have a job; right now I am the only Instructor he has and since I have been here he has had only eight different ones. He just fired another one last week, but you know me, I can get along with anybody and as for having trouble with him— I'm not worried. I just laugh at him when he gets mad about something. I guess that's why we get along so good. Now the second thing that has made me feel like there was hope is the fact that I learned the other day that they were considering employing women as co-pilots in Miami with the Pan American Ferry Company. This would really be a government job because it is under the supervision of the government and the type work they do is ferry ships to South America. They pay their co-pilots *only* $900.00 per month which isn't bad. I have made application for the job with them and have interviewed the man down there plus writing to Washington to their headquarters asking for consideration for the job. After all, I have quite a bit of time now, 1600 hours which I think will help.

No, I never intend to go back to office work or anything else as long as they make airplanes. I wouldn't be happy doing anything besides flying and hanging around a hanger and talking flying all day and night. That is the one thing that is really in my system and I believe it is the thing I am best suited to do and I intend to stick with it no matter what happens. That is of course if you approve, and I'm sure you are for me 100% cause you always have been. You know I think I at last have found what I was cut out to do when I started flying.

By the way, the other day I was sitting around the hanger and who should walk up but Caroline Hart and her mother. She said they had bought a home down here and were down for a few days. I think Caroline had been sick again per usual. That is one girl that I don't think will ever marry, she is very nice but oh so awful ugly.

Well, so much for this time, just thought I would answer your letter a little sooner this time. I know I am awful when it comes to writing as I should but— Give my love to all and take care of yourself and write when you can....

A copy of Hazel's application for the English Ferry Pool Service would seem to prove that her ambition in early 1942 was to be accepted in the Air Transport Auxiliary, recently formed by Jacqueline Cochran who would be significant in Hazel's life. By 1942, Jacqueline Cochran had already made a name for herself in the field of aviation. She won first place in the women's division of the Bendix Race in 1937 and broke the international speed record for men and women in 1939. In 1941, Jackie became the first woman to pilot a bomber across the North Atlantic from Montreal to England."When they heard the news, the male pilots already flying for the ATA threatened to strike. She was sure to be shot down by Germans, they argued, and the ATA would be blamed. Some even grumbled that their jobs were belittled by a woman." (Elizabeth Simpson Smith, *Coming Out Right,* 1991.)

Jackie's ambition was to prove that American women could fill the same roles that the female pilots in England were already doing—that was ferrying all types of aircraft to RAF squadrons. This released the male pilots for combat and England was desperate for qualified pilots. Not only would her plan advance the cause of women in aviation, but would be a helpful war effort with Great Britain. Jackie found the needed, (if not controversial) support from President Roosevelt and General "Hap" Arnold, working out the details with the British Air Transport Command officials.

The telegram from Jacqueline Cochran arrived in early March and Hazel described her excitement:

It all came about way down South in Georgia. I was teaching flying when the telegram from Miss Jacqueline Cochran arrived asking me if I would be interested in flying planes in England. Whatta silly question. Me, a two bit Flight Instructor, and a gal trying to make her way in Aviation and Bang**—- Outa the blue comes a telegram, of all things, from the top aviatrix asking me, quote— 'Can you fly to New York Thursday, March 5th for interview— transportation will be reimbursed, answer Western Union.' Even tho it was my last eighty-five cents until payday, I dashed into town and sent a quick — 'Arrive New York Thursday 6:45 P.M.'

My one and only dress suit was at the cleaners. It was Monday and I had left it there on Monday morning. I stopped by the cleaners on the way back from the telegraph office to make sure I could get it on Wednesday. Although it was fast growing too small for my expanding "fuselarge", I managed to wiggle myself into same in time to make the plane on Thursday.

Miss Cochran turned out to be a grand person, even tho she did notice my too tight suit and commented on same. After a most wonderful week in New York, at her expense, I returned to Georgia to await orders to go to Dorvall Airdrome at Montreal, Quebec, Canada.

March 15th saw me boarding a train for Montreal. March 16th, I was in Montreal — Mount Royal Hotel. March 17th, Dorvall Airdrome. Physical examination, issue of flying togs, assignment of Flight Instructor and — I was on my way. With fingers crossed, luck and a fast backfield, I made the grade.

MAR 10 PM 7:38
POSTAL TELEGRAM

Miss Hazel Raines
CARE MRS MARION BERTRAM 916 NE SECOND AVE MIAMI FLA
Please Report To Dorval Airport Montreal Forthwith STOP Transportation Ticket Being Delivered Above Address STOP 300 Lbs Baggage Allowed STOP Bring Own Helmut Goggles STOP Passport Necessary STOP Confirm Date And Time Of Your Departure STOP Room Reservation Made For You Mount Royal Hotel Montreal

CAPT NORMAN EDGAR
RAF FERRY COMMAND

For Hazel, making the grade involved passing the physical exam with a history of asthma and a heart condition. This was a legitimate cause for concern. In a letter to her mother, March 18, 1942, Hazel mentions that:

the Doctors up here just don't seem to understand my heart condition and they are running some tests—- It would surely help if he (Dr. Richardson in Macon) could make a casual statement in the report to the effect that there is absolutely nothing organically wrong with my heart, but it is just a fast beating ticker——-the Doc said I looked like the picture of health——-I weigh 150 and think perhaps I'll not try to lose any more cause I need the extra weight to handle these large ships up here.

Please impress on Dr. Richardson how much this means to me, my whole future and life——- so tell him to make it sound good, if such is possible....

Hazel passes the physical and is allowed to continue her training.

Mount Royal Hotel
Montreal, Canada

Wednesday Afternoon
March 25, 1942

Dearest Mother & All;

I'll start this way cause I guess the whole family will read this— Gee but it was swell talking to you all last night. So sorry I was not in my room when you called. The gang all gathered down in one girl's room and we rented a radio from the Hotel so we could listen to some American broadcasts. We had gotten in from the Aerodrome about 5 o'clock and went out and bought some cokes and sandwiches and had a regular picnic in the room.

We certainly have a nice group of girls, we all get along swell.

Well, I did it- Saw Lt. Armstrong this morning and he said I was O.K.- isn't that grand! What a time I have had- looks like everything in the world is wrong with me yet— I am the healthiest looking one in the bunch and — after all there is not anything wrong with me. I think I must have been made out of "leftovers" and it has just taken me 25 years to get them to fit properly. I do know that up until the flying bug bit me, I was a "miss-fit", physically and socially— but now I believe I am on the right track—who knows? Keep your fingers crossed. However, I am not at all worried about my flying cause I feel I can fly the darn thing if any other girl can. I have been spending my mornings out at the hanger repair shop where I have been watching and helping work on the ship— now I know a little something about Why and How they tick. The rest of the girls have been going the way 90% of the females go —- After the tall, dark, and handsome pilots. They can have them— just give me a big shiny aeroplane! ....

Mount Royal Hotel
Montreal, Canada

Sunday Morning
March 29, 1942

Dearest Mother,

Just got up, dressed, and had breakfast, and got my mail where I found a letter from you. Thanks for the article. They sorta put it on thick, didn't they? Oh well, what the heck. I guess Mary Halliburton got a nice check out of my story.

Well, we have at last started our flight training. We took to the air Friday and I now have three hours dual. We do not fly on Sunday, that's why I'm taking it easy today. Tomorrow will be "my day". I am to solo, and believe me, I can hardly wait. I think at last I can really fly a ship that will get up and go. Of course it's only 550 h.p. and only cruises 185 and weighs 4,000 lbs, but that's something for me. However, I'm told that before I get back from England, I'll be flying anything and everything that's been made in the way of aircraft. Now, won't that be swell!

If the weather continues to be good, we will finish up the last of the week and probably leave here by next Sunday. We go from here to Halifax, Nova Scotia, and that's where we sail from. We got a cable yesterday from England saying the first group of five girls had arrived O.K. I'm still not sure I can call you from here. If I do, I won't be able to tell you when I am leaving. However, when I do call, if I can, you may know that we will be leaving in a day or two. Then— don't expect to hear from me for at least a month, cause they make us wait several days when we get to England before we can send you a cable. My letters from England may be short and not much news in them, but you will understand why. Our letters will be censored.

Guess the stockings will get here O.K. and thanks lots. I have bought my uniform shirts and enough material for two uniforms to be made when I get to England. They give us two and I think with having two made, I can make out O.K. The material is very pretty and it only cost me $43.00 for enough material and lining for two. My shirts were $3.00 each and I got six. I think I'll get two more before I leave. Also, I am stocking up on canned goods, such as canned meats and fruits. Don't worry about me not having enough of everything, cause I will have plenty of clothes, medicines and money.

By the way, the $25.00 per week will start when I arrive in England. I writing Mr. Fleming today...

Mount Royal Hotel
Montreal, Canada

April 1, 1942

Dearest Mother:

Received my hose today and sure do appreciate them. I am well supplied now.

Today has been another awful day, in fact it has been snowing and raining since Sunday and we haven't been near an airplane since last Saturday. This will delay us about another week so I doubt very much if we get away from here before the 10th. I'll wait and call you next week now since I see we won't be leaving here as soon as I expected. I have really been taking it easy, stayed in bed all day today just resting and reading until four this afternoon when I got up, took a bath and dressed for dinner.

I have learned that we will be from ten days to three weeks making it across and will more than likely stop in Iceland to put off supplies. Looks like I will really see some cold weather, but I don't mind at all because I have decided that a cold climate as this is certainly agrees with me much better than Florida. I feel so much better since I have been up here in this cold atmosphere, not one time have I felt the least touch of asthma as I was constantly feeling definite signs of while in Florida. I believe if I had stayed down there much longer I would have definitely started having asthma again. I am used to this clean cold air now and I love it. A couple of the girls are having visitors from the States this weekend and I think we are going north about 100 miles and try some skiing and bob sleighing. One of the girls from New York is having Ursila Parrot, guess that's the way you spell her name, up for the weekend. They seem to think that's something just cause she is quite an author and writes stories for the *American Magazine* and *Colliers* etc. To me she'll be no more than the maid that cleans my room, but I'll go along with them just to have something to do. People like that are usually dull and never know how to do but one thing but— to me most people are dull anyway, guess I'm too stuck on an airplane.

For the want of something better to do, several of us found a spiritualist yesterday afternoon and had our fortunes told. The uncanny part of it all was she told me practically the same thing the spiritualist in Florida told me. Oh, I'm gonna be quite famous and stuff and a big success with my flying and specially with this English deal. She also said I was going to marry an Englishman with lots of money which will help me succeed with my flying career. You can tell Frankie if you like; it might ease her mind a bit and help her overcome her fear of being disgraced with an old maid sister. Personally, I'm not worried about the matter; you know me. Well, so much for this time. Take care of yourself as I am doing and I'll write again in a day or two....

Jacqueline Cochran's standards were high.

"The women who were chosen were not only highly skilled but also of upstanding character. Cochran did not want to risk failure because of personality problems or the appearance of less than exceptional moral behavior."(Deborah G. Douglas, *U.S. Women in Aviation, 1940-1985* p.30). Out of the forty women who were chosen by her, fifteen failed to pass the test. Twenty-three of the pilots were Americans, but Polly Potter failed to pass the medical exam in Britain; leaving twenty-two Americans and two Canadians, Helen Harrison and Gloria Large. Hazel was in the second group of five female pilots who would make their way slowly to England as the transportation became available. Leaving from the mouth of the St. Lawrence River in a convoy of ships, it took 27 days to reach the coast. (Three ships in the convoy were sunk.) The twenty-two pilots recruited by Jacqueline Cochran would be the first American women to fly military aircraft. They were: (Ibid. p.115)

Myrtle Rita Allen (Carter)
Opal Pearl Anderson (Averitt)
Dorothy Rita Bragg (Hewitt)
Emily Chapin
Catherine Del Van Doozer
Virginia Farr
Mary Estelle Hooper Ford
Suzanne Humphreys Ford (de Florez)
Virginia Garst
Una Goodwin
Evelyn Hudson (Richards)
Margaret Elizabeth Lennox (Drown)
Nancy Jane Miller (Livingston Stratford)
Mary Webb Nicholson
Winnie Rawson Pierce (Beasley)
Hazel Jane Raines
Helen Richy
Roberta Sandoz (Leveauz)
Louise E.M.Schuurman
Edith Foltz Stearnes
Grace Stevenson
Ann Watson Wood (Kelly)

The following narratives of the trip over were found in Hazel's hand writing:

Top Secret

It was as much of a mystery to me as it was to my three new pilot friends, but without question, we carried out our orders and directions feeling quite like important somebodies embarking on a mission— "Top Secret."

We had waited 8 days for this day of all days, when the telephone in my room shook us all of a sudden—quick alarm. It was our friend, Mr. A., instructing us to meet him in the lobby of the hotel in 45 minutes. He asked us if that would allow us enough time to get ready. He didn't know we had hardly unpacked more than a toothbrush since we had been here and even that was in the proper place when he called.

We each breathed a sigh of relief in anticipation of our new adventure and the thought of at last leaving our God forsaken last rendezvous of bleak, bitter, cold countryside where the people seemed as tho they might be refugees from civilization, also waiting passage to an unknown destiny.

I began to see here just why we had been restricted to a limited amount of baggage. At least that is, I thought I understood, when we were taken aboard ship and found every bit of her packed to the fullest with bacon and aluminum (the British call it alu-min-imum).

Disappointment must have been fairly oozing from my face as I stood on the Lighter that took us out to the "S. S. Tetina" for our escort, Mr. A., said to me:

"What's the matter, Miss Raines, you aren't getting homesick already?"

"Oh no," was my reply, as I strained my words through a terrific lump in my throat. "But is that (pointing to a small 6,000 ton what-used-to-be British fruit boat) the ship we are sailing on?"

It was, and we soon found ourselves being helped aboard via rope ladder, where a bewhiskered British Merchant Seaman greeted us with a 'Cherrio Miss, I say we are lucky to have you fair lassies coming aboard.'

Somehow, I managed to produce a false smile and a 'thanks,' as I tugged frantically at my too tight girdle and scratchy wool skirt that had also done a bit of climbing as I scaled the seaman's ladder.

Once on deck, we four were shown to our quarters by another merchant seaman, a red-headed Irish lad, who I later learned was just 17, but had already seen service with the British Merchant Navy since the beginning of the war.

Our quarters were below the main deck, just aft of the dining room and within sound effect of the kitchen.

The cabin was small. Two bunks, a wash bowl, and a small cupboard, that scarcely held our top coats and a change of clothes. To walk between the bunks, was a single file procedure. The community bath, which was next to our cabin, always reminded me of the kitchen due to its proximity of location and the constant smell of boiled cabbage and sour pudding.

Our first night aboard ship was dull and very calm sailing, due to the fact I awakened the next morning to find we were still anchored to our yesterday spot of embarkation.

Breakfast at eight was typically American, much to my disappointment. Fruit juice, eggs, bacon, and coffee. Lunch, quite the same with peace time rations of cold cuts, pie, and milk. I was beginning to doubt those rumors about spam and brussel sprouts even before we weighed anchor, not realizing my anticipation of food shortages and rationing, was but a matter of hours from my American-humored stomach.

After breakfast and a turn around the deck, we went below to our cabins to find a notice from the Captain asking that we join him for a cup of tea at 11:00 in his quarters.

The tea turned out to be gin and bitters, served by the Captain's Tiger (his personal valet, buss boy or what-have-you), while we waited for the Captain to join us from his routine duties.

We four were sitting on edge, when the door opened with a bang and in walked our host. Just a suddenly as he arrived, he stopped his 5'5 stocky seaman statue and said:

"Good morning ladies, sorry to keep you waiting. I'm Captain Bill. Orders say I am to take you to Jolly old England and that I will do, long live the King."

We each stood immediately. There was a dead silence, then Sue, thank God for Damn Yankees, introduced us. It was only a matter of a couple of gins and bitters before we were all good friends and ready for anything, come hell or high water, and believe me, they both came.

Just after four o'clock that afternoon, while I was deeply interested in the operation of an anti-aircraft gun on the port side of our ship, I suddenly realized we were slowly moving down the bay. In my moment of excitement to get below deck to tell my comrades we were under way, I lost my footing on the steep descent, and arrived ahead of schedule, to find my pals already aft ship watching the last bit of the North American Continent fade away into an Eutopia.

Sea Legs
"What time is it Sue?"

"Er-what-going where?"

"Wake up-what time is it? I forgot to wind my watch."

"Aw, go to sleep, it's only-say, it's 8:15. We were supposed to eat breakfast 15 minutes ago."

With that, came a knock on our cabin door. "Miss, are you eating breakfast this morning?"

"Yes, sure, be right there," Came my reply. With a leap, I was out of my bunk, into my slacks and breakfast bound.

The thought of "first day out" kept running through my mind, together with, "Am I going to be seasick?" Of course I had already told myself no. I was right for a change. At least for the beginning, cause I was up and at it, ready for anything, I thought. Oh well, why worry, I told myself. It's only for a few days. Make the best of it.

Those few days turned out to be weeks. Those weeks, almost a month.

"Water, water everywhere" and not a drop of fresh water to take a bath in.

We were rationed on fresh water to wash our faces, underwear, and for drinking purposes!

Me get sea sick? Oh no, I was an old hand at this sort of thing. Why, I used to go out day after day in Fort Lauderdale deep sea fishing. I couldn't possibly get sea sick.

"It was too much sweet pudding," I said one morning when I just couldn't make it for breakfast. Lunch and dinner, the same old story. The Captain was a wise old owl, even if he didn't sit in an old oak tree, cause that night, there came a rap tap tapping on my cabin door.

"Come in."

"Well, well, little lassie. How are you tonight? Too much British food, er too bad. Oh well, I have a sure cure, believe me."

"Sure cure— you have what?"

"Just you keep still. I have an old remedy right here." Doubting Hazel looked up to see the Captain peering through a barrage of freshly laundered long handles, so arrayed for fast, sure drying at the foot of my bed, which incidentally was directly in line with the one and only entrance and exit to our abode. He was just reaching to elevate his woolen obstruction, as I mustered enough courage to view the man in my room.

Many times in comic strips and in the movies have I seen situations of this type but, this was my first experience coping with strategy of this nature.

His bald head was but one third visible through the barrage. His struggle was mild and simple, with one big salty hand, he brushed aside a leg of underwear to find the other, dangling in his mustache. His attitude of 'You can't defeat me' burst forth with a left to a right flank leg of underwear to reveal he had won on the count of two. He was in the ring.

"I say, little lassie. This hot buttered rum is quite good you know, and will have you up and around in no time."

After two generous potions of the Captain's nectar, I was up and around. Time was then no element. The long, strong drawers did it. The hot buttered rum, well, it was wonderful medicine too.

The next day found me up and around to enjoy one of the three days that were pleasant enough to sit on deck and appreciate the wonderful work and protection our corvette and destroyer escort was giving us.

Since time was no element, we spent most of our shipboard days playing cards. Of course, we would have an occasional lifeboat drill. This was a novelty and I thought fun, but was always given to understand by my life boat captain that I would not be allowed on a life boat in case of emergency, unless I had my necessary passport ticket, which consisted of one quart of scotch and a carton of cigarettes. From then on, I appeared for lifeboat drill with bulging pockets.

Columbus Versus Hazel

I was wrong. Columbus sailed the ocean blue, to settle a land for me and you but, he didn't back tract. We did, and many times.

To me, it was a simple matter crossing the Atlantic, but with hurdles to jump, evade, and pursue. I had not considered it was a problem of war. In fact, not one of us had given it a thought of serious concern.

Weigh anchor, full steam ahead, a bee line for dear old England, that was our simple thought. This was war—war, what did we know about war? We were born in a new, free, peace loving country. We were children of World War I. We were babes of A New Era—New World. Little did we realize that our diapers were still wet with a stench not our own. Nor did we realize that odor was haunting our very own generation. We were World War I babies, still innocent of a fate that would claim our children, still carrying on with that true American spirit of "It can't happen to us." We were going to England to do our bit— our part, all because America, the land of the free and the home of the brave, would not give us a chance to prove our worth for our own land of "spacious skies and home of the brave."

We knew our country would not give us passports. We knew if we left, it was for the duration and six months. We knew we had no letter from an American Consul to see us through. The British also knew this too, thus a letter from the Canadian Ministry saying "To whom it may concern etc."

In brief, it was what we needed to see us through, to get us to our destiny, to place us where we could serve our country, even if our country didn't want us.

My Trip O–Var

It took only a wee five weeks for me to get my three hours dual and three hours solo before shipping off to Halifax, Nova Scotia. We were in Halifax only one week, thank goodness. Saw the same movie five times. Then, very secretly like, we were taken out to a boat "lighter". When we went aboard this boat, I thought it was just another "lighter" that was going to take us on out to the big boat we were going to England on but—no, this second boat was "it". It was a British fruit boat laden with aluminum.

Twenty-seven days in normal times isn't too long. But twenty-seven days on a British fruit boat laden with aluminum is a long time. Especially on the high seas in the North Atlantic in the Spring of '42. I was one of seven passengers. There were five of us bound for England for duty with the RAF ferry group and a British counsel and his bride. All of us shared a common bath, salt water, all the way over. That was O.K. with exceptions. We five Americans washed out long-handles in the salt water we were allotted and hung said long-handles in the common bath. We received complaints when said long-handles froze and hit said bride in the head. We were of the opinion she was jealous cause she was cold and did not have long-handles alike unto ours. The trip was most eventful. With long-handles to the right of us and subs to the left of us. We discharged many depth bombs and surface bombs in those twenty-seven days. The sweet pudding served was taken to stomach by me. For two days I was bed-bound by same.

But, even so, upon arrival in England we were met by a contingent of officials that snapped us thru customs in short order. After debarkation, we were escorted by train to London to the Savoy Hotel where Miss Cochran was waiting to give us a warm reception.

Soon after checking in at the Savoy, I found myself soaking in a good ole fresh water bath for the first time in 27 days. The tub was a junior size swimming pool, some three by six in size with enough nobs and tabs to keep one busy an entire evening. In fact, one would almost hafta have an instrument rating to be able to take a "barth". The towels were King size, could have been used as a "long white robe."

Although Hazel mentions the discomfort of the salt water baths, there was only a slight allusion to the danger of the voyage, but "By June, there were 40 U-boats on daily patrol off the eastern seaboard, sinking an average of three ships a day." (Winston S. Churchill & Life, *The Second World War,* 1959 p.246) The U-boat battles in the Atlantic were "our worst evil" according to Winston Churchill. "It would have been wise to stake all upon it. Between January and October 1942 the number of U-boats had more than doubled. One hundred and ninety-six were operational, and our North Atlantic Convoys were subjected to fiercer and larger packs than before." (Ibid., p.239)

However, Captain "Bill" succeeded in his mission to deliver his passengers to "Jolly Old England" and a note to Hazel, signed by the entire crew reads:

FYFFES LINE
S. S. "Tetela"

May 1942.
Miss Hazel Raines

Dear Miss America,
    The first stage of your journey towards your great adventure is over.
    That you came in this ship and that we have been able to assist in delivering you safely we consider an honor.
    As you land in England full of enthusiasm for your task, may you also soon return to your homes in the United States full of the same zeal for the strengthening of the ties of friendship between our two great nations which is so necessary to ensure a more peaceful world in the future.
    We trust you will be favoured with good luck, make many friends and that when you eventually depart, you will leave a small part of your heart in Britain.

Happy landings,

A copy of the English Ferry Pool Service contract stated that the applicant would serve for a period of twelve months or a minimum of six months. The remuneration would be: "Salary is $150.00 per week, American money, and is exempt from British taxes. Transportation paid by England and return from point of origin, and $10.00 per day living expenses during transportation period out-bound. On return, a flat $100.00 expenses. If employed for one year—$500.00 cash in U.S. money bonus.
    The nature of the work is entirely civilian, and U.S. pilots do not lose their United States citizenship, nor are they required to take the Oath of Allegiance."

Some years later, Jacqueline Cochran had other comments to make about "her America women" who served in the British Air Transport Auxiliary:

> The 'going off to war' giddiness probably originated in Montreal, where the American women were checked out in powerful, complicated aircraft. There was a feeling of exhilaration among the forty girls. Fifteen failed to pass. That's how we ended up with twenty-five.
>
> Small groups of three or four together left for England by boat from the mouth of the St. Lawrence River. Organizing the American women was a tough assignment on all fronts. The British Ferry Command was unprepared for us when the first group arrived.
>
> Some of the women in the American group had Master's degrees, and I didn't see the need for general retesting. When it came to understanding the English battle scene, that was a different story, of course. There was a lot to be taken in. Flying air corridors set off and hemmed in by captive balloons was tricky, particularly in sticky weather. Navigating both new and disabled aircraft wasn't going to be easy. I finally convinced the English to adjust the period of indoctrination and testing to accommodate the special needs of my American women. (Jacqueline Cochran and Maryann Bucknum Brinkley, *Jackie Cochran, An Autobiography*, 1987, p.189.)

Hazel was in the first group of twelve American female pilots to join the Air Transport Auxiliary. By the time she reached England in May of 1942, the major air battles over Britain had already been fought and won by the Royal Air Force, but German aircraft still roamed the skies over England. These ferry pilots would fly without ammunition, ferrying planes to RAF squadrons and back to factories for repair. They would be trained at White Waltham, ATA Headquarters near London. The Spitfire and the Hurricane were the great defenders in these battles. In a period of four days in August of 1940, 236 aircraft were lost to the Germans. Factories worked around the clock to replace the airplanes that now attacked the German Reich, Malta, North Africa, and Asia. These were the airplanes that the Air Transport Auxiliary in England was ferrying to the fighter squadrons or returning to the factories for repair. After returning from England, Hazel related an incident when German planes were strafing an airfield. She took cover behind some paint cans but dismissed the incident with a comment about the Germans being poor shots. Many of these facts do not surface in her letters, however, for her life was a "military secret." Caught up in the middle of World War II, Hazel tried her best to reassure her mother that all was well.

May 12, 1942
Maidenhead, England

Dearest Mother and All,

After a very nice trip we arrived in London yesterday and spent last night at the Savoy Hotel with Jacqueline Cochran. It was really a treat to get a good hot bath again and a big soft bed. We had to take a bath in salt water on the boat and the bunks were not too comfortable. However, the people and officers on the boat were swell to us: they were all English. There were only eight passengers: we four girls, one American boy, one Canadian, and a British Counsel and his wife. Last night we were guests of "Jackie" at the Savoy in London and she had a very special dinner party for us. Of course "the people" were present such as Major Beasley, U.S.A. Air Corps and past president of Lockheed Aircraft in the States; Capt. Leonard Plugg, member of Parliament, House of Commons, owner of British Broadcasting stations; Dr. and Mrs. Oberhalt, he being a well known chemist and—several others that are among the "well knowns" but that is not interesting I am sure.

We had our uniforms fitted today— or rather measurements taken then reported here at Maidenhead. This is a very lovely and beautiful place—the flowers are in full bloom and everywhere you look you see tulips, sweet peas and etc. I am sure you, Frankie, and also Gene would go crazy over the flowers over here. Never before have I seen trees and grass so green. Also, we saw the same sights in Ireland and Scotland. Also, don't believe all you read in newspapers, things are not half so bad as you would think, quite the opposite and the people are all swell— you would think they came from the South when it comes to hospitality.

Tomorrow we receive the rest of our equipment and settle down to work. We will be at another pool for several weeks for ground and flight training then back here.

Well, I must turn in, cause I am tired and will get off another longer letter to you in a few days. Just wanted you to know I am well, safe and happy. Give my love to all and to those that asks about me, I am doing fine. Don't worry for there is nothing to worry about, really. Remember—I love you,

Hazel Raines
A.T.A. White Waltham
Maidenhead, England

The Air Transport Auxiliary pilots were trained at White Waltham, which was the A.T.A. Headquarters. According to Diana Barnato Walker, (*Spreading My Wings,* p. 66) there were 14 original pools. Hazel would be transferred to many of these pools as she trained to ferry various types of aircraft. The first fourteen pools (there wasn't an 11th or a 13th) were:

1. White Waltham
2. Whitchurch, Bristol
3. Hawarden, nr Chester
4. Preswick, Ayrshire
5. Luton, nr Thame
6. Ratcliffe, Leicester
7. Sherburn-in-Elmet, Leeds
8. Sydenham, Belfast
9. Aston Down, nr Stroud
10. Lossiemouth, Scotland
12. Cosford, nr Wolverhampton
14. Ringway, Manchester
15. Hamble, Southampton
16. Kirkbride, Solway Firth

Thursday Morning
May 28, 1942

Dearest Mother:

Today was a red letter day for me— got two letters from you. It seems that it only takes about 11 days for your mail to get here. Again I want to remind you there is no need to worry about me; I am feeling fine and have an excellent place to live in an English home with a swell couple who treat me like a Queen. They think American girls are wonderful and seem to think so much of us for what we are doing. Believe me, I have been doing some serious studying since I have been here and believe me, these people are truly thorough and make sure you know what you are doing before they put their O.K. on anyone. This type work is within itself a college education, for we are being taught the technical and theoretical side of flying as well as practical. Had two days leave this week, Tuesday and Wednesday, and went to London to relax a little. Saw a play, "Doctor's Dilemma" that Vivien Leigh was in. It was very good and she is a beautiful girl. Also, saw a new British picture just produced about A.T.A. and the late Amy Johnson, girl British pilot— the name of the show was "We Fly Alone", and if it comes to America and to Macon, don't miss it cause it will give you an excellent idea of the type work I am doing. Also it is about her husband, Capt. Jim Mollison, whom I know very well and have had several dates with him. He is also an A.T.A. pilot and holds a number of world records. The radio program comes on at 9:30 Sunday Nights here and I too listen to it. It is very likely they will have us on that broadcast in the near future so— keep on listening!

The gloves were only $3.00 per pair, I checked up to make sure. Are they depositing the money every week and when did they start? I was notified it had been started, but want to make sure it is coming thru as it should. Listen, I want you to use that money for not only my bills but for yourself. If you don't spend what you need of it, I will stay over here an extra year! You better do what I tell you or I'll turn you across my knee when I get back. By the way, my knee isn't as big as it was. I've lost about 20 lbs.—getting back to normal size again, thank goodness. You know Dr. Richardson said I would do that. Did I tell you I bought a bicycle— it's either that or walk about 10 miles a day, and you know me and walking.

Well, I've got work to do as usual so this will hafta be all for this time. Tell Jeaneane hello for me and to learn lots of new dances for me and the soldiers. Give my love to Frankie, Rege and the kids— Hope they are well now. Will write Frankie next week. Also give my love to Martha and Gene but keep the most for yourself ....

Friday Night
June 5, 1942

Dearest Mother,

At last we are having some nice weather here for a change, thank goodness! I have at last gotten warm again, took off my long-handles the other day and now it's almost like summer time in good old Georgia. I am getting quite a tan from the sun and wind cause at present we are flying open equipment. This country is quite different from ours, it is thickly populated but so pretty from the air. I am truly getting a good view of the British Isles from the air, an unusual way to visit a new country but I must say it is very interesting.

We are all still in school and studying like the very devil. I can truthfully say I am studying my head off and liking it. We expect to complete our basic training in another couple of weeks when we get our wings plus another promotion and better pay, then a few days leave after which we go back to school to learn how to handle bigger and better equipment. Wish I could tell you all about our aircraft we are flying but— I can't. My instructor, by the way, is an English woman and we are forever at odds with each other; yet she really doesn't worry me cause I have really shown her a few things about this business of flying. Most of the people are quite nice while as for those who are not it's awful to have to hold my temper down. I have managed to do so thus far and only hope I can continue. If I go thru 18 months of this I'll be the best natured person in the world when I get back. Guess you all will be glad cause I have been bad, haven't I?

They tell us they are planning to let us broadcast from London back to the States in several weeks. Wish I could say just what time and when but I don't know. Just continue to listen to all the broadcast you can from London and maybe you'll hear me before too long. If I should find out in time to let you know, I will....

Saturday Night
June 6, 1942

Gee, but I feel better tonight- got a letter from home. Sister sure is good about writing and I'm gonna answer her letter in a few days. Honest, we stay so busy until I really don't have a chance to write as often as I would like to cause at night I am so tired all I can do is go to bed. I am at last getting used to my bicycle— it almost killed me at first, not being used to so much exercise.

We get our uniforms Tuesday and will send you a picture when I get my wings. The lady here where we are living is knitting me a sweater, a blue wool, to wear under my tunic with my uniform. I think she is very nice to do this for me cause I really needed a sweater— it is cold weather here about 80% of the time. She is making it V neck and long sleeved. A good sweater cost about $15.00 in stores which is awful, that's three pounds English money.

Time for bed— so until next time remember,

I love you,
Hazel

Excerpts from these first letters from England were published in the *Atlanta Journal,* July 5, 1942 under the headline:

MACON GIRL FERRIES WAR PLANES
By Mary M. Holtzclaw

Mrs. F.G. Raines, of 212 Riverdale Drive, Macon, Georgia, has the distinction of being the first Georgia mother with a daughter in England's Ferry Service.

Mrs. Raines is a tall, slender woman on whom the years have settled lightly, but she confesses to having felt the weight of them recently more than ever before. When I interviewed her for *The Journal's Magazine,* she said:

"No one, more than I, appreciates the fact that it is a wonderful thing to have a daughter who is capable of working in our first line of defense. And I don't oppose Hazel's going over, not audibly, as she had her heart so set on it, but it seems to me it would be an unnatural mother who could work up enthusiasm over such an undertaking. Hazel said, 'If you tell me I cannot go, Mother, I'll give up the thought, but it will break my heart. So, you see, I couldn't say 'no', I just didn't say 'yes'. Then Hazel loves to do a hard job well, and this business of being in the Air Transport Auxiliary calls out all the ability a pilot has. She has to move aircraft that is very valuable and thousands of dollars are entrusted to her every time she takes off. Many of these planes have been damaged having just returned from a bombing expedition over Germany, and she must carry them back to the factory for repairs. Sometimes the territory over which she must fly is dangerous because of enemy planes, and ferry pilots must learn to fly without benefit of radio beam or any weapons with which they might protect themselves. Hazel is subject to call at any time, and she must know how to pilot all types of aircraft, and how to get to and from all factories, 'pools', or stations anywhere in the British Isles. In fact, the slogan of the A.T.A. is this:

'Any aircraft, any time, any address.'

We hear from her so rarely and there's not very much she is allowed to tell. But it is enough to know that she is alive and well, and doing the thing that she would rather do than anything else. Now I'm going to read you some excerpts from her letters.

"Mrs. Raines took them from the table beside her, adjusted her glasses and began reading:"

'Mother, if you only could know how happy I am when I fly a plane! I never feel so completely close to God as when I'm up in the blue. So if you ever get a message that I've been in a crackup and have been killed, don't grieve for me any more than you can possibly help, just know I died the way I wanted to.'

Mrs. Raines wiped the mist from her eyes and smiled bravely. "Hazel carries a silver dollar in her pocket with her all the time," she said, "and just before she takes off, she touches with her finger tips the words, 'In God We Trust', and she says them softly to herself. In fact, she said one day when we were talking it over, that if we trust as though everything depends on us, then we will beat the Germans and Japs before long. And she's doing her part, don't you think?"

Sunday Night
June 14, 1942

Dearest Mother,

Just received your letter written May 27th and was so glad to hear from you. The information in regards to the money was correct. If ever it fails to come thru each week as it should, let me know. Also I want you to use it for the work on your teeth—let the other things go and take care of yourself first with it.

Hope this letter reaches you on the 26th, if not just remember I love you and am wishing you the happiest birthday ever and will be thinking of you specially on that day. Just take care of yourself for me cause after all you are still a young lady to me and always will be. After all you can still beat me walking and taking exercise even if you still can't manage to turn me across your knee.

Yes, I am very happy. Of course I do get homesick at times, but I am still glad I came over here. Just as I have written you before, this is an education itself. I am not only learning flying from A to Z but I am meeting people from all over the world and at the same time seeing the British Isles from a point of view that very few people have seen it. It is really a beautiful country from the air and I can hardly wait to get back to tell you all my experiences. In fact I am going to have so much to talk with you about until I am afraid you and I will have to spend three months in Florida on a vacation, instead of two. Yes, you and I are going to take a little time off when I get back and have some fun— yes indeed!

Just took a hot bath and washed my hair and am now sitting in front of the heater drying it while I write to you. Had a busy day today, took a final flight test on some heavy equipment and passed O.K. Never did I dream I would be flying the stuff I am on now. It's lots of fun and at the same time quite safe so there is no need for worry. These people really make sure of your ability before they let you go off in a new type machine. As for other dangers, it's really a joke, it's as quiet and peaceful here as living 100 miles from the nearest human being.

Guess I had better hit the hay cause I've got lots to do tomorrow. Tuesday is my day off and I'm going to London to get my uniform and a few things. By the way, the two pair of long- handles I bought in Montreal have saved my life, you can't get them here and I sure hate it cause I need some more....

Chapter 3
"ANY AIRCRAFT, ANYTIME, ANY ADDRESS"

Sunday morning
June 19, 1942

Dearest Mother,

Well, at last we have finished our primary training, received our wings, and have been promoted to the rank of Third Officer. I am now on three days leave before being transferred for Class II technical and conversion course. Besides resting and taking things easy, I am trying to pack my things cause I am moving Tuesday. Gee, but I hate to move cause I really like where I am now but— that's part of this game I guess; time one gets settled in one place, they are posted somewhere else.

For the next two weeks we will be on the ground going to ground school again—then we go back to the type equipment we were flying in Montreal— stay on that a couple of weeks, then we at last get to fly some sure'nuff stuff (Hurricanes and Spitfires) for about 4 months— that is delivering equipment for that length of time then— back to school where we check out on twin engine equipment— and that will be the day for me! That is the phase I am really going for cause I think the time and experience will do me the most good of all.

Got a letter from Frankie last week enclosing the newspaper story. The story with the picture was correct information about our work. So many stories you read in the newspapers are not true; but this one was. I don't like that picture they continue to use. It is not like me now. Just as soon as I can, I will have one made and send it to you. Did I ever send you the pictures we had made in Montreal of us — the ones by the aeroplane? If I didn't, let me know. I have some extra ones I'll send you.

Wish I was there now to enjoy those fresh vegetables you write about. We do have some, mostly peas and cabbage, one egg per week and *some* meat. You all might think you have been put on a strict ration basis but really— you don't know what rationing is. Anyway, I'm doing O.K. and not going hungry, so don't worry. The only thing I get tired of is this business of drinking tea 4 times a day. I usually just have a glass of water. And by the way, we found an American restaurant here in London yesterday where you can get an honest-to-goodness hamburger with onions and a coke. That was the first coca cola I have had since we left Montreal and did it taste wonderful. Wow!

You asked about my weight— well, I am down to 135 now. I weighed 159 when I left (censored). Won't be long before I'm back to normal. Well Mother, there's really no news of interest, so, 'til next time ....

P.S.

Hate to admit it but I have been so homesick lately till I have almost gone crazy. So, I decided the best thing for me to do was get me a dog. You know me and how I love dogs. So, I have bought a little Scottie and we call him Fritz II. I am going to keep him and bring him back with me. So, love me; love my dog. I never intend to be without one as long as I live. If you ever get a chance to see Coke Connary, ask him what happened to Fritz. If he still has him, I want him too when I get back.

Hazel's reference to the newspaper story "which was correct information about our work" was probably the following article from the *Atlanta Journal*

(June 18, 1942). It was originally printed in London and reprinted in Atlanta with an added caption about Hazel:

MACON GIRL FLOUTS DEATH TO FERRY RAF PLANES

Miss Hazel Raines One of Pilots
Who makes Giant Air Raids Possible
By Kathleen Harriman

London, June 18.-(INS)- Behind the recent 1,000 plane Royal Air Force raids on Germany, and the smaller scale attacks which resumed Wednesday after a two week layoff because of weather, are the pilots of the British ferry service. They are the ones who make possible the RAF performances that have astonished the democratic world, raising the hopes of the war-weary world that the final scene- Germany's defeat- grows even nearer.

I went back stage today.

I got a picture of the "stage-hands" at work— the ferry pilots taking back for reconditioning the bombers unlucky enough to have been caught in the great searchlight belt over Germany, unlucky enough to have felt the weight of the ack-ack guns hurling their metal skyward...But lucky enough to have gotten home.

Women in Service

Down at Air Transport Auxiliary Pool No 1, pilots—men and women— moved hurriedly to and fro through the long corridors of headquarters, checking in— checking out— always on the move.

Twenty pilots needed at such and such factory...one pilot to Wales immediately....another needed in Scotland....still another in Devon...

But all must be ferried home again.

The mechanics of the ATA are bewildering enough to any civilian.

Commodore D'Erlanger, the man who organized the service when the war broke out, tells me that Britain's ATA is larger than all the U.S. commercial air lines together.

Pilots, too, must be trained to keep up with the ever-increasing production of aircraft here and in America. The ATA has its own school of instruction. Here peacetime fliers must be taught the ins and outs of fighting aircraft. Their training must be thorough. A precious aircraft worth thousands of dollars is intrusted to each ferry pilot every time he, or she, takes off.

Invalid Pilots Used

Here at the school are crack RAF pilots, invalided out of the air force for varying reasons. Men too old for operational flying are whipped back into shape—women too.

Outside the navigation class I met Jacqueline Cochran, ace American aviatrix.

"I'm back in flying school again," she has two and a half stripes on her Navy ATA uniform, a ferry captain.

Captain Cochran is the first woman to fly a bomber across the North Atlantic. She accomplished this feat last fall, made a quick tour of England; then foreseeing a shortage in first-class pilots hustled back home to organize as American girls branch of the ATA.

"Three hundred girls right off the bat," Captain Cochran told me. "From those three hundred, I hand picked 95. Twelve of those girls are already here. The rest are on the way.

"I think I got a good bunch of girls. The rest are on the way."

She introduced me to the twelve. They were a smartly turned out lot. Some wore navy slacks, others the skirt adaptation of the ATA uniform. Each one had ATA wings on her jacket.

There was Miss Louise Schuurman, daughter of the counselor general of the Dutch East Indies, now a resident of New York City; Miss Virginia Farr, West Orange, N.J.; Miss S. Ford, New York City; Miss Dorothy Furey, New Orleans; Miss Virginia Garst, Kansas City; Mrs. H. Harrison, Toronto, Ont.; Miss W. Pierce, Mineola , N.Y.; Miss P. Potter, Portland, Ore.; Miss Hazel Raines, Macon, Ga.; Miss Helen Richey, Pittsburgh, Pa.; Miss G. Stevenson, Tulsa, Okla; Miss A. Wood, Waldoboro, Me.

Saturday Night
June 20, 1942

Dearest Mother:

Well I feel as though I have been back home tonight, got four home town papers today and despite the fact that they were May 6,7,8,9 editions, I enjoyed them thoroughly, even the advertisements. I took my papers in and let Mr. and Mrs. Hinton, the people I live with, read them and they nearly had a fit over the grocery adds. You see fresh vegetables and meat, specially chickens, are delicacies and to be able to buy such things and without food rationing coupons is something. Anyway, even if the papers are 6 weeks old when they get here, I truly enjoy them. Thanks a lot for having it sent to me.

At last I have finished my primary training and am actually doing what I came over to do. This work continues to be quite interesting and I am beginning to like it better, thank goodness, and it is just as I had it pictured in my mind. This is indeed the best type training anyone could ever hope for, cause after my stay over here, I will indeed not only be qualified but capable and experienced in flying any machine ever built, which I think is not bad at all. It will be one of the answers to my flying ambitions. The second and last as far as flying goes is acrobatic competition, which is incidentally what I would like to do when I return home should there be a field for it. If not I guess I will go back to instructing for awhile until I find another phase of flying that will offer new fields to conquer. I never intend to grow up and settle down, for I am sure there will always be something new and interesting to do that at the same time will be constructive and educational.

After reading all about gas rationing, I have been quite concerned over Reginald and his business. How is he getting along? Is there any chance of Gene having to go into the army? I certainly hope not.

Now when I tell you this, don't faint—but— I have taken up knitting. Yes, I am knitting myself a white scarf to go with my blue uniform for dress. I knit a little every night before I go to bed. Hope to finish it before winter gets here. I'm not doing too bad with it either.

How are the children getting along now? I think of them so much and hope they won't forget me. Guess they will grow so much before I get back till I won't know them.

Well Mother, there seems to be no more news that I can write and really that is all the news I know. Nothing interesting or newsie happens around these parts, just routine work and that's all. So, until next time....

Tuesday Morning
June 23,1942

Dearest Martha,

Know you must think I am the world's worst about writing, well, to tell the truth- I am. Seems as tho I can only find time to work all day, and actually I am working hard for a change, and then scribble a few most uninteresting words to Mother about once a week. Thanks for your wonderful letters, keep up the good work. Mail means so darn much to me over here.

Sunday Morning
June 28,1942

Well- here I go again, maybe I'll finish this, this time. Have been given two days leave to do a bit of resting up. Goodness knows I needed it cause we do stay on the fly. I stayed in bed all day yesterday and just got up for lunch today. I am feeling O.K., just seem to get tired too quickly due to the complete change in the mode of living and then too, I have lost about 20 lbs., thank goodness. Anyway, the Doctor says I'll be O.K. after these couple of days rest and I'm sure I will too.

You should see us all in our uniforms: we do look quite nice and mine makes me look very slim. Soon as we finish our basic training period here and get our wings I'll have a picture made and send it to you all. This work continues to be most interesting and I have now seen the whole of England from the air. This is truly the most beautiful and interesting country I have ever seen, however; nothing can ever surpass the good old U.S.A. and Georgia. I am now receiving the paper every day and even if it is a month old when it gets here, I enjoy every line in it. Whether the *Telegraph* realizes it or not, they have quite a number of fans here in England, for I pass my papers on to others at the Aerodrome when I have finished with it and about 200 people out there have read it. I bring it home to my landlady who in turn reads it and then trades it to her local grocer for an egg or a couple of ounces of butter. So, you see they should be proud to print such a far reaching paper.

Say, your idea about our friend, Phillip Morris, is excellent, and if you can work out a deal, please do so at once for it will certainly be appreciated. Get Mother to reimburse you.

Cochran is still over here with us and looks after us all as if we were her children. She has invited me and Sue, the girl that rooms with me that's from New York, to have dinner with her Monday night and spend the day with her Tuesday which is our day off. So, when we finish work tomorrow night, we are going to London and stay with her for the night and day. She is really a very nice person and I have invited her to spend a few days with me when I get back to good old Georgia and she said she would like to. Hope you don't mind. After all, she's just a poor country gal what's done well and had good luck. I am sure she will be quite helpful when I get back cause she has promised me an excellent job in aviation in the States when I get back.

Well, I am afraid I have run out of allowable things to say except, I hope all of you are O.K. and don't forget to write as often as you can....

Hazel's description of Jackie Cochran as a "poor country gal what's done well and had good luck" reveals an awareness of the hardships that Jackie overcame to become "the worlds leading aviatrix in 1937, 1938, and 1939." As a young orphan, Jackie lived in poverty, sharing a one room shack with her foster family. At the age of eight, she went to work in a Georgia cotton mill for 6 cents an hour, working from six at night to six in the morning. Jackie struggled through her teenage years with little education but managed to become a beautician and a nurse. Her good luck began while working at Antoines Beauty Salon in Florida and New York City. Through this connection, she met and later married Floyd Odlum, a wealthy businessman who encouraged her to learn to fly so that she could sell cosmetics around the country. Jackie became consumed with flying and entered races that had been closed to women. She was the first woman to enter the Bendix Race in 1938 and the first woman to win it. Hazel would eventually follow Jackie into the W.A.S.P.s or Women Airforce Service Pilots, which Jackie organized in 1942.

In later years, Jackie broke the sound barrier (1952), received the International Flying Organization's gold medal (1953), the Legion of Merit and the Distinguished Flying Cross. She was also voted the 1953 Business Woman of the Year after founding and successfully running her own cosmetic firm.

The letters continue. In early August, 1942, Hazel is in class again at the Air Transport Auxiliary school of instruction:

All day today I sat in class writing on exam papers; we have had 6 so far and 4 more to go making a total of 10 that will finish up this particular course. I must say this is truly excellent training we are receiving and I have truly been doing some studying. After this is all over we take to the air once again and believe me that will be a relief after sitting in a dull classroom all day for three weeks...

Tomorrow I am moving again- at present I am by myself but have decided it will be better to be with some of the other American girls. I am moving in with Virginia Farr, one of the girls in the first group that came over. She seems like quite a nice girl and I think I'll like it better with someone rather than living alone. She has a very nice billet (that's the term they use for home or living quarters) on the Thames River and we can go boating and fishing whenever we want to. She has a car which will be swell for going out to the field and back. That's as much automobiling as we are allowed to do since we have such a strict rationing of petrol. You asked how much we paid for our room— I pay per week two pounds 17 shillings which is approximately $14.00.- This gives me in addition to the room and plenty of hot water for a bath each night, two meals per day, breakfast and dinner at night. My mid-day meal I eat at the Aerodrome and it costs one shilling (25¢)....

Virginia Farr's description of her work with the A.T.A. was "flying anything and everything of two motors or less, and trying desperately to keep them all in one piece." (Deborah G. Douglas, *U.S. Women in Aviation, 1940-1985*, p.13)

Thursday afternoon
August 13, 1942

Dearest Mother,

Gee, but it was great getting your swell letter yesterday. It was such a sweet one too and I do enjoy your letters so very much cause I know you really mean each little word you say to me and each letter I practically memorize, cause I put it in my pocket and read it every day 'till the next one comes.

You know I really think you are worrying too much about me and how I am getting along- Please stop it! I'm feeling swell and getting the best of attention in a medical way. I stop by to see the doctor quite often and he checks me over about every three weeks. You see we have a Doctor and a small hospital at each Airdrome and you know me— I have made friends with the doctor and nurses here and they really treat me swell.

The cheese arrived a couple of days ago and tell Frankie thanks a million. You all would have had a fit if you could have seen what happened when I got it. You see we do get a little cheese over here, but it's not as good as ours. Well, a couple of the other girls were with me when I collected the package and when they found out what I had, of course I had to open it right then and there. The three of us sat down out on the Airdrome and ate half of it just so and believe me it was excellent— tasted like chocolate cake. Can't wait to get the ham. However, I'm gonna save the ham till I really need it. Right where I am living the food isn't so bad. In fact, it's good.

As for the cigarettes— well I think that's swell of you to send them to me. I do hope you won't feel too badly about that. I know you had much rather not think of me using the things but I really do enjoy a good cigarette occasionally and remember this- I don't use them to excess nor out of place and I'll always be a lady in the use of them. Now that you know- I feel much better about the situation. Of course I am sure you have known all all along, but you just didn't mention the subject to me. Now that we have gotten that off my chest I feel like a different person. Believe it or not, I do like to please you in the things I do and I can do a much better job when I feel I have your approval of even the smallest things I do such as smoking. There is something else I want to assure you of and that is you'll never have to worry about me taking too many cocktails. I do join in and drink one and sometimes two just to be sociable, but that's as far as it goes. I don't feel bad about doing that either cause I honestly don't think there is any harm done just as long as it isn't a habit and it doesn't hurt me.

You know some girls do these things just cause they think it's smart and their mothers don't know about it. I am so glad it's not like that with you and me.

Remember I told you about buying a bicycle– well, I kept it about six weeks and I have sold it. I didn't like it so – I thought the best thing to do was sell it. Where I am living now I don't really need one cause Virginia has a car and I ride with her. She is the American girl I live with and is very nice. She is Virginia Farr from New Jersey. She will be posted again in a couple of weeks and when she leaves I think I'm gonna buy me a motor bike— a light weight motorcycle. The rest of the girls are all buying one. You see they will allow us enough petrol to travel back and forth on. We really need something like that cause transportation is indeed a problem. I think I can get a good second hand motor for about 30 pounds which would be $150.00. I have already saved 15 pounds to go on it. Don't think I'm doing so bad really cause to save anything over here is indeed a problem. As a rule it take every penny one makes to live. Things are very expensive.

By the way, is my money still coming thru O.K. and how is my debt situation now? Thank goodness I'll soon be clear again. What a relief!

Please tell the children hello for me and to be good and I'll take them for a ride when I get back.

Well Mother, so much for this time, I gotta go get ready to fly. Will write again in a few days....

The following letter from Hazel is to a family friend, Lee Wood. (He made a lasting impression upon me even at the age of four because when he visited us in Macon, he always brought Hershey bars, a real treat during the war.)

Lt. William L. Wood, Jr. (0-438080)
414 th. Bombardment Squadron
A.P.O. # 875 U.S. Army England

Thursday Night
August 20, 1942

Dear Lee,

It was indeed a surprise to me when I received your letter today, and needless to say, it made me feel quite happy. Although I have only been over here four months, it seems like four years— therefore, getting a letter from someone that's from good ole Macon, Georgia really puts me on top of the world again.

This is indeed a strange world, isn't it? Never did I dream such a thing as this would ever happen to me — to say nothing of us meeting in England under the existing circumstances. Just the same, I must say I love the type work I am doing now, and hope this little part I am playing in this dreadful show will help in a small way to hasten the end of this silly business of war.

Now to tell you something about my work — At present I am stationed here at White Waltham for what is called Class II Conversion. At present I am only ferrying light equipment such as Masters, Hurricanes, and Spits but hope to make twins in a couple of months. This is truly wonderful training for me — never would I have had the chance to fly such equipment in the States.

Of course the best way to tell you all about my work and to hear what you are doing is to get together when we both have leave. That I imagine is going to be a problem. I have two days leave every two weeks and my next leave is week after next. In the meantime, should you have a chance to do so, you might tell them you need some practice cross-country flying and drop in White Waltham. You can always contact me thru A.T.A. White Waltham Airdrome, Maidenhead, Berks.

By the way, I have also heard from Liveley Armstrong since I have been over here but we too haven't been able to get together. You can contact him by writing P/O Liveley Armstrong, American Eagle Club, 28 Charing Cross Road, W.C.2, London.

Thanks for the newspaper article as well as your swell letter. Looks like the *Telegraph* could find something worth while to write about.

Lee, please keep in touch with me and drop me a note whenever you can find time. Also, let's see what we can do about getting together soon. I too go to London almost every time I have a day or two off so that idea would be excellent-

Keep up the good work, lots of luck- and let me hear from you again soon-

Always,
Hazel

Friday Night
August 28, 1942

Dearest Mother:

Gee but I've been happy this week — Four letters from home. All of a sudden the mail service has been extra good, the last few I've gotten have come over in 8 to ll days which is excellent. Also I received the ham yesterday and have put it away in my trunk until I really need it. Thanks lots for sending me these nice things. Tell Martha to please continue sending Camels once a week cause you can't get them over here and I truly enjoy them after a hard days work.

Well, this week I finished up another stage of training and have been promoted from Third Officer to Second Officer which means another stripe on my shoulder as well as added responsibility in regards to flying still faster equipment. Once again I am now out on the job and I sure do love my work. Tonight I am in Scotland in the most interesting little village. Had to deliver a ship up here and have another to take South tomorrow. One of the other American girls had a trip to make up here also and we are spending the night here. After dinner we went for a walk- it still being daylight, and we visited the home of the Scottish poet, Robert Burns, where he lived and died. We then walked down a cobble stone street to the Church where he is buried. It was really quite interesting. This is a wonderful education for anyone and something I'll never forget.

Again I say, I have never worked quite so hard before and loved it. I had a long talk with the "C.O."(Commanding Officer) at my pool the other day and was told if I continued to make a good record I would make twins in a few weeks. That will be the day! I have always wanted to fly twins and I am sure now I will soon be doing so. When I make that grade I will get another promotion to First Officer.

Well Mother— I'm very tired and must get a bath and go to bed cause I've lots to do tomorrow. Don't forget- I'm feeling fine and very happy and don't for goodness sakes believe all you read and hear over the radio— this is the quietest little Island in the world- I really don't think Germany knows where England is. Give my love to everybody and specially the children. Fritz II sends his love also, you just should see him! You will, of course, cause I'm gonna bring him home with me....

P. S .
I have lost 25 lbs. but feel so much better.

In a letter of September 9, 1942, Hazel has bought the much discussed motorcycle (of which I am sure her mother disapproved, having never learned to drive a car).

By the way— about the motorcycle— Well, we did hafta have something to get about on— all the rest of the girls have bought 'em so Grace Stevenson and I bought one together. We rode it to London Sunday— me on the back cause I haven't learned how to run it yet. You should have seen us going down the middle of London on that motorcycle— me holding on to Grace with one hand and a big suitcase in the other. I found out the next day that riding on the back of that thing is worse than riding a horse so— now we have decided to save our money and buy a side car.

Chapter 4
A VISIT FROM ELEANOR ROOSEVELT

September 14, 1942
Monday Morning

Dearest Mother:

Just a note to let you know I am still O.K. Last week, as I wrote you, I took a little cold that settled in my chest and the station Doctor sent me away for a couple of weeks rest. He said I had been working too hard and needed to just do "nothing" for a while but sleep and stay in bed and that's what I have been doing for the past week. When we first came over we met a man, Wing Commander Cotton is his title, and is quite well known over here. Well, he has a beautiful apartment in London that practically overlooks the entire city and he has given it to us American girls to have as our head-quarters when we are sick or want to stay in London. He also has a big estate near Maidenhead on the Thames and he lives back and forth between the two places. Well, anyway, to make a long story short, that is where I am now, in London and have been here for the past week resting up. One of the other American girls, Virginia Garst, from Kansas City, is here also. She had her appendix removed a couple of weeks ago. We are planning to go down to the estate in a day or two and stay down there in the open air and sun-shine for a few days, then it's back to work for me. I guess I did need the rest after all, then too, when I go back I am starting out on my conversion course to twin equipment and will need all the energy and strength possible.

Thanks for sending the money for the motorcycle, guess you think I am crazy to buy one but it is lots of fun and make it much easier to get around. Don't worry about it, I'll be careful.

I am enclosing a picture of me with some of the other girls. It was made about a month ago when we all got together to celebrate one of the girls' birthday.

I do wish I could write you the things I would like to for there is really lots to talk about, but as per usual they are the things that can't be said, so you see my letters must continue to be dull repeti-tions of "I'm still safe, well and happy." However, these many things will keep till I get back then we will have a long session of doing nothing together but talking and catching up on the happenings of the past few months...

Sunday Morning
September 20, 1942

Dearest Mother:

Yesterday was truly a red letter day for me, not only did I get a letter from you, Martha, and Aunt Claudia but, I also received your package containing the scarf and socks as well as the candy from Martha. It was almost like Xmas getting so much mail and the packages. Thanks so much for the scarf; you have no idea how useful it's going to be this winter cause it's just what I needed to use when flying. The socks were very nice ones and just the kind I like, however, should you send any more make them black ones then they can be worn with my uniform. I am going to dye the ones you sent me. It seems a shame to do it but I can't use them otherwise and they are just what I needed. As for the candy, well, I almost fainted when I saw it. That was exactly the amount we are rationed for three months, except what we get isn't half as good and without nuts. It is impossible to make you realize how much all the things you all send me are appreciated; it's not because of the lack of things over here, it's the quality of American goods that's so outstanding and make them priceless to us over here.

You mentioned something about rationing and you don't see how the people here would get along this winter as far as food is concerned. Really, I hope you believe me when I say this, it's a shame the way they print such nonsense in the newspapers back in the States. Of course things such as foodstuffs and clothing are rather strictly rationed over here, but— not to the extent where anyone will actually suffer. After all, this is the first war I have ever experienced, and the last I hope, but at the same time I haven't found the little sacrifices I am making to be what one would term a hardship. Of course you see we have our breakfast and dinner at night in our billets, that is where we live, and we are given the very best because we are in the forces; while at the different aerodromes we always eat in the Officers mess and there again the food is not too bad. You see, there is really no cause for worry so stop believing all you read in the papers.

You know when you keep writing me about the different people that call and ask about me as well as the things they think and are saying in reference to my job, it makes me feel so little. After all I am doing no more than those people would be doing should the opportunity present itself. Through God's help I hope I'll never let those people down but will always to the best of my ability be able to execute the duties entrusted to me however small or great they may be. Thank goodness you never did oppose me in my plans, even tho everyone else did think I was crazy and would never amount to a hill of beans, you always stood up for me.

Well, I go back to work Tuesday after two weeks of doing nothing. I can assure you I am ready to get back on the job although I guess the rest has done me lots of good.

Guess you have seen the news in the paper about the newly organized Women's Auxiliary Ferry Squadron there in the States of which Jackie is in charge. That is the result of her efforts of some time and I wouldn't be surprised if eventually we were re-called for service with that group. That would be swell if they did do that. If not, I guess when my time is up over here that is what I will get into. I just can't get away from the fact that the sky is my home as long as there is a place up there for me....

"Somewhere"
September 26, 1942

Dearest Mother:

While I'm sitting here waiting, I'll start this letter to you. At present I am at an Aerodrome waiting to collect a ship to deliver " Somewhere " in Scotland. I am at an aeroplane factory where they make the type ship I am to deliver and it's quite an interesting place. This is my first trip here, however, but I do like coming to this particular place because we always get new equipment to fly. I have been very lucky so far with the equipment I have been given to deliver, most of it has been new stuff which of course does make the trips more fun when you don't have to worry about your ship and how it's gonna behave.

You know, I really do wish you could be with me at times when I get a nice new machine and have a long hop to make. I am sure you would truly enjoy not the aeroplane ride so much as you would the view you would get of this little Island. It's different from anything I have seen before— so green— a deeper and fresher looking strictly from any I have ever seen before and it all seems to have been laid out according to well made plans thus giving you a beautiful patchwork quilt effect when flying at about 3,000 feet. I would love to make pictures of this but- since there is a war on the only pictures that can be recorded are mental ones.

Tuesday
Sept. 29, 1942

Once again I will try to finish this letter that I started 3 days ago— Since then I have delivered my ship, came back by train and am now sitting and waiting on the weather to clear so I can go again.

The weather over here is beginning to get cold and wet and believe me the scarf you sent me is already being put to good use. I fly with it around my neck by day and wrap my feet in it at night. I do hope you can send me the hot water bottle cause that is what I need most of all now.

I am feeling exceptionally well now after my 3 weeks leave. Guess I did need the rest. I am taking my vitamins and think I have plenty to last me. Also I am taking ultra- violet-ray treatments 3 times a week which the Doctor said I needed since I have been use to lots of sunshine and— sunshine is one thing we have very little of over here.

Well, how is Jeaneane and school- I think of her so much- I I know she is going to be smart as a whip and truly whizz thru her studies— I know Martha will never hafta make her study like you had to keep after me. Those must have been awful days for you when I was "just getting by" in school. Sometimes when I think back over those days I don't see how you had the patience you did have with me. I really wasn't dumb tho—I just didn't like what I was doing, oh well....

Tuesday Morning
Oct.13, 1942

Dearest Mother:

This is truly a life of living out of a suitcase— I have been seconded (transferred) for a period of two weeks duty at another pool and that's where I am now. After my two weeks here I go back to my home base. Where I am stationed now it's entirely a woman's pool— it's commanded by a woman and we only have women pilots working out of our base. It is however, quite a nice place and I like it for a change. Another one of the American girls was posted down here with me and we have found a very nice place to live— it's a large country home, plenty of heat, hot water, good food and the people are lovely to us—a middle age couple. This is really the nicest place I have lived since I have been in England.

You would have had a fit had you seen us on the way down here Sunday— you see I am now the proud owner of a motorcycle with sidecar— So, We packed our luggage in the sidecar on top of the other girl, and away we went. When we got about half way here we ran out of petrol and after walking six miles and doing some fast talking we managed to promote a pint, enough to get us to the next town where we were lucky enough to buy a gallon which was plenty to finish our trip on. But— as luck would have it, when we got within eight miles of our objective the chain broke on the bike and— We had to finish the trip by transport. Some fun !! It's fixed again now !!

Received the cheese last week, and thanks lots. I haven't forgotten about the picture and will have one made the next time I have some leave and can go to London.

The letter you received from Scotland was written while I was on a trip- I do write once a week but I am sure you do not receive all my letters.

So far, the weather has not been too bad— a bit damp and foggy but I think I am getting used to it. Believe me, I think if I ever get back home I'll go to Florida for the rest of my days. Maybe I won't freeze to death down there.

Well Mother, as usual- there is no writeable news. I'm still well- safe- and happy...

There is no way to know what gradually begins to change Hazel's mind about serving the full eighteen months in the A.T.A., but the re-occuring asthma and the prospect of another cold winter in England, seems to weigh on her mind. She mentions that her work is "sorta tough " and at the same time speaks of the newly organized American Ferry Command as a possibility for her to continue flying. There is no doubt that Hazel's health is a real problem for her and is belittled in her letters to her mother. Cold shots, ultra-violet- ray treatments, and sick leaves are only casually mentioned.

Saturday
Oct. 24, 1942

Dearest Mother:

Just came in from London where I spent three days leave at an American Red Cross Club. It was simply wonderful being with a group of Americans, eating peanuts and drinking Coca Colas once again. The Red Cross has set up this Club in a big house just for members of the American forces and A.T.A. girls. It is an Officer's Club and they have a number of bedrooms fixed up to accommodate American girls only that are over here in the services. All of the girls that stay there are either Red Cross workers or nurses from the States and they have made special arrangements to take care of us should any of us get sick. One of our girls has been there for the past couple of weeks with the flu and you not only have nurses looking after you but they call in American Doctors as well. Believe me it sure is swell to have a place like that to go.

The weather has started to get cold and wet so I bought me a pair of fur-lined boots to wear with my uniform as well as to fly in. The boots they issued me are so big until I can get both feet in one boot. They don't make the flying boots small enough to fit me, that's why I bought a pair— had to have them made up specially for me and I had to pay a pretty price of $30.00. That's the way everything is over here now tho— sky high. Just cause they know they can get whatever they ask. It's a darn shame!

Even tho things are sorta tough, I still like my work and wouldn't take anything in the world for having come over here. Maybe by next Spring the American Ferry Command for women will be better organized and have something to offer— if so I'll come back and go to work for them. I understand they are only flying light equipment right now- Well, that's what I have been doing for the past five years, that's why I came over here. Maybe by next Spring they'll give them Sho-nuff aeroplanes to fly, if so I'll come home.

Doesn't time fly— do you realize I have been flying five years in January ? It has taken a lot of work and worry but I think it's been worth it. I just hope that some day I may be a success with it and I think maybe I will if I keep on trying.

Well, Mother, I hope you are well— I'm O.K. I am taking cold shots now in hopes they will do me some good this winter. I'm also taking ultra- violet- ray treatments to take the place of the lack of sunshine over here...

Tuesday Night
Oct. 27,1942

Dearest Martha:

Thanks so much for your letter received yesterday- it came over in record time- 12 days. Most of my letters are from 3 weeks to a month getting here. So you have changed jobs, well, just as long as you like your work and the pay is good I guess that's all that really matters. As for me, I really don't give a darn about pay, it's the work- if I am really interested in what I'm doing then I know I can do a decent job if I try, and believe me I'm trying to the extent of a bit of overwork now. I wrote you about being on the "sick list", so to speak, well, after three weeks complete rest I am back on the job again but- as per Doctors orders I am taking things a little slower now. There was nothing seriously wrong with me, just the usual thing of asthma, which incidentally I fear is slowly coming back, plus the old heart business— all of which is not organically wrong but can be taken care of by lots of rest. So, I am slowly turning in to be a veritable old maid whose life consists of an eight hour work day, twelve hours sleep, and, an occasional quiet evening at the movies. It's simply shocking to think of how I have suddenly settled down and completely resigned myself to a sane and simple life of doing nothing but a few hours flying each day and spending the rest of my time waiting for old age to creep up on me.

Tonight I am in Scotland— delivered a ship up here this afternoon- 475 miles in 1 hour 45 minutes. And- I'm taking a sleeper back tonight where I came from which, will take only 14 hours for the return journey—"the slow freight". What a way to travel!! Give me the sky any day!

Yesterday was a most eventful day for the American A.T.A. girls. We had the unusual honor and pleasure of having Mrs. Roosevelt and Mrs. Churchill visit the Aerodrome for an inspection. As luck would have it, it was a typical English October day, cold and raining up a storm. They lined up the different types of ships that we fly and in the awful rain we had to stand outside by the ships while Mrs. Roosevelt walked by and was introduced to us. She asked me where I was from and I told her Macon, Georgia, near Warm Springs. She smiled a big smile and said, "Oh yes, how well I know where that is." After the review of all the girls, we went to the Officer's Mess where we had a cup of tea with her, Mrs. Churchill and Mrs. Hobby, head of the newly organized W.A.A.C. back in the States. I had quite a long talk with Mrs. Roosevelt and she was quite pleased with our type work over here and said she was sure the U.S. would soon find need for us in similar capacities. She certainly is a swell person and truly beams with personality and is most gracious and friendly in manner. We all assembled in the hanger where she was introduced by the Minister of Aircraft Production, Col. Lewellyn, and she made a short talk. Even tho we did hafta put on skirts for the occasion, stand in the rain for half an hour and almost freeze to death, I guess it was worth it.

About those items mentioned in your letter that you were sending to me: don't worry if you can't send much, just the cigs, candy and peanuts. If you can't do that, I'll be O.K. anyway cause we are well taken care of as far as food goes. The cigs would mean an awful lot to me cause they can't be bought over here and believe me I do enjoy a good American cig whenever I can get it.

Yes, I have been thinking about the American Ferry Service that has recently been organized. Guess that is what I will do when I get back to the States. Of course, I came over for 18 months service but- I might just make it a year and come home about April or May. It just all depends on me and how I make out physically and with the work. So far, I have advanced right along and am due for another promotion as soon as they have room for me on a conversion course.

I will take more training on bigger types and I am sure I will be able to handle the equipment without any trouble.

So Jeaneane likes school, I knew she would and am sure she will always be the outstanding one in her class cause she is smart as a whip. I think of her so much and really do miss her and the other two children. Give my love to Gene and Mother -take care of her and let me know how she is all along. Must go now and have my dinner for I've gotta go catch that slow freight....

Lotsa Love Always,
Hazel

In a later letter to her sister, Martha, (December 16, 1942) Hazel presents a more colorful picture of Mrs. Roosevelt's visit to the Aerodrome:

I saw an article in the *Telegraph* about Mrs. Roosevelt visiting us over here. It said she was making a speech when we had an air raid— Well they are all wet— She had finished her speech and we had had tea with her in the Officer's Mess and had just told her goodbye and she had driven off from the Aerodrome when the alert sounded. I never shall forget it for more than one reason— the first being we all had our skirts, shoes and stockings on and had to go down in this air raid shelter that was ankle deep in water— It was very funny— there we all stood for about 30 minutes freezing and puddling around in the dark in all the muck and water trying to check up and see if all the American girls were accounted for. Then we sang songs to the top of our voices until it was all over. So you see— we don't work all the time, we take time out for a little fun and song once in a while even if it is forced upon us.

Chapter 5

IN PRAISE OF THE ENGLISH PEOPLE

Tuesday Morning
November 3, 1942

Dearest Mother:

While I sit and wait on weather I'll try to get this note off to you just to let you know I'm still O.K. and happy over my job but— a wee bit homesick. Together with shorter days and bad weather I now have more time in which to do nothing but read and write.

Once again I have been transferred to another "pool" for a period of three weeks duty. There's one thing about this work, when

I finish my time of service over here I'll know this little Island better than my home state of Georgia.

As I travel from one part to another I wish more and more for you, Frankie and Martha because of the extremely interesting historic places, old English homes, and people. At present, while I am located up here, I am living in a very old English home which is really an estate. It is a huge place about two miles from the Aerodrome and seven miles from town. It is the home of Sir Lindsay and Lady Everard. The Aerodrome was their own private Aerodrome in peacetime. Really the surroundings and atmosphere remind me of a typical Southern plantation. The house itself sits back off the road with a long gravel drive among evergreen trees leading up to the front of the house then circles back down the road. The house proper is nothing less than a small hotel and although I have been here now 3 days, I haven't seen one third of the place yet. There must be at least 40 rooms in the place apart from the fact that there is a huge room equipped with ping pong table, a ballroom for dancing with a Radiogram providing dance music, and yet another specially constructed room in which the old famous English game of Squash is played. The room is sound proof, specially lighted, and a spacious balcony for spectators is provided at one end of the room. As you can see, this is quite an Estate and still carries with it much of the true English air of formality. We have maid and butler service and all meals are served with pomp and ceremony that one would expect to find in a place of this type. I must say I do like it all and wouldn't mind staying here for the rest of my time in England, however, that will not be possible, I fear.

Off on one side of the house are located the garages which can accommodate no less than 25 automobiles, and which is incidentally now full of cars most of which have been stored for the duration. Above the garages are about twenty small rooms very clean and nicely furnished with lavatories in each room and steam heat. This is where I am living, two other girls and myself. About 500 yards from this part of the Estate is located the stables in which they now have only about 8 horses. Believe me this is quite an establishment!

Well Mother, outside of telling you about where I am living, there is no writeable news. I will say that I am making definite plans to return to the States in April— then I will have served a year which I am beginning to think is about all I can take over here right now. I'll no doubt go back and get in the American Ferry Service which I think would really be the best place for me due to the climatic conditions over here....

Mary Holtzclaw who wrote for the *Atlanta Journal* seems to have followed Hazel's progress in the Air Transport Auxiliary. The following description was written for a requested article to be published in the paper. Some of this letter was censored, leaving a few gaps as to times and places.

Thursday
November 5, 1942

Dearest Mother:

Had just posted a letter to you this morning when I received two from you, September 23 and 30th. Although there is really no news of interest to prompt my writing this letter, I thought I would try to give a brief picture of my work so that Mrs. Holtzclaw would have something around which she could build her own story. I do hope she will not attempt anything until this reaches you. Also, in regards to pictures, I am afraid such shots as would be preferable for newspaper copy is out of the question, since pictures cannot be made of us while we work. Then too it is practically impossible to get films to make pictures with. However, I am having a picture made this week at a London studio which I do hope reaches you before too long. Maybe she will be able to use it.

Really, you know the things I would like to write cannot be written, so— it is quite difficult to try to outline my activities so that there is anything interesting. Just the same here goes, hope she can find something worthwhile in it. Understand, this is just an outline- she'll hafta rewrite it.

It was on [censored] that we disembarked at a [censored] coast Port after spending [censored] on a British Boat, having left the Continent by convoy from [censored]. The crossing itself was very quiet and we were four of the eight passengers on board. (The passenger list was: we four American girls- Grace Stevenson, Oklahoma; Virginia Garst, Kansas City; Sue Ford, New York City; and me. There was a British Consul and his wife. They said they were on their way to China via England, why, I can't imagine. Then, there were two Canadian boys coming over to join the Air Force.)

We were met by a captain with A.T.A. and escorted to London by train. Here we stopped at the Savoy Hotel where we were guests of Jackie Cochran for a couple of days. We then reported to White Waltham Aerodrome, Maidenhead, which is only 30 miles from London. This is headquarters for A.T.A. Here we met the well known Pauline Gower, Commander Women's Section A.T.A. and incidentally one of the first to organize A.T.A. three years ago. We then met Commander D'Erlanger; he is the "big boss" of the 540 pilots in A.T.A. of which 100 are women (22 American women). We were then issued with flying equipment, maps, etc. and taken to another "pool" about 70 miles away for our primary training. Here we were located in homes (billets as they are called). We had to start our training by attending ground school for a month studying navigation, meteorology, aircraft instruments, map reading, and code. We then took to the air once again in a small low wing trainer similar to our Ryan S-T. In this we learned to navigate and read our maps and got used to finding camouflaged Aerodromes. Incidentally, I had no trouble spotting the Aerodromes due to the fact that I am color blind. We also flew our own Fairchild-24 on some of our cross-country trips.

With reference to flying cross-country over here- it is quite different from flying back home. This little Island is so thickly populated until you are never out of sight of a town or village. The whole land is covered with a net-work of railroads and highways that weave in and out in most curious fashions among the small green farms and hills. Another interesting fact is that no matter where one may go on this Island, they are never more than 70 miles from the coast. When flying you are always within 10 minutes of an Aerodrome. Never have I seen so many Aerodromes in such a small space.

While taking our primary training, which lasted 3 months, we were cadets. After passing flight and navigational tests we had earned our wings and another stripe which made us Third Officers. We were now allowed to ferry all types of Class I Aircraft which were the lighter type ships.

Right here I would like to tell of my first real job. I was given two chits (order slips) for delivering two planes. They were Tiger Moths (same type as at Great Lakes) and I don't mind saying I really felt important. On this particular morning, we had arrived at the Aerodrome at the usual time for reporting-9 o'clock. We received our chits about 9:30, I dashed off to collect my flying suit and kit bag from my locker, ran down to the parachute room and collected my chute. It was at this point that I looked at my orders again to make sure of my destinations then off I went to the "Met" (Weather bureau or Meteorology office) to check the weather along my routes. Then- off to the "Maps and Signals" Office to check for balloon barrages along the proposed routes and got the signal of the day. By this time it was 9:45 and they were calling me over the "blower" the P.A.,(public address system or broadcaster- whatever one rather call it), for Third Officer Raines— so-in-so to report to Taxi Plane No. 2479 which was waiting outside of Operations to take us to our Collection points. So, in a wild hurry, I snatched my kit up, pulled out the maps I needed for my job, quickly plotted my courses, and away I ran to the waiting taxi plane. It was one of the usual taxi ships which is a twin engine ship that will carry about 14 people. I tossed my chute and bag in and almost fell in after them in haste. After pulling myself together I stood up and looked around at the seven other pilots- all women- then I looked up in the pilot's seat- my goodness- another woman. It was quite an odd scene for me, here we were - 8 females starting off on a day's work and no men to worry with. Capt. Crosley, our pilot, and one of the best in A.T.A., taxied the ship out to take-off position with as much ease as tho it were only a Cub. The engines and instruments were checked, then into wind and off we went with the greatest of ease. In 20 minutes we were circling the Aerodrome where I was to pick up my first ship. After going to the Collection department where I picked up the log books I walked out to my machine to find it was a new one just assembled by the factory at this station. After getting into my flying suit and chute, I crawled in the Ship and found everything in perfect order except the rudder bars which were so far away until I almost had to lie down in it to reach them. There was absolutely nothing that could be done to shorten them so- I knew I had to fly it in that way. Just the same, I started my machine up, set my compass, taxied out, and into the air I went feeling quite proud and most important. After turning "on course" and checking my first check point (land mark), I settled down in the cockpit for my 30 minute trip. Because of my "prone" position in the ship I could not see where I was going, therefore, after about 20 minutes, I pulled myself up and looked out to check my position to find out I was only 12 miles off course. I immediately corrected my error and 20 minutes later reached my destination. My second job was more successful, the rudder could be adjusted- therefore, not one time did I vary off course because I could see and keep check on my check points. After reaching my second destination and turning over my log books, chit and aircraft to the receiving station I had to wait a couple of hours for the taxi ship. It finally picked me up about 4 o'clock and we were back at our base at five- my first day's work successfully completed.

Due to the fact that most of us that came over here have had quite a bit of experience, we were not kept on the light ships but a few days. Just long enough to learn ferry procedure. We were now sent back to White Waltham for Class II Conversion which is a period of training for flying fighter type aircraft, usually single-seaters ranging from 800 h.p. to 2000 h.p. Again we had to attend ground school for 3 weeks after which we had ten written examinations to pass on such subjects as— Aircraft Instruments, Propellers, Aircraft Construction, different types engines, fuel systems, superchargers, boost control, Mixture Control and Carburetors. I am sure I did more studying during these three weeks than I ever did as long as I was in school. However, I must say I did enjoy the course and did not mind having to burn the Midnight Oil, which is most unusual for me.

After passing the ground school tests, we were put on Harvards (A-T-6 as they are called back home- this is the ship we took our flight check in while in Montreal). I put in 4 hours in this ship and was then passed out for the single-seater fighters. Never shall I forget the first flight in this type machine. It was almost as thrilling as my first solo five years ago in a 40 h.p. Taylor-craft. This time I knew it was up to me entirely since it was impossible to be given any dual on this ship. There she sat— to me, the largest aeroplane I had ever seen, and as I looked at her from about 50 feet, I slowly walked up and said "Good Morning Chum." She looked at me and made the most gosh awful face and seemed to laugh out loud at the tune my knees were playing. I fooled her tho by getting in and showing her who was boss. After three weeks of circuits and bumps, we were the best of pals and just getting to like each other when they passed me out of the school back to ferry flight with a promotion to Second Officer and two Yank stripes on my shoulder.

This just about brings me up to date for my job now, as it has been for the last two months, is ferrying this type equipment. This I can truthfully say is the most interesting job I ever had— breezing along at 250 miles per hour over Scotland, Wales and England.

The other day I was informed that I would be re-called to the School again for further training on all types of twin engine equipment. This I am looking forward to, for after I complete this course, I will have flown practically every type Aeroplane that has been built by the United States and Great Britain. Of course, there are the four engine Ships which I never will fly because of my size— but that's O.K. with me. This job I'm doing now is really the realization of a dream I've had since I first started flying—a dream I had no idea would ever come true because it was too fantastic. But, it just proves the fact that one never knows what they can do until the opportunity is presented to one. Maybe after this is all over I'll know a little something about flying, I hope so anyway!

This, I am afraid, is about all I am allowed to say in connection with my work. Later perhaps when this is all over maybe I will be able to share with you some of the most exciting and interesting experiences I have ever had in this flying world.

In regards to the people over here and life in general on this little Island, there is quite a bit that could be said, however, if I really started on that phase of my experiences over here, I could write almost twice as much as I already have. I would like to say I have found the people most hospitable and friendly. Of course, it must be understood that the English people are quite reserved and are not as quick to make friends as we Americans however, after the ice is broken, so to speak, they are much the same as we. The spirit of these people is most amazing considering all they have gone thru. It also surprised me very much to find life going on in a sane and normal way. As for bomb damages, there is quite a bit in certain areas and even that is being immediately cleared away and made ready for rebuilding. As for air raids, well, as a general rule the people take about as much notice to a siren as a telephone ringing and go on their way just as tho nothing at all was happening. Really, it all is most amazing the way these people carry on- only we who are here and can see- know how to appreciate these people who certainly deserve all the praise and respect in the world for doing a swell job that I am sure we would have found very very hard to take had such blows and hardships been thrown in our face suddenly. Personally my hat is off to each and every person living on this little Island. They can truly take it! Also, each and every person is doing his or her bit toward helping win the War. There is not an idle hand, no matter how young or old— there's a job to be done and believe me these people are doing one and I am sure some day they will be rewarded not thru ultimate victory alone, but through and by One that hold the fate of us all in his all powerful and justifiable hand.

And so— I feel that I have had my say— at least all that I am allowed to say because, as I have told you before, my true life is none less than a military secret.

Best of luck in translating my scratch....

Hazel's praise of the English people sounds somewhat like that of Winston Churchill after the War:

"There were times he said, when the English, and particularly Londoners, who had the place of honor, were seen at their best. Grim and gay, dogged and serviceable, with the confidence of an unconquered people in their bones, they adapted to this strange new life, with all its terrors, with all its jolts and jars." (Leonard Mosley, *Battle of Britain.* p. 136.)

The issue of the motorcycle is finally resolved. In a letter to her mother, Hazel decides aeroplanes are easier to handle:

Friday Night
Nov. 20, 1942

Dearest Mother:
Here it is almost Christmas once again and another year gone. Believe me, this past year has truly flown by and I don't really feel as though I have accomplished a thing. Oh, it's true, I have seen a bit more of this wicked world in which we live, and have flown a few more hours as well as new types, but other than that, I can't see

where I have done any real good. Guess I'll have to see what I can do about it during the coming year. Something tells me my outlook on life is getting too serious—maybe I'm getting old.

Well, it's almost moving time for me again. I'm supposed to go back to the "old home base" Monday after three weeks here. I think I wrote you about the home I am in. It has been a very comfortable billet with the exception of no heat. They do usually have a big log fire at night in the drawing room but-that's all. I must say, however, I haven't found the cold weather so hard to take. They tell me I haven't as yet seen any cold weather. The only thing I do know is-it's already as cold as it gets at home. So, I can't imagine what the winter will be like.

Today was quite a day for me. Again I would like to tell you all about what I did but the only thing I can say is— I flew another new type aeroplane, one I have never flown before but always wanted to fly. It was a wonderful ship — a single seater fighter and one you perhaps read about every day in the papers as having taken part in a raid over Germany— an English fighter. It is really a lovely aeroplane to fly and we cruise along at about 230 miles per hour. This is indeed just the type flying I always dreamed about, never thinking for a minute I would ever be allowed to fly such equipment. I always thought you had to be a super person to handle such ships but — it's really the easiest job one could have. Our biggest problem is weather over here, and that's what we have to watch so closely. We are not allowed to do any instrument flying, although , I have been caught several times where I had to go on instruments due to the fact that all I could see was my instrument panel.

Sunday Night
Nov. 22, 1942

Received a letter from you today written Oct.31 saying you had not heard from me in a month. It must be that one of my letters has been lost because I do write at least once a week and most of the time twice.

From the questions you asked, you must not receive all my letters cause I have written all you wanted to know. However, I will answer your questions here and hope you receive this letter.

First of all, I have received two cartons of cigarettes within the past three weeks from Martha. Tell her thanks so much and please keep on sending them- at least three cartons per month.

Yesterday I received the fruit cake and believe me, I am glad it did not get lost. I haven't unwrapped it yet cause I am saving it for Christmas. Thanks so much for sending it to me. I know I will enjoy it- I'll feel like I'm home when I'm eating it.

You asked how much I weigh now. Well, I now weigh 135 and am not loosing any weight at present.

The climate is O.K. I can't say truthfully that it fully agrees with me because it's so cold all the time but it's not bad. Yes, my contract went into effect the day I signed it in Montreal which was April 14th. That means my time will be up over here next Oct.14th. However, my plans are now to make it just a year. I can't say definitely just what I will do. It all depends on how I get along over here with my work and physically. Also, it depends on the war situation, and what my chances in flying would be if and when I return to the States. There will be a lot to be taken into consideration, because just as long as there is the least thread of hope for a place for me in the flying world, I intend to not only stay in it, but keep on going forward.

In regards to the motorcycle, I only kept it a month and sold it for just what I paid for it. You see, I first started out with a half interest in one, then sold out to one of the girls and bought me a cycle with a sidecar. After riding it a month, I got fed up with the thing. It was so cold and windy riding it and with wet roads, ice and snow, I thought I had better sell it before I spun out on it. It was lots of fun having it but I decided it was not too safe...

Hazel neglects to mention the hazard of the balloon barrages to her mother but Diana Barnato Walker, who was a British pilot in the A.T.A. from 1941 to 1945 mentions them:

The reasons for making us do so many cross-countries were for us to gain general flying experience, become familiar with the country, and see for ourselves the actual whereabouts of the many hazards such as balloon barrage areas. These were enormous hydrogen gas-filled silver balloons on very heavy cables which went up to cloud base or to 5,000 feet, placed around sensitive areas such as factories, certain aerodromes, town and cities to keep German aeroplanes high up, accurate bombing being difficult through cloud or from altitude, nor could their fighters' ground-strafing come off. It was also easier for our early radar tracking and anti-aircraft defences to target higher flying intruders. We marked these barrages on our maps in heavy red pencil so that we could decide routes to give them a wide berth. The cables were dangerous to fly into; I think they got more of us than the Germans. (Diana Barnato Walker, *Spreading My Wings*, p.51)

She also described other daily hazards of the A.T.A. pilots:

"When I was delivering aircraft to some of the forward fighter bases along the south coast, I would often see the V 1s (flying bombs) coming in over the sea from the direction of France. Sometimes they would fly across in front of my aircraft." (Ibid, p. 157)

Up until November 20, 1942, Hazel's log book recorded that she had been flying mostly Hurricanes and Fairchilds. However, on this date, she flew a Spitfire from Desford to Lichfield.

MO. DAY	FROM	TO	TYPE OF AIRCRAFT	TYPE OF ENGINE	H.P.	LICENSE NUMBER	DURATION HRS.	MIN.
11 18	Ratcliffe	barse	Fairchild	Scarab	175	KV 200		15
11 18	barse	Waddington	Fairchild	Scarab	125	KV 250		20
11 18	Waddington	Ratcliffe	Fairchild	Scarab	175	KV 250		20
11 20	Ratcliffe	Dishfield	Spitfire	Merlin 45	1250	KS 179		20
11 20	Dishfield	Lichfield	Spitfire	Merlin 45	1250	KS 179		10
11 26	Lichfield	Aston Down	Hurricane	Merlin II	1200	HV 603		20
11 26	Aston Down	Little Rissington	Master	Mercury II	885	HV 922		20
11 29	Rissington	Ledden	Fairchild	Scarab	175	HK 341		30
11 29	Ledden	Ratcliffe	Fairchild	Scarab	175	HK 341		20
12 2	Ratcliffe	W.W.St.Mary	Hurricane	Merlin II	1200	KV 922		30
12 14	Halfworth	Brill Avington	Hurricane	Merlin II	1200	V 268		45
12 27	Win Avington	Moret Farm	Spitfire II	Merlin 61	1500	EN 299		10
12 29	Moret Farm	Blawbarden	Spitfire II	Merlin 61	1500	EN 299		45
12 29	Blawbarden		Spitfire II	Merlin 61	1500	EN 299		15
12 30	Locon	Brden	Spitfire II	Merlin 61	1500	EN 299		15
12 31	Brden	Willavington	Hurricane	Merlin II	1200	KX 236		20
12 31	Willavington	Lyneham	Hurricane	Merlin XI	1200	KX 221		20

YEAR 1942

TOTALS 1448 00

Page from Hazel's Log Book
1942

Chapter 6
CHRISTMAS WITH LADY ASTOR

Saturday night
November 29, 1942

Dearest Mother:

Although there is no news at all to write about, I will drop you a note to let you know I am O.K. I am back at home base again and from the looks of things right now I will be here for several months. I was supposed to start back in school again this week for twin conversion, but will not be able to do so for a couple of more weeks due to the fact we have had so much bad weather lately they have got us all out on the job ferrying whenever the weather is good. As soon as we get caught up on our work, and there is room for me in the school, I will start in on twin equipment.

Another one of our girls left for the States several days ago. She was Virginia Garst from Kansas City. She had her appendix removed two months ago and since then hasn't been well at all, so they decided it was best for her to return home. That makes three of the girls that have gone back, we only have nineteen now.

All of us have received Xmas packages from home and we are planning to get together Xmas if we don't have to work and have a little party. I think it will be lots of fun to get our group together; we have only had one party when we were all present since we have been over here and that was just before Jackie returned to the States.

I am very lucky in having a good warm billet for the winter. The people where I am living are swell to me. I have been with them since the first of July. Their names are Mr. and Mrs. Roy Littlehales and she was at one time quite a famous singer on the stage in New York. She is 43 and he is 53; her mother lives here with them as well as her married daughter who has a child three years old. Her husband is in Egypt and has been for three years— he has never seen his son. They are truly a swell family and call me their daughter, and— treat me as tho I really were. So, don't worry about me, I am getting the best treatment and food. I don't know how they do it but the food is very good. Of course we do have brussel sprouts and potatoes almost every night but they get very good steak and veal for me which is a real treat. I also have a big glass of milk and some fruit every night. The fruit is usually stewed apples or pears but, I have learned to like a lot of things I would never have thought of eating before I came over here.

Just to give you an idea of how ridiculous some of the prices are, I must tell you of my experience in one of the stores yesterday. We got away from the aerodrome rather early so a couple of the girls and I decided to go to a show. We were walking down the street looking in shop windows and saw some white grapes for sale. Immediately we thought we would buy some to eat in the show. We walked in and asked how much they were a pound, well, I almost fell over backwards when she told me thirty-four shillings per pound, (seven dollars). We just smiled, said thank you and walked out the door. Of course everything is not quite so unreasonable but that will give you an idea how unreasonable most things are.

By the way, I have had a sudden spell of bad luck with stockings. If you can still get them back home I could use a couple of pair of tan ones.

I am sending you a picture I had made in London the other day. It isn't very good cause I was tired and not feeling too good when I had it made. Also, I am sending you a picture of me with Mrs. Roosevelt when she was over here. It was made in front of one of the aeroplanes I fly and isn't a bad picture even if it was made out in the rain...

Hazel's letters continue. She is receiving packages from home and saving them for Christmas with the Littlehales. A letter of December 1, 1942:

"I wrote you about the people I am living with and how swell they are to me, well the other night they wrote you a letter. I thought it was sweet of them to write you. They are really good people and believe me they treat me as tho I belonged to them. They do all they can to make me happy and comfortable. Mrs. Littlehales, I call her Olga, is a very good cook and she cooks me a hot meal every night when I come in. So you see you have nothing to worry about as far as my welfare is concerned. In fact, there is nothing to worry about at all."

The following letter is from the Littlehales:

"Harefield"
River Road
Taplow. Bucks.
30. 11. 42

Dear Mrs. Raines,

I thought you might like to hear from me- as your Hazel Jane is staying in our house. She has told us such a lot about you and the beautiful Georgia.

In the first place- I must tell you that Hazel Jane is very well and full of "Pep". We think she is a lovely girl and just as sweet with it. I know she is happy with us and I am sure you will be glad. I do hope the weather won't be too bad for her. Our climate is rather treacherous.

We are going to try to make it a Happy Christmas- but many loved ones will be away.

I hope you will have a Peaceful Christmas- you will miss your Hazel- as she will you. Hazel looks fine in her uniform-we do so admire her. In fact, my husband calls her his second daughter- I think he wants to write a little here.

I think I will butt in here to say she is just the sweetest and swellest girl that the United States could send over, and we are indeed lucky to have met her. If you should lose her, you will know we can't part with her. To crown it all, come over and see us, as we are quite sure such a grand little woman must have as equally charming Mother. Au Revoir, and here's to our meeting in happier times.

My daughter Jill- who is 23 years old - now wants to say something.

The only thing I want to say is that I think she is 'just swell'.

Do not worry over your Hazel Jane- I love her as my own daughter. I will write to you from time to time- telling you about her.

With very best wishes-
Yours very sincerely,
Olga Littlehales

Saturday
December 5, 1942

Dearest Mother:

Just received your letter written Nov. 19. Also received the package with the hot water bottle etc. Thanks so much for the nice things, they really will come in handy, 'specially the hot water bottle. Tell Jeaneane and Martha thanks so much. Haven't received your package yet with the ham and nuts but guess it will be here in a few days.

I do wish you would not worry about me so much. I am feeling fine now and resting lots. Just had 4 days posting leave- that is I have now been posted to a definite pool where I will no doubt stay as long as I am in England. Due to bad weather, I have not as yet started my twin training but expect to start any day now. I am so glad they posted me here cause then I won't have to worry about moving back here when I go back in the school for my twin time. I have really been lucky cause some of the girls have been sent all over the place.

Now about coming home. Well, I think I will stay at least a year. You see my year is over April 14 which is only 4 months from now. The contracts were signed for 18 months which would make the contract expire Oct, 14th. So—if everything continues to go O.K., I will definitely stay until April and maybe next October. I don't like the idea of breaking my contract. Three of the girls have already done so and returned to the States, but I like sticking to my end of the bargain cause I do want my record to be clean and straight. It will be a darn good record to fall back on for reference for another job— in fact, the best and it never hurts anyone to have as many good references as possible— specially in this flying world.

Again, I say- please don't worry about me and my health. I am feeling fine, getting lots of rest, staying warm and the food is not bad at all. Olga and Roy, where I am billeted, make me eat all the time and they give me the best of everything. Sometimes I worry for fear they are saving me their ration, for I get steak at least three times per week and a big glass of milk every night before I go to bed. Olga is simply wonderful to me, she treats me like a baby, just like you do. She wraps my pajamas around my hot water bottle and puts them in the bed every night after dinner so they will be warm when I am ready for bed. " Uncle Roy" wakes me every morning at 7:30 with a hot cup of coffee. So, you see I really will be a spoiled child when I get back.

We American A.T.A. girls are planning a Christmas party about December 16 at a place in London where we can have turkey and all the trimmings. Olga and Roy are also going to get a turkey for Christmas so- you see I will be well taken care of.

Well Mother- guess this is about all for right now. Have to see about writing you more letters than Martha! Take care of yourself, Give my love to all the family ...

Apparently Hazel waited about three weeks to write her next letter because she spent this time in a Canadian Hospital near Maidenhead. However, this unfortunate event resulted in a unique experience for her.

December 23, 1942

Dearest Mother:

Another Christmas is almost here and once again I find myself far away from home; in a place more distant and strange than anywhere I have yet been privileged to travel. Although this will not be the happiest holiday I have ever spent, it has all indications of being the most interesting and educational.

So that I may give you as graphic a picture of my present surroundings, I must digress a bit. I had not planned to tell you of my past ten days experience until I returned home for fear you would worry- but since there is absolutely no need for any undue concern and worry on your part, at this point I can say I have been on sick leave again. About two weeks ago the doctors decided I needed a rest and general check-up. They found me a bit run down. So, I remained in the hospital until yesterday, just resting, sleeping, and eating and I must say I do feel better now. They have suggested that I take it easy until the first of the year when I plan to return to my work. So, by the time you receive this letter, I will be hale and hearty once again and back on the job. So- you see you have no legitimate cause for worry.

Now, to get back to my original story. While spending this time at the Canadian Hospital, I had quite an experience. Last Saturday, I was sitting up in bed talking with three of the American girls who had come in to see me, when, like a shot out of a shell, this middle-aged woman came bursting into my room and said- "Where is that Gal from Georgia? I want to see some good old Southern blue blood." I sat up in amazement and said: "Here she is —so what?" With that, this little woman who was moderately dressed, said, "Well, honey chile, I'm from Virginia and I know all about us folks from the South and if you are from Georgia, I know I'm talking to a lady." In the meantime the other girls had gotten up and were standing almost at a stiff attention and were looking rather ill at ease every time I made a remark. Just the same this unusual visitor started talking about the South and started making slight remarks about the fact that a Southern girl would come off her dignity and do such an unladylike thing as fly. Well, that was enough for me, so I started in and told her just what I thought of flying, as well as the people who do, and that I was of the opinion that the women of today were doing a man's job in a woman's world with unfaultering ability and finesse, and to me if a woman of her integrity could not see it in that light, she must be a very narrow-minded person. With that remark, she stopped and looked at me- then said: "Well, that's the first time in my life I have ever had anyone speak to me in such a frank manner, but- Georgia, I like you." I said it didn't really matter to me whether she did or not, that I was just expressing my inner self. She finally said she had to go but would see me the following day. Not having remembered her telling me her name, but thinking she was just another Red Cross worker, I said, "Say, what's your name?". She smiled and said, "Georgia, my name is Lady Astor." I just laughed and said, "So what!", thinking she was still joking. She laughed with me and said she would see me the next day. When she left the room, the girls almost had a fit. Seeing nothing funny to laugh at, I asked them what was wrong. They said, "Well, even though you would not believe her- that was Lady Astor." Gee, how was I to know? They had seen her before, I had not.

She kept her promise. For the next day, she did come back and in quite the same mood. She brought a friend of hers in to see me. He was Ambassador Phillips, President Roosevelt's personal Representative from the U.S.A. to India. He was enroute to India, having stopped in England on official business before going to his post. She informed me she had talked with my Doctor, Col. Walton from Canada, and had been given special permission to have me over to her home to spend the day with her on Monday. On Monday morning, I got up, dressed, and was taken over to the Astor Estate, which is known as Cliveden. The day passed much too quickly, for I had a wonderful time, not only talking with Lady and Lord Astor, but looking around the Estate. I was told that Cliveden is one of the largest and most historical estates in England. I will tell you all about the place in my next letter for I am afraid I won't be able to get all I want to say in this one.

Both Lord and Lady Astor were lovely to me and treated me just as though they had known me all my life. I have never been made to feel so much at home during a first visit to a new and strange place as I was that day with them. When I started to leave that afternoon after tea, Lady Astor called me into her study and informed me she had made arrangements with the hospital for my discharge to her care, and I was to come to Cliveden the next day and spend a week with her (from Tuesday, December 22nd to December 29th). And so- yesterday, I came over here for my week's visit and that's where I am now.

I do wish I could write and tell you all about everything but it is just impossible to do so....

                                                        Thursday Morning
Well, I'm still having a wonderful time being treated like a queen here at Cliveden. Yesterday after lunch I went for a walk in the gardens with Lord and Lady Astor where we made some photographs. Soon as they are developed, I will send you some reprints.

Lady Astor and I had quite a time teasing each other. She informed me last night that the real reason she invited me here for Christmas was she wanted her four eligible sons, who are here for Christmas, to meet a lady from the South in hopes one of them would fall for me. I told her that was a good thought on her part but I didn't think I was interested or ready just yet to even contemplate falling in love with anyone- not even an Astor- because I came over to do a job as yet my job had just begun. Although I was frank about the situation, she seemed to like me all the more. She said it odd to find a young girl these days who wouldn't jump at the chance to marry someone with money and a name. I told her that was not what I was looking for in life. Oh, we had quite a talk which I will have to tell you all about when I get home....

December 28, 1942

Dearest Mother:

Well, another Christmas has come and gone and for some reason I am glad this one is over, even tho it was quite a nice one for me. I wrote you about going over to Cliveden, Lady Astor's estate, well, I stayed with her until Christmas Day and then came back to my billet to spend the rest of the holidays with the Littlehales. Lady Astor insisted that I stay with her but I just couldn't because I had promised the people I live with I would be with them; and then too I knew they had not only planned to have me with them, but they made such a special effort to get everything possible so that I would be happy and would not get homesick. We had a twenty pound turkey with all the trimmings, then I dug down in my trunk and got out some nuts along with the delicious fruit cake you had sent me. So you see I was well provided for, and am sure I will always be taken care of in the best sort of way as long as I am with these people, and that will be as long as I am in England. I do wish you could see what they gave me for Christmas, one of the most beautiful yellow gold cigarette cases I have ever seen. They had engraved on the inside, "To Hazel Jane with love from all at Harefield—1942". (Harefield is the name of the house here. All English homes are named and have the name of the place on the front gate, and they all have gates cause they all have fences around them.) I hope you note the Hazel Jane, that's what they have always called me, in fact that's what everybody calls me now. By the way, why not have Martha type out a letter as coming from all the family in appreciation for all they have done and are doing for me.

It is almost impossible to write you all about my visit to Cliveden. I must say it was a most interesting experience and the palatial mansion fairly reeks with a historical stench that can be detected time one passes through the massive gates which form the entrance to the one mile drive up to the mansion. On Christmas Eve, I went for a walk with Lord Astor all over the Estate at which time he told me the entire history. We also made some pictures which I am sending you as soon as they are developed.

Lord Astor told me that the original Cliveden was built in 1650 by the Second Duke of Buckingham who, in 1668 ran away with the Countess of Shrewsbury and brought her to Cliveden. While they were in the act of running away, they were overtaken by her husband who fought a duel with the Duke and was killed. When they arrived at the mansion, he buried his sword he had killed her husband with in the garden by the east wing of the mansion and the date 1668 he had patterned into the grass with cross swords running thru the date. From that time on the grass has been kept cut so that the date and pattern can be plainly seen and that's the way it is today. The original house was burnt down in 1795 and a second built but pulled down where a third was built in 1830. This third was also burnt and yet a fourth built in 1849 by Lord Astor's father and remains as we see it today. It was built from designs by Sir Charles Barry.

I wish I could describe the inside of the place, but since I can't as it should be done, I will mention several interesting things I noted. In the great hall, where you find yourself when first entering the house, are huge tapestries that were put there in 1700 by the Duke of Orkney. They are truly wonderful works of art. At the end of the hall is a massive fireplace of stone, which comes from the great Spitzer collection, and was installed by Lord Astor's father in 1890. To the right of the fireplace hang two of Sir Joshua Reynold's paintings. At the other end of the hall, which is about 400 feet in length, is a beautiful oak staircase. As you walk up the steps, there are carved effigies of past owners and people that were connected with Cliveden in some way. At the top of the stairs is a carved figure of Jack Shephard who was a notorious English highwayman.

Oh, I could go on for pages telling you all about the place but since I am no good at writing descriptions, to say nothing about my spelling. We'll just reserve the rest till I get back, then we'll sit and talk for hours. The pictures I am sending will help make up for what I have not written.

Now for a few words about me. I went over to the hospital this afternoon and had a final check-up. The Doctor said I was O.K. and has recommended that I go back for a month's duty then return to the hospital for another physical. I can truthfully say I am feeling much better after my three weeks rest, and intend to do everything they tell me to do, such as get plenty of rest and drink lots of milk. I am drinking a quart a day, go to bed at eight and get up at eight. Now don't worry because I am perfectly O.K. All the rest of the girls have had the same trouble due to the fact that for us all it has been quite a drastic change; English weather and diet, and we had just been rather slow in getting used to it, but I'm sure we are in the groove now.

By the way, I am enclosing a picture that was made when Mrs. Roosevelt was over here. I am also sending some larger ones under separate cover that may be used by Mrs. Holtzclaw if she so desires....

The following letter is from Lady Astor:

Miss Raines
Air Transport Auxiliary
White Waltham Aerodrome Nr. Maidenhead, Berks.

Cliveden
29th. December 1942

Dear Hazel,
I am so grateful to you for the wonderful parcels. It really is much too kind of you. And such nice things.
I shall not eat everything myself, but will take some things along to an old lady whom I know will appreciate them very much, and to whom I like to give something.
I do hope you behaved yourself on Saturday night.
With all best wishes for 1943.
I hope we shall see you soon.

Nancy Astor

When Hazel visited Cliveden in 1942, both Viscount Waldorf Astor and Nancy Astor were sixty-three years old. This was the same year that Waldorf offered Cliveden to the National Trust. "Its upkeep had become ruinous and he felt very deeply that it had long since ceased to provide a family centre."(Derek Wilson, *The Astors,* 1993, p. 328). This was the end of an era for Cliveden which had been the site of political activities and house parties in the 1920s and 1930s. "Cliveden was an enchanted kingdom and Nancy was its queen." (Ibid. p.247.)
One wonders if "the old lady" to whom Nancy Astor refers might be the same one in the book, *The Astors,* p. 213.

Once, riding with the children near Cliveden, she (Nancy Astor) encountered an erect, elderly woman dressed in black. Nancy accosted her. 'You shouldn't be walking on the road. Where are you going?' The stranger, obviously very poor and very proud, intimated that her destination was none of her ladyships's business, but Nancy persisted and eventually learned that the woman was destitute, had no family and was on her way to the workhouse. 'No you're not,' Lady Astor ordered. 'You're to go along this road until you come to the big gates. I'll meet you there.' Having issued her instructions, Nancy hurried back to make impromptu arrangements for the reception of her new 'guest'. The end of the story was that the old, woman spent the rest of her days at Cliveden-fed, clothed and comfortably housed.

As to why Nancy Astor would invite Hazel to visit Cliveden in 1942, no one will ever know. However, Nancy had succeeded in a man's world as Britain's first female Member of Parliament and had played a prominent role in women's' reforms such as equal opportunity with men and equal pay. She was known for her humor and perseverance; both traits were prominent in Hazel's character and Nancy seemed to assume a motherly role with Hazel. Hazel was trying to succeed in the field of aviation by becoming one of twenty-two women taking part in the British Air Transport Auxiliary in 1942. The male pilots and many military figures were opposed to this plan, even though the jobs these women did, freed a British pilot for combat duty. So 1942 came to a close, and was a memorable year for Hazel. Her ambition of "adventure, new worlds to conquer" and wanting to "meet new people" was coming true. And to quote Hazel, "above all, I have discovered the sky is my home."

Along with the letters written in 1942 was a poem sent to Hazel by her sister, Martha:
"By the way I got poetic the other day and wrote a poem to you. From some things in your letters, I imagine that you feel just as I have written."

"To Hazel"

I have a wonderful feeling
when I'm flying alone High above the clouds,
In the Sky- my home.

As I fly along
and look down from above
I can't help but feel
God's wonder and love.

All of my sorrows,
my troubles and care,
Seem to vanish completely
when I'm flying up there.

I am merely an atom
on the large world below,
But when I'm in the sky
I always seem to know

That He cares for me

As He loves every man
and even I have my Place
in His Infinite Plan.

And when that day comes
that I vanish from sight
I know He will be waiting
when I make my last flight.

Chapter 7
"JERRY" PAYS A VISIT

Saturday Night
January 9, 1943

Dearest Mother,

Today I received three letters from home- one from Martha written Nov. 23 and two from you, Nov.28 and Dec.1st. These are the only letters I have gotten from you all since the last of November. I have been told the reason for such delays in the mail now is, there is not any more air mail to the States or to England. Haven't received your last parcels yet either but imagine they will be here soon now. They should have come over when your letters were sent.

About the pictures in *Life*, I haven't seen a copy but I guess that was me. I was standing behind the platform while she made her speech. I'll never forget that day because the weather was awful and we had to stand out in front of the hangar by the aeroplanes we fly while she reviewed us. Hope you got the picture I sent you that was made while Mrs. Roosevelt was talking with me about Georgia just after she left the aerodrome. The worst part of it all was I had on a skirt and nearly froze to death! After being so used to wearing my long-handles and slacks all the time, it felt as tho someone had left the back door open.

Lady Astor seems to be quite fond of your daughter. I wrote you about my experience with her at the Canadian Hospital, then spending a week with her at Cliveden, her Estate. Since then I have received two letters from her inviting me back to see them again. I have two days leave coming up the last of the month and I think I will spend it with her. She has arranged to take me to see George Bernard Shaw as well as the House of Commons where I can "sit in" on a session. You see, she and Lord Astor both are Members of Parliament.

Haven't done so much flying lately due to bad weather. We washed out 3 days this week due to snow and rain. They say we will get lots of snow and bad weather now thru March. Had a job today from a field that was completely frozen over with snow and ice everywhere. Saw my first snow storm the other day too. Had a plane to deliver from "Point A to Point B" and ran into a heavy snow storm. As you well know, it was the first storm of that type I had ever seen. Therefore, as I was approaching it, I thought it was just low white clouds and I would climb on top and continue my trip. Well, I started climbing as I ran into the stuff and found it not to be soft fluffy clouds but snow and hail. Immediately I turned and started back the way I had come and put in at the nearest aerodrome and got on the ground just in time. They all had a good laugh at me when I got back for not knowing the difference between snow and clouds- but how was I to know, I am the only one in the group that has never seen a snow storm.

Looks as tho I will be stationed here for the rest of my stay in England, however, that suits me fine cause the people I am living with are swell to me and my billet is warm and comfortable, which is a lot more than the rest of the girls have. I don't think I could have found a better place to stay if I had looked all over England.

Well, I'm still ferrying single engine fighters and guess I'll stay on this type of equipment until Spring. I had hoped to go on twins this month but my C.O. said he had rather I stay on singles a while longer because I had such a good record: no crack-ups or damages to any equipment as yet and I hope not any at all ever— so keep your fingers crossed. I never thought I would get used to flying along at 250 miles per hour but now it seems easier than flying a Taylor-craft and I think it's a lot safer.

By the way, does Wes Raymond still have a school out at Herbert Smart Aerodrome? Believe me, that's one guy I'll never forget or forgive. I think I still owe him about thirty dollars, but that is one debt that'll never be paid and if you see him, you can tell him I said so. And, speaking of debts, thank goodness I am in the clear again. I never intend to have another charge account as long as I live, it doesn't pay.

Well, Mother, looks like I am out of news again. Hope this letter doesn't take forever to reach you. Take care of yourself and give my love to all the family....

In a letter in late January, Hazel reassures her mother about all the war news:

Have just finished listening to the 9 o'clock news from London and I imagine the way you look at it back home it wouldn't be too good to be over here now. Well, don't you worry, things are not as bad as they seem. We pay as little attention to it all as possible and just continue with our work as per usual. It's odd the things one can get used to that one never dreamed they could.

Tuesday Morning
February 2, 1943

Dearest Mother:

Just finished reading the swellest letter from the sweetest person in the world, the letter you wrote Mrs. Littlehales. Last week I wrote you about being transferred from here. Well, I came back here yesterday to spend four days leave. They insisted that I spend my leave here, so rather than going up to London or staying in Southampton, I thought it best to come back here where I can do just as I please and rest lots. I will be here until Thursday— then back to my pool for duty Friday Morning.

Yesterday I stopped by White Waltham to see the M.O. (Medical Officer) and had a thorough check-up. He said I was O.K. in every way but to stay on the safe side, he suggested that I see him once a month for a complete physical. I must say they really look after us but then it is no more than they should do because after all, we must be even more fit for this type job than was necessary for the kind of flying we were doing back home. The aeroplanes are so different in speed, handling and navigation and in case of emergency, you don't have time to sit and debate with yourself what you will do- you must decide immediately and act accordingly. But it's great fun and I love every minute of it.

Olga, (Mrs. Littlehales) has read your letter about a dozen times already. Never before have I seen anyone appreciate a letter any more than they seem to appreciate the letter from you.

It was such a swell letter and I must say I was so proud of you when I read it. It was so sincere until I could almost hear you saying those things in person. It's a darn shame it has taken me 26 years and 3,000 miles between us to make me fully realize what a swell Mother I have. Oh well, we'll have a great time when I get back— won't we? You bet we will! There will be so much to talk about until I'll just hafta take at least a two months vacation.

Don't know exactly what to say in regards to my returning home. After all, you know I did sign up for 18 months and since things are going O.K. at present, it looks as tho I might stay until my time is up which will be next October. Of course lots can happen between now and then, so time alone can tell. We won't worry about that but will just let the situation take care of itself......

Harefield
River Road
Taplow Bucks
Eng:

10th Feb. 1943

My dear Mr. Raines-

In the first place I must thank you for the beautiful letter you sent me. I shall cherish it. Secondly, to receive such a lovely parcel almost took my breath! You really are a Dear and I cannot thank you enough.

Hazel Jane was here when your letter arrived- she was spending four days leave with me. You can imagine how pleased she was, too. Hazel Jane looks very well and is. Do you like the photograph she sent you? I have one and I think it is beautiful.

I expect you will be rationed for everything soon- though I don't suppose quite as much as we are. The clothes are an awful nuisance- 20 coupons for six months do not go far. I have not worn stockings for about a year. All through the winter I wear slacks most of the time- but the wind still blows up one's legs most of the time. I must say, we have had a very mild winter. I am so glad, for the Americans feel the cold dreadfully.

The floods have now subsided and we've only had one lot of snow so far.

We took some snapshots of each other- Hazel, Jill, and I (Uncle Roy never seems to be there), so will send you some if Hazel does not. We must get Uncle Roy, Nan and Baby in next time.

Through Hazel Jane, I feel as though I have known you for years. She has told me all about you and how you looked after her and did everything for her, and you have from her a great love- she adores you. Perhaps one day we shall all meet- who knows? I think we shall be rather overcome if we ever do.

Once again- thank you so much. I must tell you before I close, that Hazel will be coming here again March 4th and this time, I think permanently.

God bless You. I'll look after your Hazel.

With my love-yours very sincerely,

Olga Littlehales

In a letter to her mother dated February 18, 1943, Hazel presents an amusing picture of the A.T.A. group:

You should see us in the morning when the weather is too bad for flying; some play cards, some knit, some read and others write letters as I am doing now. The room is a continuous buzz of feminine chatter and sounds more like an over crowded parrot shop than an Officer's Mess. The topics of conversation would slay you—Anything from the discussion on the technique of how to fly such-in-such type machine to how many children so-in-so is going to have after the War.

Conversation about how "to fly such-in-such- machine" was not surprising, for many times they "had no experience flying many of the aircraft types, but they would read the pilot's manual for the plane and do their best." (Vera S. Williams, *WASPs*, p. 21)

Possibly a more realistic picture of what was happening in England is written in a letter to her sister, Martha, dated February 18,1943:

We had a bit of excitement the other day. Just as we started out to go to work 'Jerry' paid us a visit [censored] that'll teach us to pay more attention and heed Air Raid Warnings from now on cause as a rule we take no notice of them but just go on with our work. The other day I delivered a Spit to an aerodrome and after landing and getting out of my ship, I looked around for someone to turn the papers over to but couldn't find anyone. Thinking they had all *gone out to tea.* I just sat down by my ship and waited but not for long— I soon found out there was a raid on so— I still sat and waited till it was all over. Some fun! What burns me up is—- they give us the best fighters built to fly but minus ammunition. How I would like to take a shot at one of those so-in-sos!

Hazel later stated that the German plane sprayed machine gun bullets across the field and "that the German's aim at them was not so good, but (he) damaged the equipment they were to use that day and killed three men."

The newsy letters to her mother continue. Hazel had been posted to Southampton in a March letter. What she fails to mention until later in the month, is that she has been in an English Hospital for ten days. On March 2 while flying in a Spitfire IX, she crashed when the engine quit after taking off from Hamble. This is recorded in her log book but not mentioned until the news has traveled to Macon.

YEAR 1943		AIRCRAFT		PILOT, OR 1ST PILOT	2ND PILOT, PUPIL OR PASSENGER	DUTY (INCLUDING RESULTS AND REMARKS)
MONTH	DATE	Type	No.			
—	—	—	—	—	—	—— TOTALS BROUGHT FORWARD
2	13	Spitfire XI	EN347	"		Colerne — Benson
2	13	Fairchild	FK333	"		Taxi
2	14	Fairchild	FK179	"		Hamble — Portsmouth
2	16	Fairchild	EV789	"		Taxi Pilot
2	18	Hurricane	KX461	"		Hullavington — Kemble
2	19	Fairchild	HM174	"		Taxi Pilot
2	24	Seafire	NM927	"		Chattis Hill — Wroughton
2	24	Seafire	LR635	"		Wroughton — Lee on Solent
2	25	Spitfire VIII	BF327	"		Eastleigh — Brize Norton
2	25	Fairchild	EV789	"		—
2	26	Spitfire VIII	JF334	"		Eastleigh — Brize Norton
2	26	Spitfire V	AB392	"		Brize Norton — Swindon
2	27	Seafire	NM934	"		Hamble — Wroughton
2	27	Fairchild	Hm174			Taxi
				Summary for February, 1943		1- Spitfire
				Unit : #15 F.P.P.		2- Hurricane
				Date : February 28, 1943		3- Master
				Signature Hazel Raines		4- Fairchild
				Aircraft Types :		5- T-Moth
3	1	Spitfire IX	EN490	"		Eastleigh — Cosford
3	1	Spitfire V.B	AB366	"		Cosford — Swindon
3	2	Spitfire IX	EN205	"		Hamble — (Crashed Collingbourne Kingston)
				Summary for March 1943		
				Unit : #15 F.P.P.		1- Spitfire
				Date: March 31, 1943		
				Signature : Hazel Raines		

GRAND TOTAL [Cols. (1) to (10)]

.................Hrs.................Mins.

TOTALS CARRIED FORWARD

Hazel's Log book on crash.
1943

Chapter 8
DROPPING IN FOR TEA

Hazel received many letters while recuperating in the Canadian General Hospital. This one was apparently written by an employee of the Ferry Pool, possibly a cook. It is obvious Hazel is not only a favorite but also a tease.

March 11, 1943

Dear Miss Raines,

We were so glad to hear that you hope to leave hospital at the end of the week and I just thought I'd like to send a message myself.

I miss you very much and have to remind Mrs. Clark that you do not allow her to bully me. I think she'd help me to make a fuss of you , if only you were back; anyway she wouldn't grumble over stained knives.

I'm not getting on very quickly with my cabbage patch, but I've optimistically planted parsley and radishes, now I have to pray for rain and lots of luck.

Mrs. Salmon has started digging a patch for herself, so I'll be left in peace with my little plot. I can picture my crop and as a result can now understand how it is possible to have such lovely drawings on seed packets; they are done by gardeners and it is wishful thinking. Anyhow, even if I don't know as much as Mrs. Middleton, I can dream.

Miss Stevenson occasionally comes in with a hungry look in her eye— you see, you've got to get well quick, you feed her and inspire me.

There is another nice American here now—Miss Nancy Miller, but I'm still waiting for your return. I feel sure you ought to get lots of milk and everything you fancy to eat, like nice sandwiches with lots of French mustard!

Anyhow, I am concentrating on you and hope you will soon be back amongst us. I don't have anyone to tease me and I miss it so much. Best wishes for a quick recovery.

Yours sincerely,
Helen Clemmitt

In corresponding with Nancy Miller Stratford, who was a member of the A.T.A from July 1942 until July 1945, she stated that "It's good to know (Mrs. Clemmitt) thought me nice!! It's strange that we Americans did not know each other better. I was fairly shy, and one of the youngest. Primarily we were not stationed together as a group— as Hazel mentions, she was moved to different pools (stations), as were most of us were at various times. Also we were billeted in different houses with British families."

Wednesday Morning
March 17, 1943

Dearest Mother:

This business of writing is getting to be more of a problem each day due to the fact of limitations as to writeable subjects and, you well know my one subject of interest, whether writing, talking or sleeping is—Aviation, and that is the most restricted of all topics in this day and age.

Instead of 4, they are giving us 6 days leave per month and I'm now taking a couple of days off to catch up on my letter writing and try to mend a few socks. Grace, one of the girls from Oklahoma that lives down here with me, is also on leave and we two have been busy doing nothing together. She and I are living with Mr. and Mrs. G. A. Porter who are a couple about 40 and extra nice to us. They have a lovely home down here right on the ocean front and only five minutes walk from the Aerodrome.

I have once again taken up my childhood hobby of planting radishes. Two weeks ago, I planted two beds of radishes which have met with "foul" play. The birds seem to like them better than I and have scratched them all up. So— yesterday I replanted and put some wire mesh screening on top of the bed. This should protect them O.K. Yesterday afternoon when Mrs. Porter came home, of course I was feeling quite proud of what I had done, so I invited her out to see my new effort. Well, you should have seen the look on her face when she saw what had been one of her choice flower beds. I thought they were just weeds so I dug in. How was I to know?

Grace and I are going in to Southampton this afternoon and take in a movie for a change. I have asked Mrs. Porter to go with us to sorta help make up for my mistake yesterday.

By the way, the new picture of me that I sent you for xmas came out swell in the *Teleqraph*. They made a mistake about my rank however, I am a Second Officer instead of First. However, by the time you get this letter, I will probably be a First Officer. Second Officer is the same thing as a 1st. Lieut. and First Officer is the same as Captain in the U.S. Air Corps. As for stripes on my shoulder, I now have one wide and one narrow which means Second Officer. First Officer stripes are two wide ones. The lighting on my picture made it look like 3 instead of one and a half.

Well Mother, it's almost lunch time so- I'll say so long for now. Hope you all are O.K. Give my love to all the family, specially the children. Hope they won't forget me. I'm sure I won't know them when I get back....

Hazel finally mentions, to quote Hazel, her "funny experience" of having crashed, but only in a casual way at the end of the letter. A more accurate description is written to her sister, Martha in a later letter.

Sunday Morning
March 28, 1943

Dearest Mother:

Yesterday I received a letter from you written on March 10th. Gee, it was swell getting a letter from home in just a little over two weeks. By the way, next time you see Mr. Willis, please tell him I asked about him and send my love and hope to see him when I return home next fall. I'll send that card to Mrs. Tinsley this week. It was swell for her to ask about me.

Did I tell you- I got a long letter from Emma Lovejoy about 3 weeks ago. Also, I got a nice letter from Aunt Mattie in Dublin. She told me about Martha getting married and said she was living in South Carolina where she and her husband were working.

Gee, I do feel as tho I am getting quite old when I hear about all my younger cousins getting married and joining the Army, Navy, etc. Really tho, you know I don't feel any older than I did when I was 17 and here I am almost 27. I just can hardly believe it!

Last Monday I went up to London and spent a couple of days sitting around the American Red Cross Club drinking Coca Colas and eating ham sandwiches. They have truly been swell to us since we have been over here. They have fixed up a house for us so we have a place to stay when we go to London. The house has been given to just us twenty American A.T.A. girls and we also have the use of the Club which is open only to American Officers and Nurses. That's the only place you can get a "coke" in England and the food is real good too. They try to fix things American style but somehow they don't quite make the grade. No fried chicken— in fact, I haven't seen any fried chicken since my last Sunday at home last March. So— here's wishing you lots of luck with your chickens cause the very first day I'm at home when I get back, I want some fried chicken and lemon pie.

By the way, while I'm thinking about it, I think it will be best to cancel my subscription to the *Telegraph* as of August 1st. Send it on to me thru July but after then you might as well stop cause it usually takes about 2 months for it to get here and you see I'll be coming home in October if not sooner. That was certainly a good idea to have it sent over to me and I have been enjoying keeping up with all the home town news. It was interesting to note that at last the public schools have waked up enough to incorporate a simple course in Aeronautical Science at Lanier Hi for Boys. Guess they have the

silly idea that such a subject should not be taught to girls. Maybe
they'll wake up in another 50 years. I also noticed an article about
Wesleyan College publishing a brief book telling all about their up-
to-date varied departments of study for the young women of today
but— no facilities, as yet, have been arranged for a simple ground
school course in Aeronautical Science. If they could only see what
the young women in England are doing now, I am sure they would
wake up and alter this biased curriculum. I hate to think of the possibility of my three nieces going thru high school and college
without a chance to learn something about Aeronautical Science.
But here— let me stop before I get strung out on something I don't
know much about myself.

By the way, now that it's all over, I'll tell you all about a funny
experience I had some time ago. I would have told you sooner but
was afraid you would worry, now, there's nothing to worry about.
On March 2, I had a (censored) to deliver from "A" to "B" but, after
leaving "A" and getting half way to "B" the thing got tired and just
refused to run any longer; so not having enough altitude to jump, I
stayed with it and had quite an interesting ride thru a house and
wound up in somebody's front yard right in the middle of their
newly planted flower garden. No one was hurt 'cept me and I only
got a bump on my head and two beautiful blue knees.

The people that lived in the house were thrilled to death over
the fact of having a (censored) take off the top of their house, and
were yet more·excited and pleased when they saw it was a girl flying
the machine— and an American at that! They were certainly swell
to me— they took me in what was left of the house and cleaned me
up a bit and sent for an ambulance to take me to a near-by hospital.
I was only knocked out for about 15 minutes, had a slight concussion, and a small cut on my forehead. You would really laugh if you
could see me now— they had to shave off half my hair on the right
side of my head and I now look like a prisoner from Sing Sing. The
only reason they cut off so much was cause they thought I was hurt
much worse than I really was. Anyway, it's growing back now and
will be good as new by the time I get back home. They took 13
stitches in my head just above my right eye but- my eyes are perfect-
didn't hurt them at all. Saw the Doctor at Maidenhead yesterday and
he said I could go back to work next week. I've been up 4 times
since the accident and can hardly wait to get back on the job. Won't
be allowed to fly anything but twins tho cause I can't wear a (censored) yet but I don't mind cause I like twins much better than
fighters. I was only in the Hospital 10 days- an English Hospital and
to top it all off, they put me in a Maternity Ward cause they had a
full house and couldn't accommodate otherwise.

I've never had so much fun in all my life. You should have heard me giving advice and comfort to expectant mothers. You are right, I will have lots to tell you when I get back. Don't forget there is no need to worry now that it is all over, cause anyway, time you get this I will be on the job again. They did find out the cause of the engine failure and I was held *not responsible* for the accident. So, everything turned out quite O.K. Yes, never a dull moment!

Well, Mother— guess this is about enough for this time. Now please don't worry cause I'm O.K. Just take care of yourself and please do what Dr. Chrisman tells you.....

Among Hazel's memorabilia, is an ashtray made from the propeller of an airplane, which Roy Littlehales gave to her shortly before she crashed. The inscription reads:

To Hazel Jane, the Spitfire Queen
With love from Uncle Roy
January, 1943

Saturday Night
April 3, 1943

Dearest Martha:

Guess I've neglected you lately, haven't I? So sorry, but the reason has been a good one. I wasn't quite sure what to do about writing Mother about the accident I had last month but finally decided I had to mention it to her just in case it got back to the States and got in the papers. Of course I didn't tell her what actually happened for fear she would worry unduly. By the way, I had rather you would not tell her you received this letter from me.

Yes, Sis- I was sure (as we say in the Air Force over here) "I had Had it." But Lady Luck was truly with me on March 2nd. I was flying a (censored) when the engine quit— went thru a house, lost my wings, aeroplane a complete write-off; of course I don't remember anything after seeing the houses coming up in my face until I waked up in the Hospital. I was darn lucky, only got a rather bad blow and cut on my head. They had to take 13 stitches in my forehead above my right eye. The cut runs back in my hair just where I part it about an inch like this—— (picture drawn) 'cept it was on the right side. They had to shave off all my hair on the right side cause of the cut and I thought I had a fractured skull but I didn't— thank goodness. The stick beat up my knees rather badly and my right one is still rather stiff and sore but will be O.K. in time. Only stayed in the Hospital 2 weeks but- I'm still off duty due to a bit of eye trouble. The blow seems to have affected my right eye. My vision comes and goes but they tell me it will be O.K. in time. I'm going back to see an eye specialist in London Monday and see what he thinks. If they decide that I won't be able to fly again for a few months, I guess I'll come home. It sure is a tough blow for me but— I guess I can take it. If I do get O.K., I am planning to renew my contract for another year. If I do, I hope to get a few weeks vacation and try to arrange to fly back home. I'm not too keen on going back on a boat.

By the way, have you ever changed my account at the bank to a savings account? I see no need in having a checking account. Now, if you need any money for anything, you can always make a withdrawal. What's the balance now?

Well Sis— so much for this time— I know so little news to write cause all I do is sit—read only a little cause I can't use my eyes too much , and walk over to the Aerodrome occasionally. Kiss Jeaneane for me and write soon. Let me know how Mother is getting along….

Lots of Love Always,
Hazel

Hazel continues to write her mother, leaving out that she is grounded due to head injuries. She is not allowed to fly for three months from the date of the crash.

Friday Afternoon
April 2, 1943

Dearest Mother:

Due to the high winds we washed out this morning so Grace and I came back to our billet and have been doing a bit of nothing today. Told you about re-planting my radishes after the birds dug them up— well, my second effort was not in vain cause they have at last come up. The next time we wash out I'm going to plant some more radishes plus some corn. You know the people over here don't know what corn is —they call any grain that grows, corn. Well, I found some sweet corn packets in a flower shop and bought all they had. Mrs. Porter told me I could plant some in the back yard but I think she is a bit doubtful as to the results of this new effort of mine as well as this "funny vegetable" I want to grow. Isn't it awful, I think these people have missed half their life, never having eaten corn on the cob and fried chicken. We have also been trying to pull a few strings and promote a chicken of some description so we can show her what's good. Don't worry, we'll get one somewhere. If one is lucky enough to get one they charge about 12 shillings for it ($3.00). It's hard to believe isn't it?

We have invited a few of the girls around tonight for a little party we suddenly decided to have. I have been busy this afternoon making sandwiches- tongue- cheese- and watercress. Guess we'll have a game of cards, play the victrola and perhaps dance a bit. You see, we have learned how to amuse ourselves in a quiet and simple way but then we have to do something now and then cause there's no place to go and even if it was, we wouldn't have any means of transportation. Then too- going out at night isn't the best thing to do because of the blackout. You see everything over here is always blacked out from sundown to sunup. The cars that do run have the faintest sort of light and unless the moon is shining you can hardly see them. It will indeed seem odd when I get back and see the lights at night again on the streets and thru the windows of houses.

Now back to a bit of talk about my job. They have asked me to sign up for another year when our contracts expire. Personally I don't know what to do about it. My contract is not up until Oct. 14th and even tho that is 6 months from now it will soon be here. Several of the girls are going to renew their contracts, but plan to fly back to the States the last part of the summer if it can be arranged. They will return only for a month, then back to England. Somehow I feel that is what I should and want to do. I am not keen on returning by boat but if it can be arranged would fly back. A.T.A would give me the money it would cost on a boat and I could make up the difference. It would be rather expensive, but much the safer way to travel I am sure. I think they will allow me 80 pounds ($320.00) and the fare would be about 120 pounds ($480.00). Well, I can save the difference— What do you think about this idea? You see I could be at home longer if I traveled this way. Then too— if things look good for me over there, I wouldn't have to come back. It's just that I feel at present that the opportunities are greater for advancement over here. If they would only realize that "that it can be done" by a woman in the States the same as they are doing it over here! You see if I do decide to make it another year, I'll no doubt come home earlier than originally planned. I'll probably try to arrange something for July or August. Oh dear— I never could decide things for myself— guess I've always depended on you too much.

Planning to go back to Maidenhead in a couple of weeks for a conversion course and will be with the Littlehales while I'm there. They were certainly good to me when I was in the Hospital last month. They have a duck that lays an egg per day and they sent me that egg every day while I was ill. I spent seven days with them before I went back to work...

Several articles about Hazel were published in 1943: One in *Mademoiselle,* "The Magazine for Smart Young Women",(February, 1943) and a newspaper article about her crash in the *Macon Telegraph* (June 20, 1943). It is unfortunate that we do not have a record of Hazel's comments on the article in *Mademoiselle,* for she would certainly have made some. It read as follows:

DIXIE CALLS THE ROLL

It's out of hoop skirts and into dungarees and denims for southern belles! War has come to Dixieland, and these girls of the deep South are in it.

There was a time when their background below the Mason Dixon line was a romantic combination of ruffles and moonlight, magnolias and nostalgic melodies of the Land o' Cotton.

But today the southern belle stands against a wartime background of airplanes, riveting machines, test tubes and codes. She rises before sunup... she's greasy and tired before sundown. She's tight-lipped, determined, but she's enthusiastic. She's at work...at work on a war job.

For women to do their part in wartime is as traditional to the South as corn bread and turnip greens, Aunt Pittypat and you all. Our great grandmammas before us, during the War Between the States, melted their prize pewter so their fighting men could have more bullets.. and that is just one example of how southern women will stand behind their men at war.

But you are wondering where all these southern girls are working— in what war plants— for the land of Dixie has never boasted of as many factories as farms. The answer is: a boom has swept southward! Furthermore, it's a woman's world in Dixie now. The women are wearing the pants— and literally.

Georgia, you know, is proud of its "firsts" and "onlys," so this state boasts of the fact that Hazel Raines, 26, of Macon, Georgia, is the only girl from the entire southeast in the British Air Transport Auxiliary. Hazel graduated from the Wesleyan Conservatory in '36 and was the first woman in Georgia to secure her commercial pilot's license. She was one of the few women in the country chosen to be an instructor in the Civilian Pilot Training program, and she held that post until a call came from Jacqueline Cochran, asking if she would join other American women aviators as flight instructor in the RAF. So Hazel took her place in the first line of defense. Her duties as a member of the Air Transport Auxiliary in England are exciting and varied. She moves costly and valuable aircraft; ferries wounded planes fresh from bombing in Germany to a factory for repairs; flies without the aid of radio beams, pilots all types of planes, flying them from factories and stations anywhere in the British Isles...

The *Macon Teleqraph:*

Macon Girl Is in Crack-up
While Flying in England

When Macon's Hazel Raines crashed in England recently she made just as much of an impression by her efficiency as she has in her work as a ferry pilot.

There are not many who have heard of her crash, so I will tell you at the start that she has recovered and is now back on duty. The following story came through the American Red Cross.

"London— 'Guard that plane' muttered Second Officer Hazel Raines, Air Transport Auxiliary pilot, to the amazement of two broad-shouldered Britons who rushed to 'dig out the dead man' from the wrecked Spitfire.

Instead of the expected corpse they found a tiny, self-possessed girl who spoke in the soft accents of her native Georgia. She crawled out of the wreckage, took off her 'chute unaided and gave the required order, stressed in ATA pilot's training.

"Then, without further comment, she allowed herself to be taken off to the hospital.

'It's funny, but I don't remember a great deal about what happened,' admitted Hazel, pushing back her little leather skull cap to show the rapidly healing scars, where the curls had been shaved off.

"She was having mid-morning coffee at the American Red Cross Nurse's Club, her 'other home', where she meets all the gang on leave, before reporting back to duty. And she was frantic to get back at the controls again: sitting on the ground 'is a bore.'

'It was my first crack-up, too, in five years of flying,' Hazel continued 'And I'm glad I said "Guard that plane" like I was suppose to, even if I don't remember saying it. That shows training accounts for something in a crisis!'

'What happened? Oh, the Spitfire engine quit on me. There really isn't much to do when that happens. Nor much time to think things over, either. It was frightful weather but I figured I might be able to get down without tearing up the plane.'

'Well, I was wrong. Took the second story off a thatched house coming down, too. The family was peacefully having tea. As it happened, they had wanted that house rebuilt for years and now they'll get it done free. So they weren't complaining.'

"Hazel, who is the daughter of Mrs. F. G. Raines, 212 Riverside Drive, Macon has flown since college days, when she took to air as a hobby. She is a graduate of Georgia's Wesleyan, oldest woman's college in the United States and alma mater of China's Madame Chiang Kai-shek.

"After a year as a ATA pilot in England, Hazel still thinks that the 25 American girls chosen by Jacqueline Cochran to join the ferry pilot service in Britain were the luckiest in the U.S. Flyer Cochran 'hand picked' the candidates on the basis of personal interviews and type of flying done.

"These American girls in navy blue fly equipment for the RAF and the USAF from factories to fighter and bomber stations all over the British Isles. Their hours: sun-up to sun-down with six days leave a month. " The ultimate aim is that every pilot be able to fly any type of aircraft, any place at any time. Hazel herself was just due to go on bombers when she crashed. That would be a new thrill she added, though it's 'lonesome up there alone in a giant airplane.'

"It wasn't necessary to ask about her morale after the crash: not when she kept one eager eye on her wrist watch in fear of being late reporting for duty.

Morale? You can't keep a girl like that on the ground!

Hazel wrote to her family about the crash and her life while recuperating. She was pretty badly hurt, according to Mrs. Reginald Trice, her sister, and it was three months before she was able to resume her flying. The accident occurred on March 2, and it was June 1 when she returned to duty. She is planning to come home for a month in the fall.

In her next letter Hazel celebrates her twenty-seventh Birthday with a unique party and also tries to explain to her mother what is like to be a "small part of it all" in the war.

Chapter 9
MOTHER, I'M FINE

Friday Afternoon
April 23, 1943

Dearest Mother:
Tuesday I received your cable asking about me and my accident; immediately I went to the Post Office and cabled you right back. Several weeks ago I wrote you all about it and I do hope you have received my letter by now. Had you received my letter when you sent the cable? It was really a very funny incident, or should I say accident and I saw no reason for writing sooner about it since I was not hurt. Just a simple case of engine failure but I got out O.K.

with only a simple little cut over my right eye. They took me to a hospital and sewed me up—13 stitches worth- plus shaving off half my hair. Just in case you might have some doubt about how fit I am now, I am enclosing a picture one of the girls took of me just a month after the accident. It's an awful looking picture but she took it while I was sitting talking to one of the girls and I didn't know it until I saw the picture. They truly cut all my hair off didn't they!

Well, I wish you could have been here Wednesday night. Mrs. Porter, the people I am now living with, gave me a Birthday party and believe me it was a swell one. She invited all the girls from the pool over and most of them came- in fact, we had 25 in all. Mrs. Porter was certainly swell, she had a big Birthday cake made for me and Wednesday night she invited three of the girls, that we run around with, in for dinner before the rest of the gang came around. Then she had a woman that is a whizz bang of a piano player to come in and play for us while we rolled back the rug and cut a jig— Then we had plates of sandwiches sitting around with lots of awful English beer but it was fun. We held forth 'till about one o'clock when they all decided they should struggle forth in the blackout and try and find their respective billets on their bikes. It was indeed great fun and a party I'll always remember. Mr. and Mrs. Porter gave me a white and blue scarf as well as a very nice pair of gloves. Also I was given some cards, handkerchiefs, lipstick, cigarettes etc.

Haven't received the package you wrote me about yet but guess I will get it soon.

We truly have a house full here now— I wrote you that two of us, Grace Stevenson and I live here with the Porters— Well, we have another one of our girls posted down here now, Kay VanDoozer from California, and Mrs. Porter has taken her in too— so, we have quite a house full but it is great fun.

Going back to Maidenhead tomorrow for another conversion course and will be with the Littlehales again, but only while I am taking this training which will take about two weeks, then I'll be back down here.

Well Mother, I'm not sure, but I think I have finally decided to stay here until October when my time will be up—Oct.14th to be exact. Then I will come home for awhile. Just what I will do then— I haven't decided— I am thinking seriously of re-signing up over here— if I do, then I'll come home for a month then back here again. I have all reason to believe my efforts over here are more useful and appreciated more than they would be back in the States. You see, you have no idea what a wonderful feeling it is to deliver a Fighter Aircraft to a Fighter Squadron of Boys that are really just standing there waiting for you to bring them something to fight with. You then feel that you are truly a part of it all. Specially when the boys all come dashing up to the plane and before you have time to get out of it they are all asking "How does she fly?" "How fast is she?" "What do you cruise her at?" You see what I mean about feeling as tho I am a small part of it all?

Mother, I'm sorry if I caused you any undue worry about the little accident, but you can now rest assured I am O.K. I do hope you are feeling better now after your operation. I hope it does you as much good as it has done me. Let me know how you are getting along and if you have any more trouble. Were you in the Middle Georgia Hospital? Glad Dr.[   ] didn't do the work.

Must get this finished cause it's dinner time— Take care of yourself and for goodness sakes, stop worrying about me— You can see by the picture I am in perfect health—

[censored] Aerodrome
May 6, 1943

Dearest Mother:

After a rather hectic train ride yesterday from Maidenhead down here, I'm in no mood to write a sociable letter but- here goes.

Have been at White Waltham again for more training and while there stayed with the Littlehales. Was only there 10 days this time and I must say I'm am more than pleased to be back down here at work again. This is such a lovely spot to be in this time of year- much warmer than any part of England I have been in yet, and I guess I can say I have been in about every part of this little Island. Found a letter from Martha waiting for me written March 16th. That was a bit of luck winning a War Bond. I think Martha should have it tho cause I didn't do anything to earn it.

While I was in Maidenhead a friend of mine gave me a little black Persian kitten. It is the cutest little thing you ever saw, it's 9 weeks old and was born on the day I had my accident, so I have named it "[censored]" after the type machine I was flying. You should have seen me coming down here on the train with "[censored]" sitting up big as you please in a fish basket. That's why my trip was so hectic. I had to change trains twice and in the process of doing this, I lost my suitcase which was packed beyond capacity as usual, and of course my passport was in it. Well, I almost went mad when I discovered my loss. I didn't have my name on it either, only a sticker with Southampton on it. Well— I tried to trace it— but no suitcase. This morning about 8 o'clock the phone rang and it was the Parcels Room Clerk at the station calling to say he had found my bag. Immediately I went in to Southampton and sure enough, there it was-nothing missing. Gee was I lucky to get it back. It reminded me of when I left home and left my case in Macon and you all had to dash up to Atlanta and bring it back to me. Guess I'm just getting old and absent-minded, but thank goodness as yet I'm not toothless. Guess I can now be called a genuine, died-in the wool old maid. Me with my cat, dog, and having passed another milestone. How do you like being the Mother of a bald-headed Old Maid! You do have a consolation as yet tho- even if I am in England I haven't as yet acquired the tea drinking habit, nor do I have any desire to add a parrot to my collection of animals.

Next week I have a couple of days leave due me so I'm going to Oxford with Mrs. Porter. Many times now I have flown over the Spires of Oxford and viewed this Educational Centre of the World from the air, but now I want to get the ordinary layman's or travelers prospective.

The days are fast growing longer- it's hardly dark now at 10:30 at night. Last night when I got in , Grace, Kay, Mrs. Porter and I went out in the back yard about 8 o'clock and made some pictures with the animals. If they turn out O.K. I'll send you a copy. By the way, just in case you never did receive the pictures I sent you that were made Christmas at Lady Astor's Estate, I'm enclosing a couple in this letter....

Time to get a move on and do some work for a change— Take care of yourself and write as often as possible....

"The success of the British ATA convinced the U.S. Army Air Force to organize its own women's pilot program and recall Jacqueline Cochran from England to become director of women's flight training." (*National Air and Space Museum,* Smithsonian Institution, 1981.) The following letter is from Jacqueline Cochran:

Fort Worth, Texas
May 20, 1943

Dear Grace, Hazel and Kay:

I received your very nice cable of greetings, and how very nice and thoughtful of you to send it. What I would enjoy even more than your nice thoughts on my birthday, is to have a really long letter from each of you as to what is going on. I have hoped that for such a long time that I could get back, but now I know it is literally impossible.

The day after I arrived back from there, I took over the job of the women's flying training program for the Army Air Forces, knowing it would take approximately six months to graduate the first group and even longer than that to tell what the Army would permit them to fly. Naturally, I didn't write you girls anything about it. At first they were sure they were only going to fly very light equipment, but after much persuasion, I finally got included in their · course of instructions, two motored training aircraft.

The first group of girls has just been graduated two weeks and the usual struggles are going on as to whether they are going to ferry primary trainers or advanced trainers. It will be sixty to ninety days before we will be able to actually tell how far they will permit them to go on their ferrying operations, but at least something has been accomplished. We are going to turn out several hundred graduates this year- more than six times the number flying for A.T.A., and with that many females turned loose in the Army Air Forces, all clambering for privileges. I can't help but feel that they will get somewhere. I am convinced that if you girls hadn't gone to England, and were not doing the grand job you are, that this program would never had gotten started, so, in my opinion, I can't overestimate how much I feel that you have contributed to women in aviation.

I am stationed out in Fort Worth, Texas, the headquarters of the Flying Training Command (which is the largest command in the Army Air Forces) and I have found all of the Army extremely cooperative and pleasant to work with in almost every instance, but I can assure you, it isn't very nice to live out in the middle of the country so far removed from the real activity of the war; and how often I wish I were back in England.

I heard about Hazel's accident, and I do hope you are quite recovered. I would appreciate it very much if you would let me know how Evelyn Hudson is coming along. I am very sorry. Will you also let me know if there is anything at all that I can do for you? I am sending two copies of this so whoever receives it first can forward copies to the others.

Again, many thanks for your kind thoughts and good wishes.

Jackie

Nancy Miller Stratford remembers why Jacqueline Cochran was concerned about Evelyn Hudson. Evelyn was ferrying a Wellington British bomber when she crashed and broke her back.

Thursday Afternoon
May 27, 1943

Dearest Mother:

Today I received two letters from you, one from Martha and one from Frankie, all around April 16th. It seems that the letters that you send by regular post arrive just as soon as the ones sent by air mail—-so, you might save a few pennies by cutting out the airmail all together. Anyway, it was swell getting so much mail from home cause it has been over a month now since I have heard from you. By the way, have you stopped the *Telegraph*? It has been almost three months now since I have received one. If you haven't canceled my subscription, you might as well do so cause it takes so long for them to get over here, then too since I am planning to return here in October, I hardly think it worth while to continue now.

Mother, I certainly hope you haven't worried too much about the accident I had and I am very sorry it got back in the papers at home. News will travel in the most mysterious ways and to think Virginia had to write you about it (Pardon the mistakes but "Spitfire," that's my cat, is sitting here in my lap while I'm typing this, and he is having great fun trying to catch my fingers as I am typing along on the keys.) I wrote you all about the accident and hope you received the letter. It was just one of those things that I knew would happen, but didn't dream of at the time because it did happen so quick. I really feel that I am the luckiest person in the world, and if I can get away with something like that, I am good for another five years of flying without anything serious happening again. Thank goodness I didn't have a single broken bone; only the head injury, and I mailed you a picture of me made about three weeks after the accident a few weeks ago. Hope you got it O.K. Of course the blow on my head was rather a severe one, but the cut is not bad at all, because the scar is only a faint line now. It did affect my right eye slightly, but even that is back to normal now. They have taken the greatest care with me, and I think I can safely tell you now without causing you any worry that I have been off flying since March 2nd., the date of the little event. I know I have written you several times saying I was hard at work, but that was only to keep you from worrying too much. The Doctors would not let me do any flying what-so-ever for three months from the date of the accident on account of my head and eyes. So, I have been taking it easy and having a wonderful time seeing England more or less on my own. Saw the Doctor yesterday and he has given me the O.K. once again for work. So, beginning next Tuesday my playing days are over and I will be back on the job. I'm going back to Maidenhead for conversion to twins. They are restricting me to twin equipment for six months due to the fact that they think it best for me not to wear a tight helmet on my head just yet. You see all twin equipment is closed cockpit and I don't have to wear anything on my head as one must do when flying fighters. Now that I have told you the truth about it all, I'll tell you what I have been doing for the past two weeks.

First of all I'll begin by saying I have spent most of my time down here with Mrs. Porter since I got out of the hospital which was the last of March. I have been up to London several times just for a change. The last time I was up there was two weeks ago Sunday. The reason I went up then was because I received a message from Helen Glenn from Macon that she had just arrived in England. She is in the W.A.C.C.S. or something like that. She and I were in high school together. I'm sure you know who I am talking about cause her folks live near you. Well, you can imagine how thrilled I was to learn that she was over here, so I immediately dashed up to London to see her. I stayed up there for two days and believe me we did some talking while she was there. She is posted near Maidenhead and I have invited her down for a couple of days just as soon as she can get some leave. Her people are Mr. and Mrs. Harry Glenn.

Week before last I went down to Bournemouth for three days with one of the English girls that is a W.A.A.F. Officer at our Pool in the Met office. She was going home for three days leave and invited me to go with her. The weather was grand and we had a marvelous time on the beach sun bathing. It was such a treat to get out and soak up a few sunbeams for a change. I actually got a good tan which is so unusual and hard to get over here. You wouldn't believe it because it doesn't sound like me but——I had a grand time walking and riding a bicycle around the countryside drinking in the unusual beauty of a Spring in England. It was really ironical to see such an array of color and life budding through and around the musty historical settings that dominate this little Isle of Tradition. Last week-end had an invitation from one of the girls in the pool whose home is in Cardiff, Wales, to spend three days with her. Saturday we met her people in Salisbury and went to the horse races. Of course I had to do a little betting , and believe it or not, I came out three pounds twelve shillings to the good. (That would be $17.50 to you.) From there we went by train to a little old place in Somerset called Langport, where we were guests of some friends of theirs over Sunday and Monday. We stayed in an old building that Oliver Cromwell used to sleep in when he was fighting his battles in those parts. Dorene, that's the girl I was with, had to go back to work Monday afternoon, but since I did not have to go back, I went down to Lime Regia where I met Mrs. Porter. She was on a business trip in her car. We spent Monday night in a quaint little village near there called Musbury, the birthplace of the Duke of Marlborough. From there we drove to Exeter in Devon, then up through the Cheddar gorge to Minehead, and on to Bristol where we spent Tuesday night. When going thru the gorge we stopped at a spot known as Burrington Combe which is the place where the Rev. Toplady, when taking shelter in the cleft of the rock during a storm composed the famous hymn—"Rock of Ages". Wednesday morning we left for Bristol, drove to Oxford then back here to Southampton. It was indeed a wonderful trip for me because it gave me the unusual opportunity of seeing part of the country I have been flying over during the past year.

That seems to bring me up-to-date now with all my news and since I must get off a letter to Martha and Frankie I'll say so long for now...

Thursday Afternoon
May 27, 1943

Dearest Martha:

Just finished writing a letter to Mother in which I have already given all the news I can think of, but just the same I want to say a few things to you.

You certainly did have bad luck with your chickens and garden. Hope your next effort turns out much better. Even I seem to be doing better than that, cause I have lots of radishes, carrots, peas and have planted some corn.

About the pin, that's O.K. I thought after I wrote you that was rather a silly thing for me to want you to do cause after all it would be taking quite a risk if you sent it over. The wings I have on my tunic would not be suitable for Mother or Jeaneane because they are gold braid on a blue cloth background and one must sew them on to wear them. However, I am buying some A.T.A. wings of a pin type and will send them over soon as possible.

Now about my account. By the time you receive this letter you no doubt will have noticed an addition of $400.00 to my account. This is part of the accident insurance compensation that I received recently as a result of my recent little accident. Since I received the injury to my head while on flying duties through no fault or mistake on my part, they have paid me this sum of money into my account at home. In reference to the war bond, I will leave that to your discretion. If you think it best to invest in a war bond, O.K. with me. Just leave a couple of hundred in cash so that I will have some money available when I return because I will be more or less broke when I reach the States due to the fact I won't be able to bring any money with me but will no doubt have to write a check when I get to New York. See what I mean? Could I cash a war bond at anytime or must one wait until after the war is over? I don't want to get my money tied up where I won't have anything to live on when I get back cause I still don't know what I am going to do when I return to the States.

By the way, there is a small transaction I want you to make for me. One of the girls that was over here and returned to the States just before Xmas left some things with me which I have sold for her. I now find that I cannot send the money to her, so the next best thing is for you to mail her a check for it, and I will write her telling her what I have done. You see we can't send any money over there except what we have deposited to our credit in our bank. So, since I have the money over here and can't get it to her, I can just keep it for my use and you can mail her a check for $50.00. Her name and address is: Miss Virginia Garst, 4707 Grand Ave., Kansas City, Missouri. Be sure and send her this check cause I have written her you would. You see that $50.00 is included in the $400.00 I am having deposited to my account.

I am writing Frankie about some china I was lucky enough to pick up the other day, so get her to show you my letter to her about it. Part of it is for you and part of it for her. Goodness knows how we'll ever decide who is to have what!

Hope I didn't do the wrong thing by writing Mother all about the accident, as well as the fact I am still off duty. However, I am going back to work on Tuesday, so there is nothing to worry about now. Thank goodness the scar on my head is not a bad one and I think perhaps it will fade away entirely in a couple of years. As for my eyes, they are good as new now and I'm sure I'll not have any more trouble with them once I start flying again.

Think perhaps I have finally decided to return home in October but not by boat— by air. That will be the safest and best way I am sure if I can arrange it. Well, Martha, I must stop and get a letter off to Frankie. Give my love to Gene, kiss Jeaneane for me and don't forget...

I love you lots,
Hazel

On June 5th, Hazel is allowed to fly again, but only twin-engines due to the pressure of wearing a helmet. Her log book records that she was now flying Oxfords and Fairchilds.

Chapter 10
SOUTHERN FRIED CHICKEN

Thursday Morning
June 10, 1943

Dearest Mother:

After spending three hectic months on the ground, I took to the air again last Saturday. Came up here last Tuesday, had a complete medical and reported back to the school for a flight check and twin conversion which I have waited so long for. Had my technical ground work on twins last Friday and Saturday then my first try at flying them. Now I have a total of six hours, three dual and three solo and I do love it. You know I have always wanted to fly a twin engine machine- now I have done it. This will be the type machine I will be flying for the rest of the rest of the summer, cause I can't wear a helmet for several months due to the pressure on my head. I have been here a week now on this course, but I imagine I will finish up and return to my pool this weekend. It'll be good getting back on the job once again.

Since I have been up here this time, I have been living in London at the Red Cross Club instead of with the Littlehales. You see her son, Jack, who is in the Navy, is at home just now on 14 days leave, and he has the room I usually stay in so- I decided to live at the Club while taking this training and travel back and forth on the train daily. There are three of us doing it, so it isn't too bad an idea. We do have to get up rather early: 6:15, so we will have ample time to catch a bus to Paddington Station where we get a 7 o'clock train for Maidenhead. It's about a 50 minute ride. Besides, it's worth living at the Club cause the food is so very good and we can buy cokes there. We usually finish up everyday in time to catch a train back to London that gets us there by 7 o'clock. I then have a good dinner, perhaps play a game of Ping-pong with the girls, have a hot bath, and hit the hay by 10 o'clock.

By the way, I'll probably be seeing you sometime in September- Can't tell you anymore but- let's hope things work out that way.

Gotta go now and fly some...

Air Transport Auxiliary
June 18, 1943

Dearest Mother:

Just received a letter from Martha written May 19th telling me about Roland Scott. This is the first I have heard about his accident. About six weeks ago I was at the Red Cross Club, that's where we all stay when we are in London, and I saw his name on the register. At the same time I saw a friend of mine, a Col. in the Signal Corps who is stationed near him, and he promised to deliver a message to him for me but— I never did hear from him. However, I am writing today to Roland, and if I don't hear within the next few days, will take a couple of days leave to try to find out what I can. If I find out where he is, I will go and see him.

Well, I finished school last Saturday at White Waltham and am now back down here on the job again. They gave me two days leave when I finished, so I went to Bournemouth and spent Sunday and Monday with one of the girls down there. Started back to work Tuesday, and believe me, it was good getting back on the job after being away for three and a half months. I am on twins now. That is all they are letting me fly for a few months, but I love them cause I've always wanted to fly them. I now have twenty hours on twin equipment: flew 4 and a half hours yesterday.

Saw Helen Glenn again last week in London and she told me you had received the picture I sent you made of my bald head. Her mail seems to get over much quicker than mine. She is planning to come down here before long and spend a couple of days with me.

Mother, you know my contract expires October 14th. Well, I have signed for six additional months which will extend it to next March. In the meantime I have applied for a month's leave so that I may return to the States, and they have given it to me— the month of September. So, unless something unexpected turns up, I hope to be seeing you about the second week in September. Of course I can't tell you the exact date, or how I will be coming over. The only thing I can do is wire you when I get to New York, and then you can come up and fly home with me. How about that?

About my cat, yes, his name was Spitfire, But— he isn't anymore. He had the cat flu last week and died. Poor little thing, we did everything we could to save him but he was so little he wasn't quite strong enough to survive. Did I tell you about the two little pups I have now? Besides my scottie, I bought two liver and white cocker spaniels, a pair; they are three months old and the cutest little things you ever saw. Mrs. Porter certainly is swell to let me have so many animals around but you know me, I love pets, so— if you want me back again you must agree to my animals too....

Friday Morning
July 9, 1943

Dearest Mother:

Just returned from five days leave and am sitting here at the Aerodrome waiting for the weather to clear, so we can start work. Had a very nice leave this time. They gave all the American girls the 4th off, so we all went to London late Saturday afternoon after finishing work. We all stayed at the Red Cross Club, where they had a wonderful party Sunday night. Lots of good food, an orchestra and dancing, and quite a good time was had by all. Monday, several of us went by the Embassy and had our passports put in proper order for our return trip home. Gee, I can hardly wait— it won't be too long now, I'm sure. I should see you by Sept. 18th anyway— so keep your fingers crossed!

Helen Glenn was in London also Sunday night, and we had much fun talking about home and things. We had a few games of Ping Pong and sat and talked until one o'clock. She is stationed near London and does manage to get in quite often. I told her about you writing me about Roland Scott, so we got together and found out where he is. We wrote him a note, but haven't heard from him yet. However, I met someone who is stationed with him, and he told me Roland was not seriously injured, and was now fully recovered and back on duty. I am hoping to see him before I leave this country.

Monday afternoon, I came back down here, met a couple of girls from the pool, and we started out on a cycling tour. I know this sounds fantastic to you that I would or could make such a trip, but we cycled 75 miles in two and one half days. It was really a lovely ride. We spent two nights down by the seaside and it was so peaceful until I felt as tho I was home again.

When I got back yesterday, I stopped by the Aerodrome to pick up the any mail I might have, and found the parcel you mailed me on May 24th. Thanks lots for everything. I am sure I now have plenty of everything to last me until I get back.

Since it's almost lunch time, I'll stop for now. By the way, I would suggest that you do not write me anymore after you receive this letter, cause I'm almost sure I'll be home again before you could reply to this letter. Give my love to all. Take care of yourself and here's hoping I'll see you before too long...

Since it's almost lunch time I'll stop for now. By the way, I would suggest that you do not write me anymore after you receive this letter cause I'm almost sure I'll be home again before you could reply to this letter. Give my love to all- Take care of yourself and here's hoping I'll see you before too long."...

AIR TRANSPORT AUXILIARY
HEADQUARTERS
Nr. Maidenhead, Berks.

Ophthalmic Specialist,
July 10, 1943
American Dispensary
London

Dear Sir,

re S/O Miss H. Raines

The above officer had a crash on the 3.1.43. as the result of which she sustained a laceration of the scalp and concussion. She had fairly marked post-concussion syndrome for some time afterwards and was passed fit on 2.6.43.

She now complains of occasional mistiness of vision in the right eye and difficulty in judging distances.

On examination: Vision is 6/5, 6/5. She has some exophoria which is easily corrected and a Bishop Harmen reading of P.D. 60/2 which is within normal.

I suggested that she should see an opthalmic surgeon and she would prefer to be seen by you, hence the letter.

The *Macon Telegraph*. (Friday, August 6, 1943):

"MISS HAZEL RAINES, who has been serving in the Air Transport Auxiliary in England since March, 1942, has landed in New York and will be back home in Macon today. A telegram to her mother, Mrs. F.G. Raines, 212 Riverdale Drive, yesterday told of her safe arrival in this country and her plan to come here this afternoon."

The *Macon Telegraph*. (Saturday, August 7, 1943):

Hungry for Dopes, Hot Dogs, Hazel Raines Returns Home

Fresh from London and hungry for Coca-Colas, hot dogs and home folks, First Officer Hazel Raines returned to Macon yesterday on leave from England where she has been ferrying planes for the RAF as an Air Transport Auxiliary pilot.

She still wore the heavy blue wool uniform of the ATA with thick black British stockings and flat heeled black shoes when she came in on the train from New York City. But she took the sweltering Macon sun with frank pleasure.

'Do you know,' she said, 'this is the first time I've been hot or even warm since I left here last year. This time of the year in England one wears a wool uniform, a sweater, and often an overcoat as well,' she explained.

But curly-haired, blue-eyed First Officer Raines was not really interested in discussing English weather or English affairs. They have become commonplace to her during the months since April, 1942, when she landed in England for ferry pilot duties as the only

Southerner in a group of 22 American women selected by Jacqueline Cochran for the ATA.

Questioned directly, she answered that the British are very much pleased over the invasion as they have wanted it for a long time.

She also commented briefly on the British reaction to American troops stationed in England. British people like the Americans, she said. But they can't get over the noise the Yanks make, or the boisterous high spirits characteristic of our troops.

But what really interested Miss Raines was a prospect of a visit in Macon with her mother, Mrs. F.G. Raines, and her two sisters, Mrs. Eugene Haines and Mrs. Reginald Trice.

'I want a coca cola and a hot dog and a good American shampoo and permanent wave,' she announced. 'Then I want some fried chicken. And then I want to rest. A rest is what I'm home for and I'm really looking forward to it.'

The little ATA pilot was laid up in England for three months this spring from injuries received when a Spitfire plane she was delivering crashed on March 3. She started flying again early in June, and since then has been piloting twin-motored craft, she said. On her homecoming, Hazel also brought news of two other Macon persons in service overseas. One of these was Helen Glenn, now a first lieutenant in the WAC and stationed in England.

'I had tea in London with Helen not long before I left,' Hazel said. 'She was looking fine and getting a lot out of her work. She told me that she had been to see Roland Scott, and of course I was interested in that.'

According to the report received by Hazel from her friend Helen, Scott is much improved, but is still in the hospital as a result of the wounds he received recently.

'I don't exactly know when I'll go back,' Hazel said as she left the station yesterday heading for home and the fried chicken to which she had been looking forward so long. 'I've been waiting for my leave a long time, and it seems mighty good,' she smiled. 'It will take me a while to get used to high-heeled shoes and orange juice for breakfast and all the eggs I want, but it will be a pleasure.'

Visiting with her friends, the Thompsons, (of the School of Aviation), Hazel made headlines in the *Fort Lauderdale Times:*

Captain Hazel Raines Tells of Experiences
Ferrying Planes in England for British.

Home from England on leave after a year and a half of ferrying fighter planes and medium bombers for the British Air Transport Auxiliary, Captain Hazel Raines explains the barely visible scar on her right temple.

At a recent reunion of local flyers, this former instructor at the Thompson Aero Corporation School recalled old times with Captain T.R. Thompson, RAF Transport Air Command, former owner of the flying school, and his wife Katherine Thompson, Ft. Lauderdale's noted swimmer and one of the first 25 WAFS in the United States. Thompson is stationed in Nassau, Mrs. Thompson is on leave from Detroit.

This Macon, Ga., girl, one of 16 American women now in the ferrying service, speaks highly of the English and their ways, is reticent about bombings she has undergone but outspoken on the attitude of Americans who 'don't know there is a war on.'

'English fortitude under air raids is remarkable, their courage unbelievable.'

Other women from Poland, Denmark, South America, Australia, Chile, Checo Slavakia and Argentine as well as English women and men of many countries form the outfit of which she is a member. Their job is to pick up new planes at factories and deliver them to operational and training stations.

She is thrilled to be back in this country, particularly in this bit of Florida where she has made many friends, and has been busy inquiring after her former students in the CPT program, dozens of whom are flying now for Uncle Sam.

Her plans? Well, her parents would like her to stay over here. 'I joined up with the British outfit before the organization of the WAFS.' Miss Raines says, 'but could no doubt find a use for my knowledge as flyer and instructor and do my bit here.' But she added, 'England's wonderful.'

Hazel also addressed the Macon Civil Air Patrol members, the Lions Club, the Civic Club, the Midville Methodist Church in Midville, Georgia, and the Macon Exchangites. It is no wonder that in an article in the *Macon Telegraph* August 30, 1943, she is hoping to take some time off "from aviation and speech making."

Hazel Raines, who is Macon's First Lady of the Air, is flying around in other ways while she is on leave from her job of ferrying planes for the RAF in England with the Air Transport Auxiliary. She has just come back from Miami where she went to attend the wedding of a flying companion and former flying pupil who was marrying as engineer from Trinidad. At present she is in Jacksonville where she is to be guest speaker at a meeting of the Ninety-Nines, a national organization of women fliers of which Jacqueline Cochran is president. After the meeting she will again go down Miami way where the flying fishes play and take time off from aviation and speech making to spend a week or so fishing and swimming and sunning.

In her mother's handwriting is a note which states: Hazel gave a talk to my Sunday School class after getting home in September, 1943 and read this poem." (It was written by a 19 year old American pilot who was serving in the Royal Canadian Air Force in England in 1941 and found in his personal effects after a fatal crash in which his Spitfire collided with another airplane.)

HIGH FLIGHT

OH! I have slipped the surly bonds of earth,
and danced the skies on laughter-silvered wings;
Sunward I've climbed and joined the tumbling mirth
of sunsplit clouds— and done a hundred things
You have not dreamed of— wheeled and soared and
swung— high in the sunlit silence.
Hov'ring there, I've chased the shouting winds along,
and flung my eager craft through footless halls of air.
Up, up the long delirious, burning blue, I've topped
the windswept heights with easy grace,
Where never lark or eagle flew.

And, while with silent, lifting mind I've trod the high
untrespassed sanctity of space,
Put out my hand, and touched the face of God.

John Gillespie Magee, Jr.

In late September, Hazel was still planning to return to England after a two month leave in the States. There is no record of why her plans changed, but it is no surprise that her next letter is from Avenger Field in Sweetwater, Texas. On August 5, 1943, Jacqueline Cochran became the Director of the Women's Airforce Service Pilots, or WASPs, and managed to move her training base from Howard Hughes Field in Houston to Avenger Field in Sweetwater. Only three women who had served in the A.T.A. participated in the newly formed WASP program and Hazel was one of these. Life at Avenger Field would not be easy, however. The program was controversial and the training would be intensive. The women had to prove themselves as pilots not only to their instructors but to the town of Sweetwater. "Although the townspeople eventually adopted the WASPs, at first they were afraid to let their kids play outside because they thought the WASPs would be crashing all over the area." (Vera S. Williams, *WASPs,* Motorbooks International Publishers, 1994. p.55) Also, they were housed in rough barracks with six women to a bay and were required to march to all functions in military style.

Hazel's arrival did not go unnoticed.

Hazel Raines, Grace Stevenson, Virginia
Garst, Helen Harrison, Sue Ford, Ann
Wood (from left to right)
England, 1942

Stewart Collings.

London. England.

The Air Transport Auxiliary uniform
England–1942

Mrs. Roosevelt inspecting A.T.A. pilots
England–October 26, 1942
(Hazel is second from left)

Cliveden

Hazel with Lady Astor,
December, 1942

Standing beside Spitfire

A.T.A pilots
Sandoz, Raines, Chapin
& Souror

Balloon barrages were used to deter low-
flying enemy aircraft. This one floats
above Tower bridge of central London.

BOOK II.
AVENGER FIELD....AS A WASP

Chapter 1
THE ORDER OF THE FIFINELLA

The Avenger, November 5, 1943:

HAZEL RAINES, ENGLISH FERRY PILOT
AMONG TRAINEES OF 44-W-4

On the train last weekend, we were reminded of our own bewildered approach to Avenger Field, when we met several bright and eager young women. Approaching them much as we do the first timid crocuses of spring, we discovered that they were members-to be of that much favored class — 44-W-4.

Of course, we immediately started to quiz them on their emotions and sensations on actually being so close to their destination. Yes, they were looking forward to it eagerly: yes, they had brought conventionally-colored shirts (tan, blue, brown, not white, because that wasn't really practical, they thought): and my word, have you really been there three months (at which we discovered we must surely be accomplished pilots by this time.)

Arriving in a fine glow of big-sisterly confidence we greeted other arrivals. One of the first to answer our questions turned out to be Hazel Raines who has given up Spitfires and Hurricanes of the English ferry command to start in PT's and come up the "hard way". She went over there at the same time as Miss Cochran and has just completed an 18 months contract. We want to welcome her most heartily back to the States, and fervently hope that she gives our check pilots some thrills...

Tuesday Morning
November 2, 1943

Dearest Mother:

Just a note to explain what happened. We had a grand trip until we got to Fort Worth. We stopped outside of town to get something to eat. Kim had my travelers checks plus gas coupons plus all her money in her pocketbook which we left in the pocket of the car. I thought I had the car locked but- when we got out of the car someone had quickly gone thru our car— got the pocketbook and my camera. We went immediately to the Police and reported what had happened. Talk about 2 sick people—Well, we were all in. I wired about my checks so I really haven't lost anything but my camera. But poor Kim lost $210.00. Well, it so happened I could not get the table for Martha— they had sold it and I still had her check which I had to cash to get some money to get out here on. Why I wired for $200.00 more was cause Kim had her return ticket to Washington in her pocketbook and had to buy another which cost $75.00. She will send me the money which I will return to you. It sure was a big mess but the police in Ft. Worth are working on it. I was lucky enough to talk a filling station operator into selling me a tank of gas without coupons which was enough to get me here.

I am in a terrific hurry, as you can see. Believe me, we stay on the run. Up at 6 o'clock and in bed at 10. This is truly Army Life, we march every where we go. Will write you more later.

Thanks again for the money— will send it to you soon as my checks are cleared and Kim gets back to Washington and can send me the money.

I love you,
Hazel

44-W-4 318th A.A.F.F.T.D.
Avenger Field
Sweetwater, Texas

Thursday Morning
November 4, 1943

Dearest Mother:

At last another spare moment and so a note home to say I'm O.K. If you don't hear from me as often as you think I should write, it's cause they keep us so busy until we have little or no time at all for writing letters. We get up at 6 o'clock, breakfast 6:35, on the Flight Line 7:30 to 1 o'clock, eat 1:15, Ground School 1:55, Physical Training 5:15, Supper at 6:40 and back to quarters by 8 o'clock in bed and lights out by 10 o'clock. There is so much to do at Ground School, which lasts 3 hours until we must study from 8 'till we go to bed at night. Some of the subjects we are having to take are Math, Physics, Navigation, Meteorology, Aircraft Engines etc. and on weekends we must attend lecture on Military Subjects.

This is certainly a rigid life and schedule. We march in flight formations to everything. It is quite good training I'm sure and I just hope I can continue to take it. Quite different from England in many ways. The food is wonderful and I don't think I'm going to need my ration book after all.

Received a letter yesterday from American Express Co. about my checks. Filled out a form and sent it back so that I can be paid for the lost checks.

There are 5 other girls in the room with me and they all seem to be swell. They all come from different parts— Missouri, Utah, Indiana etc.

Thanks again for the money and I'll send it back to you soon as possible.....

Avenger Field
Sweetwater, Texas
Tuesday Afternoon
November 9, 1943

Dearest Mother,

Just about everybody on the Post is sick today, including me. Yesterday, they gave us all shots-three at a time, Typhoid, Tetanus, and Smallpox vaccine. Today, we all have sore arms, fever and headaches. We got excused from flying and I've just had a hot shower and am in bed. Gonna try to get some sleep if possible. Other than that, I'm O.K.

Well, I've got another job—Post Bugler. Seems like old times tooting a horn again, but I like it. I hafta get up at 5:45 but I am getting use to it. In fact I'm feeling like my old self again. Started flying Saturday and even tho they are putting me thru the Mill, I love it- it'll do me lots of good, I'm sure.

Yes, I guess that was stupid of us to leave the pocketbook in the car. I had my change purse in my pocket in which was the check I gave Martha. Thank goodness I couldn't get that sideboard for her. We went down Royal Street and found the shop without any trouble but- we sure did get a scare while there. The man that ran the place was drunk, so was the woman. He said he remembered about the sideboard and tried to sell me something else in the place of it, but we got out as quick as possible. We went back the next day to make sure and found he was telling the truth.

Jackie was here when we arrived last week and was certainly swell to Kim. She took her on a trip with her down to another post here in Texas. She said she would fly Kim back out here to see me again soon.

Well, you should see us here in my Bay sweeping floors, scrubbing woodwork, making beds etc. We have a rigid inspection every Saturday and everything must be spotless- if they find any dirt anywhere, or your bed made wrong, they give you demerits and confine you to Post for the weekend. Last week our Bay, or room, was the only one that didn't get a single Demerit. Know you can't believe that. Of course we hafta stay on the Post 2 weeks before we are allowed to go to town anyway. We are all walking the straight and narrow hoping we can go too.......

Avenger Field
Sweetwater, Texas
Monday Morning
November 15, 1943

Dearest Mother:

Just came in from a flight and Gee, it was cold up there this morning. My "Long-Handles" sure felt good. I had to fly first period, from 7:45 TO 9:00, a grand time of the day to be up. There was almost a solid overcast at about 1500 feet so we climbed up to 8,000 feet where the clouds below looked like a fluffy white blanket. However, the sun soon came out and burned holes in the blanket causing clouds to slowly roll up in odd individual shapes and gracefully float away.

Saturday was graduation day for one of the classes and we had to march out on the field in formation where we stood "At Ease" thru the entire hour and 35 minute service. We were then given "Open Post" and allowed to go to the big city of Sweetwater. I took 5 of the girls in my bay with me and we had a typical Saturday Afternoon Shopping Tour. It was great fun tho, just to get off the post for a few hours and sit in the corner Drug Store and drink a coke.

Already they have started to weed out the girls in my flight. I do feel sorry for the ones that just can't make the grade. I'm really not worried about the flying but— the ground school—- Oh well, I'm having to do some sure enough digging to absorb enough to pass Math and Physics. They posted the grades for the first two weeks and mine were: Math 70, Physics 85 and Theory of Flight 90. Wish I had studied more when I was in school. Oh well, I'll make it some way.

Certainly hope you and all the children are feeling o.k. Tell them hello for me. Must go now…

Avenger Field
Sweetwater, Texas
Sunday Night
Nov. 21, 1943

Dearest Mother:

This has been a grand weekend— we had open Post from Saturday afternoon 'till tonight at 9 o'clock. Of course we went to town yesterday afternoon and did a bit of shopping. Last night we went to the Avengerette Club where we danced and had a grand time 'til 12 o'clock. The Club is for the girls here at the field and is a grand place for us to go and relax and have fun. And believe me, we need to relax and play a little after putting in 5 and a half days of sure enough work.

I was so glad of the chance to stay in bed this morning. I didn't get up 'till 11 o'clock. After lunch, several of rode out to Sweetwater Lake, a beautiful place to go boating, fishing and golfing, but—- we didn't do anything like that— we put the top to the car down and sat in the sun by the lake and studied. And by the way, my grades for the past few weeks work are: Physics-95, Theory of Flight-95, and Math-70. Gee, I have never studied so hard.

Mrs. Deaton, Director of the School here, has asked me to make a talk Tuesday Night in Sweetwater to the American Legion Post. Guess I'll hafta do it. I thought my speech-making days would be over when I got here but—no—no such luck! I don't really mind tho.

Just received my check from the American Express Co. for the checks I lost so soon as I can get the check cashed, I will send you and Martha the money..

Chapter 2
CHRISTMAS IN SWEETWATER

In a letter of November 28, 1943, Hazel tells of her successful speaking engagements:

This past week has been a full one and I have truly been working. Tuesday night I went in and made a talk before the Sweetwater American Legion Post. They all liked it— or, so they said. Then, Thursday night they asked me to talk to the girls here so— we had a Thanksgiving Service in our gym and I made the usual speech.

Doubt very much if I will be able to get home Xmas. They say we will only have Xmas Day so— I guess I'll spend another Xmas away from home but deep in the heart of Texas this time. Oh well, I don't like Xmas anyway.

A letter of December 8, 1943:
It is now definite that I won't be home for Xmas. I was just thinking maybe if you could— I would sure like to have a small fruit cake. Since we've gotta have Xmas, I would like to have some of your wonderful fruit cake. By the way, I am sending you my ration books— I don't need them here, then too maybe it will help buy the things for the cake.

You should hear all the girls singing when we get together for a meeting- sounds grand. When and if I ever graduate, I do hope you

can come out here for it. I sure would like for you to see the whole
set-up and meet the people in charge.

Avenger Field
Sweetwater, Texas
Monday Night
Dec. 6, 1943

Dearest Mother:

A free five minutes and— a note to say I'm O.K., but still hard
at it. We have just finished final exams on Math, Physics, and
Theory and today started new classes in Code, Navigation, and
Aircraft Engines. Soon as the final grades are posted, I'll let you
know how I stand so far! I know I passed everything tho. This is
truly a swell course— so good until I have just about decided it
would be best for me to take all I can get which would be about
seven months ground and flight training. It is just the type training I
have always wanted to take. If I had gone to a private school, like
Spartain Aviation School in Oklahoma, this identical course would
have cost *only* $35,000. So— you see it is certainly grand training. I
will get my instrument rating if I stay here and take the full course
and that within itself is worth quite a bit. Believe me, I should be
able to fly and should know something about Aviation some day
with my past experiences and present training.

I have been asked to speak again next Monday to the Rotary
Club in Sweetwater. Guess I will, since the Commanding Officer
here has asked me to do so. I spoke to the Student Body here on
Thanksgiving— or did I tell you before.

Time won't let me say much more cause it's almost time to play
taps so—until later.......

Avenger Field
Sweetwater, Texas
Thursday Morning
Dec. 9, 1943

Dearest Mother:

Guess you'll think I'm crazy when I ask you to do a favor for
me like make a pound cake. Well, that's what I want you to do if you
can possibly manage. You see it's like this — My Physics Instructor
is from Georgia and last night when I was in Ground School working on a problem, I bet him a Georgia Pound Cake that he was
wrong about the solution of a problem— well, he was right so— he
said if I could get a sure enough Georgia Pound Cake I could go out
to his sister's house—(she lives in Sweetwater) and she would fix

some fried chicken to go with it. If possible, whip me up one— just half or fourth the recipe. Thanks lots.

It's raining again today— If the weather clears guess we'll fly this afternoon.

I'm feeling swell these days— we have to take physical training for an hour every day and I think it's doing me lots of good. Twice a week we have drill for one hour. I am Flight Lt. of our Squadron— you should see me out drilling the girls.

Gotta go— Thanks again and if you can send me the cake I sho will appreciate it.....

Avenger Field
Sweetwater, Texas
Saturday Afternoon
December 9, 1943

Dearest Mother:

Received your package and the one from Jeaneane yesterday but haven't opened either yet— gonna try to wait till Xmas— bet I don't tho.

By the way, I am enclosing a money order for $17.00. I just don't know what to buy you or the rest of the family for Xmas, nor have I really had time off to go shopping. So— $5.00 is for you, $2.00 each for the children and take $3.00 for Martha and Gene and $3.00 for Frankie and Reginald and please try to find something for them. Don't know what it will be but— you know me, I never know what to buy anyone.

Tell Frankie thanks lots for the Xmas card and money. I will write her soon.

We are just about through with our primary training which con- sisted of 70 hours in a Stearman— Bi-plane, open cockpit, and cold as h—. We are given two civilian and one Army flight check during the course of 70 hours. I had my second civilian check today and passed O.K. Just have the Army ride to take next week. We hope to finish up by Jan. 1st. We then start out on AT 6s— the plane we flew in Canada. That should be easy for me.

Gotta go— Will write more later. Thanks again for every- thing....

Thanks loads for the pound cake.

Avenger Field
Sweetwater, Texas
Monday Morning
December 27, 1943

Dearest Mother:

Today we start back on regular schedule after three days of making merry. Went over to the flight line at eight o'clock but the weather is too bad to fly, so we are all back in our barracks trying to catch up the loose ends left over after Christmas.

They gave us Friday thru Sunday Open Post, that is, we could go to the big city of Sweetwater. Some of the girls that lived within 200 miles of here were allowed to go home but even then, they had quite a bit of trouble trying to do that due to transportation difficulties and roads being frozen over. We had rain and snow Friday and Saturday which made things very mucky. Friday night they gave a big party here on the post for the girls and had about 150 flying officers and cadets to come in from a nearby aerodrome so we would have some dancing partners. The party was held in the Gym, orchestra, Xmas tree, Santa Claus and all. Each class put on a crazy skit and of course our class had one just as crazy as possible with me in there trying to see just how goofy I could be all dressed up in crazy patched slacks and goodness knows what else. It was fun and did help us all to forget the fact that we were away from home. Seems to be a habit with me now, never to get home for Xmas anymore but then it's just another day for me.

Saturday they had a big turkey dinner for us here on the post. Several families in Sweetwater had invited me to dinner with them, but I decided I had rather stay on the post with all the girls. Saturday afternoon some of us got together and drove down to San Angelo, a town seventy miles south of here, where another party was given for us by the father of one of the girls. It was lots of fun and we got back here about eleven o'clock Saturday night. Yesterday we just took things easy, rested and went to Church.

I have now finished all my check rides, Civilian and Army, and have only 15 more hours to put in on the Stearman before going to the AT-6. This has truly been good training for me and I have learned a bit more about aerobatics which is a good thing for me since I have never been too good on such things as slow rolls, snap rolls, and all the stuff you used to see at our air shows. Maybe if I keep on trying, I will someday learn to fly.

Although I don't like to talk about myself I know you will be pleased to know that I have been made Squadron Commander of my class, the highest office a student can hold in her class.

The fruit cake sure is good and of course the nuts are just swell. All of us here in my bay have truly been enjoying the box. Tell Jeaneane I sure appreciate the stationary, I needed some badly.

Thanks again for everything and I hope all of you had a happy Xmas....

Chapter 3
FINAL CHECK RIDES AND BRASS HATS

Avenger Field
Sweetwater, Texas
Sunday Afternoon
January 9, 1944

Dearest Mother:

You know, I thought the weather in England was bad but—- we had quite a snow storm here night before last which has left everything hidden under a beautiful white blanket that is now beginning to rumple under the sun and leave the ground in a wet, soupy, slushy state. One never knows quite what to expect out here from the weather cause it's cold as ——— and the next day it is quite nice. Just the same, I have been living in my longhandles.

Well, I have finished my primary training, thank goodness. Don't know how I survived 70 hours in an open plane in this cold weather but I made it. I just told myself I could and I did. Our class was given an extension on the finishing date for our flying to the 17th. I was lucky and managed to finish last Thursday so now I have some free time until we start on the AT-6. Also, I passed my test in code last week and I am exempt from going to code class. We just started code two weeks ago, but since I had already had code in England, it came back to me rather quickly and easy. Sometimes I wonder what I have ever done to deserve so many breaks because I seem to be so lucky no matter which way I turn. Of course I do try to do things in an honest and sincere manner and put out every effort to make a success of my flying. Maybe that has something to do with it all. I know if one truly loves their work, they put more into it, and therefore, must get more out of it by trying to make good. This month marks my 7th year in Aviation, can you realize that I have been flying that long?

I'm still planning my trip to Mexico the last of the week. We will be given several days off if 90% of our class finishes and I think they will. Found out the coupons were only good for two each after all. Sure was swell of Frankie to do that.

Mother, I want you to know again how much I enjoyed the cake and nuts. It was sweet of you to send Kim a box too. No, I haven't sent anything to England yet but I'm getting up a box of things to send off this week. Tell Martha I will try to get some hose for her if I do get down to Mexico. We have open post this afternoon so several of us are going out to a ranch and go horseback riding. I have met some swell people in Sweetwater that have adopted me while I'm here and they have a very nice place out near here. Met them when I made a talk before one of the Civic Clubs. Gotta go, keep well and write often ...

Avenger Field
Sweetwater, Texas
Wednesday Morning
January 26, 1944

Dearest Mother:

Just have time to get this off before Lunch. Honest, I can't seem to figure out what happens to time around this place. Seems as tho there is a meeting of some kind every night that fills my spare time.

They finally gave us 3 days off last Thursday thru Saturday. Instead of going to Mexico we, six of us, went to San Angelo, 70 miles south of here. We decided it would be too much of a trip cause it was over 400 miles and would have taken us two days to go and come, not giving us much time to see anything and rest. We had a more restful time just sleeping and eating and taking life easy for a change.

We started our advanced phase of flying last Sunday on the AT-6 and have also started our Instrument training on the Link Trainer. We get 30 hours in the Link on Instruments (under the hood on the ground). We then have 35 hours Instrument flying in a BT-13. I'll explain what a Link Trainer is in my next letter cause it's almost time to eat.

Gotta go- hope you are all well...

Lotsa Love,
Hazel

Besides being the Squadron Commander of her class and the Post Bugler, Hazel is elected President of the Welfare Board and becomes a frequent speaker at civic meetings. She is looking forward to her graduation in May as a member of the fourth class (44-W-4).

Avenger Field
Sweetwater, Texas
February 13, 1944

Dearest Mother:

Seems as tho I can only find time to write home when the weather is bad, which it is today. They released us from the flight line just a few minutes ago and I am now planning to get this note off to you, then take a shower and go into town to church.

This past week has been a full one for everybody around the field. They had graduation exercises Friday night for class W-1. You see, they number the classes in the order of their graduation. I will be in the 4th class to graduate in 1944, that is why I am listed in 44-W-4. So after two more graduations, it will be our class, and believe me, I can hardly wait. I just hope I make the grade and, I think perhaps I shall be putting out plenty of hard work as I have been doing since my first day here. Besides my flying and ground school subjects, I have quite a bit of extra curricular activities to take care of which does keep me quite busy. I have now been elected President of the Student Welfare Board. The duties of this board being, to take charge of the management of the Avengerette Club in Sweetwater, a club for the girls from the field here which is very much like the 'Wings Club' at home but—-without the few little things happening to the girls that you had to look at up at the 'Wings Club'. Then too, we take care of entertainment programs out here at the field and just the general welfare of the student body.

I am now half way through my 35 hours on the AT-6 as well as my instrument time on the Link Trainer. Our next phase will be instrument flying which is the best part of the course. That is where I am going to truly put out some work and concentration; but then again, the Instrument time I had in Miami has helped lots and I have been getting above average grades in my Link training...

In a letter of February 21,1944 Hazel has made a speech to the Rotary Club in Abilene, Texas:

I am enclosing a little paper telling about a talk I made last week in a town about 30 miles from here. I have been kept rather busy since I have been out here making my regular little talk. Next week I am helping with a bond drive here in Sweetwater and will talk again. Oh well, if I wash out of here I guess I could go on a speaking tour....

The *Rotater,* Abilene, Texas, Friday, February 18, 1944:

EXPERIENCES OF WOMAN FERRY PILOT TOLD ROTARY

"Experiences of a Georgia girl as a ferry pilot for the American and British Air Forces in the British Isles for 18 months related at our meeting last Friday by Hazel Raines- proved to be one of the most warmly received addresses in many months.

Miss Raines, in training at Avenger Field, Sweetwater in the Women's Ferry Service, was one of 25 American girl pilots recruited two years ago and taken to England for ferry flying. She was presented to the Rotarians by Charles Paxton of Sweetwater past district governor of this district. Paxton had been billed as the guest speaker on a vocational service program. Instead, he brought Miss Raines to do the job.

A small blond girl with a warm Georgia drawl, Miss Raines gave an impressive account of her work flying every type of military plane on many hundreds of trips between airdromes and bases used by both the AAF and RAF. She returned home four months ago."

Stinson, Hair, Brooks & Duke
Attorneys-at-Law
Abilene, Texas

Honorable Charles Paxton
Sweetwater, Texas

February 11, 1943

Dear Charlie,

I want to thank you for the program you brought to the Rotary Club today. Your speaker was certainly a most charming, intellectual and cultured lady— my ideal of a representative American woman.

I was very much impressed by her personality and individuality. She is the type woman who makes America great.

With personal regards, and thanking you again, I beg to remain,

Rotarily yours,
Jim Stinson

Avenger Field
Sweetwater, Texas
February 29th, 1944
Tuesday Afternoon

Dearest Mother:

Sounds like Spring is well on its' way at home. Haven't seen any sign of new life around here yet. Trees are very few and far between and as for flowers, the only ones I've seen are the ones on those things called hats in the shops in Sweetwater.

Well, my training is slowly but surely coming to an end out here deep in the heart of Texas. If I continue as per schedule with my class, we graduate either the night of May 15th or on the morning of the 16th. However, there is some talk at present about me not taking the full time on cross country flying when I finish my Instrument training which I am on now. Even if I did do that, I wouldn't be out of here before April anyway. Oh well, I don't mind much, its wonderful training and one never grows to old to learn, specially flying. And speaking of flying, this business of learning to fly on instruments is a swell deal. It'll sure make me feel better about flying anywhere at almost any time when I know I am proficient enough to cope with weather in flight in an intelligent way. Little did I know what I was really getting into when I started flying, but, I'll never regret a day of it. If I had to start all over again I would do the same as I have done so far; choose aviation and stick to it.

I haven't said much about the program or the girls that are here in any of my letters home yet but, even tho they are doing a swell job out here, you can take it from me only the best ever graduate. We had almost 100 to start out in our class in November, well, they have checked and double checked us continuously since we first started flying for safety and proficiency and we now have about half the class left. Of course most of the girls had very little time and experience which does account for 99% of the wash outs. In our original bay of six girls we now have two left. So, I guess I am a lucky little girl. I just know I've gotta make it or else, cause, I can't let myself down to say nothing of YOU.

This has been another one of "those days". No flying due to weather. It does give us a chance to catch up on odd jobs and letter writing.

Received a letter from one of the girls in England the other day saying she is coming back soon and expects to come down here......

Hazel breaks the news to her mother that Jacqueline Cochran has advised her to complete her courses early and begin training to fly the B-26 heavy twin-engine bomber:

Avenger Field
Sweetwater, Texas
Friday Night
March 10, 1944

Dearest Mother:

A free moment, and a chat with you. Life has been steady and full of things to do from six in the morning to ten at night for the past ten days. The reason for all this - being Instruments. Yes, they have got me really working hard on this instrument flying course. It is so very interesting yet quite a strain on one's nerves; however, I suppose it's a good test for me to see if I can really take it. I am now about half way through with the course. Just think, I will be able to actually handle aeroplanes under almost any weather condition, good or bad. That will truly be a relief to me to be able to know I can do just that.

Now, for a little news for you for a change. I want you to be the first one to hear about my good break and plans. I might say here first, these plans are not absolutely definite yet but, I have every reason to believe they will be by the time you receive this letter.

Another class of girls is graduating tomorrow and Jackie Cochran is here now for this big event. This afternoon I had a long talk with Jackie about me and my plans after graduation. She has advised me to cut my training short by about two months and go ahead and finish up in about three weeks, that is, just as soon as I finish my Instrument course. So, I have decided to do just that. Then, here is the best part of it all, she is sending me to B-26 transition school, (which I think will be somewhere in Kansas) for 9 weeks. The B-26 is a heavy twin-engine bomber. Now, here is the big bit of news, but— before telling you, I want you to promise not to let it worry you, it might not happen, but I hope it does. After finishing my course on the B-26, I have my choice of serving here in the U.S. or foreign duty. If I should choose duty outside of the U.S., it will be Australia. What do you think of that? Of course I am all up in the air over the thought of it. If I get this, I will be given quite a long leave to go home before leaving the country, so don't worry about that. Gee, I can hardly believe all this, I sure am a lucky person. Let me know what you think about all this.

We had a super graduation yesterday. I told you about Cochran being here, well we also had about six Generals here. We considered ourselves extremely lucky cause General Arnold, Chief of the U.S.

Air Forces, was here and made the graduation speech. Yesterday was indeed an exciting day for us all cause we had to shine and polish not only ourselves but our living quarters. You should have seen me up at five o'clock scrubbing the floor and wood-work. After graduation, we put on a dress review. We had to march out on the flight line and pass in review before the many Army officials and brass hats. Very colorful and exciting and most impressive.

In a hurry— we are not flying today and I have been invited in to Sweetwater to go to church and have chicken dinner with a family that has been very nice to me since I have been here. Gotta go wash my neck, it stays dirty, you know that tho....

Avenger Field
Sweetwater, Texas
Monday Afternoon
March 27, 1944

Dearest Mother:

Well, I did it. Finished my Instrument course Friday and believe me, it was a relief to have that phase behind me. You know I was worried for fear I wouldn't do a good job on instruments cause I was not too sure I could, after flying in weather in England that put plenty of fear in me of bad weather. It was a grand course of training, most interesting and I truly had to work, but it was worth every effort I put forth. Please don't misunderstand me when I tell you how well I did but, I feel that you would like to know. When we finished our 35 hours we were given final check rides to determine whether or not we were capable and deserved instrument ratings. Well, I made the highest grade that has ever been given here at the field in flying of any type and, to make it on an instrument ride was most unusual and quite something. The check pilot was so pleased and excited over the ride I gave him that he read my flight report to the entire flight. It sure was a swell report, but I don't honestly feel that I deserved such praises. Hope I can live up to that report by doing a good job of flying at all times. Now I feel quite happy about instrument flying and have confidence that I can do a good job under almost any conditions.

My training here has just about come to an end. I start night flying this week, only ten hours. Then four hours of formation flying and, I will be finished. Plan to graduate with the next class that finishes which will be April 16th. After that, I guess I will be heading for Kansas for nine more weeks of Bomber twin-engine training then, home for awhile.

Seven of us finished up our flying Friday, got a three day pass, and went to Mexico for the weekend. We went down to Del Rio then across from there. It sure was fun and interesting even tho I couldn't understand half what those funny people said. The joke was truly on me. I walked up to a Mexican and stood talking with him, or rather to him for ten minutes, when someone came up and told me he didn't understand a word of English.

Sure hope you are feeling O.K. Write soon and give my love to all the family.

I love you,
Hazel

Hazel graduates, finishing two months ahead of schedule having been exempted from cross country flying. This exemption allows her to graduate as a member of the 44-W-3 class. She comments:

Working for my wings means more to me this time cause I am sure that within the next month we will be officially in the Army Air Corps and I will be commissioned. What that commission will be, goodness only knows. Does seem that I will be able to pull a rather good rank since I held the rating of Captain in England. As far as I know now, I will be going to Dodge City, Kansas from here. There was some talk about going to Orlando, Florida to Officer's Candidate School ....

Hazel's assumption that the WASPs would soon be recognized by the Army Air Corp did not take into account some of the strong opposition against them. This recognition would not actually take place until 1977. Bad press and political controversies plagued these female pilots and their role in WWII was frequently questioned. Some of them experienced sabotage, but Jacqueline Cochran continued to work behind the scenes to continue the program—sometimes covering up obvious sabotage to avoid bad publicity. "WASP Betty Taylor Young was killed when her engine failed while she was landing. They found sugar in her gas tank." (Vera S. Williams, *WASPs,* p.92). Other pilots had similar experiences with "fuel lines crossed with coolant lines." (Ibid. p. 92)

Chapter 4
TEST PILOT

HEADQUARTERS, ARMY AIR FORCES

April 7, 1944

Dear Miss Raines,

I have your very nice letter of March 28th. I am so glad to know you feel you have derived so much benefit from the course there. Naturally, we are pretty proud of the setup.

I doubt very much if I am going to be able to get out for the graduation in April due to our bill still being in the House and much work to be done in that direction. I think it will be a wonderful thing for all of the women if we can get this bill through.

There won't be a class of B-26 students going in this month.

I hope the assignment you receive on graduation will be to your liking and satisfaction. If any girls are going to be assigned to tow targets squadrons, this will be your best bet since they fly only good equipment in those squadrons.

Here's hoping everything will go well with you in the future. Kind personal regards.

Sincerely,
Jacqueline Cochran
Director of Women Pilots

Jacqueline Cochran's reference to the "bill still being in the House" relates to the proposed legislation to militarize the WASPs. Many publications like *Time* magazine turned public opinion against the WASPs. In a May 29, 1944 *Time* article titled 'Unnecessary and Undesirable', the writer said "that the WASPs experiment had been expensive and that there were men out there who could have trained more quickly and cheaply." (Vera S. Williams, *WASPs,* p. 124.) The bill did not pass.

Hazel writes her mother from Kansas on May 2, 1944:

Guess you think you will never get another letter from me, but since the day I graduated, I have been jumping from one place to another so fast until I really haven't had time to do a thing but work, eat and sleep. I was sent on a special assignment to investigate several different Stations and as a result I have been all over Texas, New Mexico, Oklahoma and now I am in Kansas but plan to leave here today for Pecos, Texas. I wish I could say more about what I have been doing but I am sure you understand.

My original plans were to report to this station for training on B-26 but for reasons which I cannot give, I am going to Pecos, Texas to another advanced twin-engine school where I think I will be located for at least three months. You see, Jackie has put me on another type assignment other than just flying duties which keeps me on the ground over half my time and which I don't exactly like. However, it is interesting work ,and I hope to be traveling quite a bit between here and the West coast, which is the remaining part of the States that I have not seen. As for foreign duty, that probably will not come up for at least six months yet.

Hazel was happy to be in a uniform again. These were specially designed for the WASPs and were Santiago blue. " When the WASPs wrote to Disney (who was known for designing insignia for other flying groups) and asked him to design an insignia for the women, Fifinella was a natural choice. Disney added a pair of goggles and some wings to the character of the book, and a perfect mascot was born."(Vera S. Williams, *WASPs,* p. 50) Hazel's comment about the uniforms was:

> "A uniform is truly a swell thing— I never have to worry about what I am going to wear— not that I ever did. By the way, I wish you would look thru my things and see if I have any more blue R.A.F. shirts and black ties. I can wear them with my new uniform."

Hazel writes that she is a test pilot and the work is easy:

Pecos Army Air Field
Pecos, Texas
May 10, 1944

The work is easy and isn't work at all. Our day begins about 7:30 when we get up, go to the mess and have breakfast then report to the flight line about 8:30. We are flying light twin-engine aircraft called UC-78 which is a twin Cessna. Our job is test flying after repairs have been made to the aircraft and engines. Usually the days work is completed by four o'clock and we have Saturday afternoons and Sunday off. It just depends on the number of ships to be tested as to how long we work each day. I must say it is quite interesting work and I love it.

MO. DAY	FROM	TO	TYPE OF AIRCRAFT	TYPE OF ENGINE	H. P.	LICENSE NUMBER	DURATION HRS.	MIN.
6 3	Pecos A.A.F.	Local	UC-78-B	Cajaos	225	874	1727	30
6 3	Pecos A.A.F.		UC-78-B	Jacobs	225	124		55
6 3	Pecos A.A.T.	Avenger Field	UC-78-B	Jacobs	225	372	1	24
6 4	Avt. Avenger	Pecos A.A.F.	UC-78-B	Jacobs	225	378	1	35
6 5	Pecos A.A.F.	Local	UC-78-B	Jacobs	225	132		20
6 5	Pecos A.A.F.	"	UC-78-B	Jacobs	225	161	1	25
6 6	Pecos A.A.F.	Deming, N.M.	UC-78-B	Jacobs	225	193	2	10
6 7	Deming, New Mexico	El Paso, Texas	UC-125-B	Jacobs	225	193	1	05
6 7	El Paso, Texas	Pecos AAF	N2-18B	Cajaos	225	193	1	35
6 8	Pecos A.A.F.	Local	UC-78-B	Cajaos	225	211	1	05
6 8	Pecos A.A.F.	"	UC-78-B	Jacobs	225	211		30
6 9	Pecos A.A.F.	"	UC-78-B	Jacobs	225	394		35
6 9	Pecos A.A.F.	"	UC-78-B	Jacobs	225	223	1	25
6 12	Pecos A.A.F.	"	UC-78-B	Jacobs	225	380		40
6 12	Pecos A.A.F.	"	UC-78-B	Jacobs	225	378		20
6 12	Pecos A.A.F.	"	UC-78-B	Jacobs	225	311		25
						TOTALS	17113	

YEAR ___

Hazel's Log testing UC-78s. 1944

Pecos Army Air Field
Pecos, Texas
Tuesday Night
May 30, 1944

Dearest Mother:

Guess you think I have forgotten about you again, but I have been busy during the past week trying to get settled here at my new base and work. Then too, Mrs. Sheehy from Washington, assistant to Jackie, has been here inspecting us for the past five days, and with her around, I have not had a free moment. I have been made Squadron Commander of the girls down here. We only have seven here; but I do stay busy trying to look after them in addition to my regular flying duties. When we came down here, they put us in Instructors school for fifty hours flying before we could start testing; but because of my past experience, they did not make me take the training, but checked me out and put me to work immediately. I am glad cause I have had enough of school and training for a while.

I flew over to Sweetwater last Tuesday to attend the graduation class that I started my training with at Avenger and had a long talk with Jackie. She had flown down from Washington for the graduation. She told me that I would return to Dodge City, Kansas July 1st for training on the B-26. However, there seems to be a good chance of me being sent to Orlando, Florida in about two weeks for training as a future officer if we go in the Army. If and when I am sent to Orlando, I am planning to stop by home for a couple of days if I can get leave. One of the girls that I lived with and went around with quite a bit while at Avenger, Peggie Parker from Portland, Oregon, flew back to Pecos with me after she graduated and spent the rest of the week. Her folks had come down for her graduation, so they drove her car down here and on to Carlsbad, New Mexico for the weekend. We drove over in my car Saturday afternoon and I came back Sunday afternoon. It was certainly swell getting away from this hot place for just a day. I have never before seen so much dust in all my life. I have decided I like English fog better than Texas dust. Peggie left Monday morning and drove on to Romulus, Michigan, which is her new base assignment. Her folks gave me quite a nice traveling bag with my name on it for graduation.

Thanks so much for sending me the shirt. The laundry situation here is awful and with only four regulation shirts plus my old R.A.F. shirts, I can hardly stay clean. I have only been able to have my shirts washed once since I have been here. Tonight I washed out two myself. That hurt worse than anything I have had to do since the war started. You know how I hate to wash clothes and iron.

Think I'll go to bed cause I am tired and sleepy. Give my love to all the family and let me hear from you soon.....

Pecos Army Air Field
Pecos, Texas
Wednesday Night
June 14, 1944

Dearest Mother:

Haven't heard from you this week, hope you are not sick. It is so hot out here until it is really all I can do to finish a days work and get home to bed. It usually gets up to about 120 in the middle of the day.

I think I wrote you about my trip to Deming, New Mexico. Ten of us took ships over there last week and were gone two days. Went out to pick up some pilots that had been out to California and had brought ships back to Deming. Well, Friday we had a trip to Santa Fe, New Mexico, and returned here Sunday night. The trip was interesting and rather fun. One of the girls that went out with us lived out from Santa Fe on a big ranch and we went out there Saturday. Of course it was my first time on a ranch and I was all eyes and wanted to try everything. We did go horseback riding and I am still so sore till I can hardly sit down. We also went fishing and I caught five mountain trout. They are grand eating fish, wish you could have some cause they are not like the trout we buy at home.

Although our job here is suppose to be testing, we are getting in a bit of ferrying as you can see. I was scheduled to go out Monday to Kansas and again today to Kansas, but talked my way out of it. I was just too tired from the two other trips. I am going out either the last of this week or the first of next to take a ship to Hutchinson, Kansas and pick one up to bring back here. Wish I could get a trip to Macon. Still don't know when I'll be leaving here but rather think it will be by the first of July. I sure hope so cause I certainly don't want to spend the summer down here in this awful hot place. It seems that I always get in a climate that is either too hot or too cold.

How is everybody at home? Has Gene gone yet? The invasion has truly affected the officers here. They are sending out quite a number of them for overseas duty.

Give my love to all the family and write soon cause-

I love you,
Hazel

Hazel's correspondence with her mother continues. She does not know where she will be stationed next but "I am not unhappy at the thought of leaving this place cause I can't picture any spot they might send me as being worse than west Texas."

In a late July letter, Hazel has been posted to Orlando, Florida.

Student Officers' Mail Room
AAFSAT
Orlando, Florida

Thursday Night
July 20, 1944

Dearest Mother:

By this time I know you will be surprised to hear from me in any part of the United States. Well, I am in Orlando. It all happened so fast, until I was really here before I realized it myself. Tuesday at noon, they told me I was to report down here Wednesday morning at eight o'clock for four weeks tactical training that they are giving all WASPs. Of course, the only way I could make it was to fly, so, they gave me a ship at Pecos and I flew it to Fort Worth, where I made connections with Delta Air Lines to Atlanta, arriving there in the wee small hours of the morning at two o'clock, just in time to make Eastern Air Lines down here. I arrived here at 7:30, Wednesday morning, reported here at the base and was in class at nine o'clock. This is a ground school course that is given to prospective officers in the Army Air Corp and consists of eight hours of ground school per day for four weeks. It is a very interesting course, and I do feel quite fortunate in being sent down for the training. Of course, it will call for quite a bit of hard work and studying, but since I never did too much of that type work, I am learning to study and like it.

If we finish according to schedule, I will complete this course August 11.

I am on orders to return to Pecos when I finish, but maybe if I can promote a ride to Macon by plane, I will be able to stop off for a brief visit before going back to Texas. Please don't count too much on that cause the Army is very funny about things like that. I will be allowed about four days to get back to Pecos, and if I can get a plane out of Macon going that way, I may be able to stop off for at least a day. I certainly hope so.

Hope you are having a nice rest up in Clayton. It sure made me homesick when I landed in Atlanta and couldn't stop in Macon.....

By August 18th, Hazel had completed her training in Orlando, had visited her family in Macon and was back at Pecos Army Air Field as squadron commander of the now 14 WASPs stationed there. This was short lived, however, for she received orders to leave west Texas and report to Kingman Army Air Field in Kingman, Arizona by September 18th, 1944:

Writing from Kingman Army Air Field, Hazel "is towing targets in the B-26 for the gunners in the B-17 to practice." One wonders if the fact that "the target is trailing behind us some 500 feet so we don't have a thing to worry about" was true.

Kingman Army Air Field
Thursday Night
September 28, 1944

Dearest Mother:

Well, I guess I am just about to get into the swing of things here at our new Post. Tis quite a swing tho, and begins at five o'clock in the morning. At least that is when we get up, cause we hafta be on the line at six, ready to go. We are taking a course of transition learning to fly the B-26. Tuesday thru Fridays, we fly tow target missions - that is towing targets in the B-26 for the gunners in the B-17 to practice shooting at. Of course, the target is trailing behind us some 500 feet, so we don't have a thing to worry about. Half of our missions are flown at 10,000 feet and half at 20,000 feet. The mission usually runs about three to four hours long. In the afternoon, we have ground school til five o'clock then - home to bed.

We are supposed to finish our course here October 12th. As yet, I do not know where we will be going from here but - rumor has it that we might be going to Lincoln, Nebraska. This id interesting work and I am still learning more about this business of flying everyday....

MO.	DAY	FROM	TO	TYPE OF AIRCRAFT	TYPE OF ENGINE	H. P.	LICENSE NUMBER	DURATION HRS.	MIN.
								1818	44
9	29	Kingman AAF	Local	TB-26		4000	28	4	05
9	30	Kingman AAF	Local	TB-26		4000	29	2	45
10	2	Kingman AAF	Local	Link					
10	3	Kingman AAF	Local	Link					
10	3	Kingman AAF	Local	TB-26		4000	31	2	30
10	4	Kingman AAF	Local	TB-26		4000	31	3	30
10	4	Kingman AAF	Local	Link					
10	5	Kingman AAF	Local	TB-26		4000	30	3	45
10	6	Kingman AAF	Local	TB-26		4000	29	3	30
12	7	Kingman AAF	Local	TB-26		4000	30	1	20
10	9	Kingman AAF	Local	Link					
10	10	Kingman AAF	Local	TB-26		4000	34	2	55
10	11	Kingman AAF	Local	TB-26		4000	31	2	00
10	19	Sweetwater, Tex	Local	BT-13	Pratt Whitney	450	124		50
10	20	Sweetwater	Local	BT-13	P+W	450	120	3	05
10	21	Sweetwater	Local	BT-13	P+W	450	121	3	05
10	23	Sweetwater	Local	BT-13	P+W	450	123	3	15
							TOTALS	1855	44

YEAR _____

Hazel's Log on towing targets. 1944

Chapter 5
DEACTIVATION AND DISAPPOINTMENT

Once again Hazel's "crazy heart actions" plague her. However, this condition seems to be more of a nuisance to her rather than a reason to stop flying. As to why the doctors let her continue, Hazel must have convinced them of her determination to continue flying. She does admit that these plans might have to be altered.

Kingman Army Air Field
Kingman, Arizona
Tuesday Morning
October 3, 1944

Dearest Mother:

Just came down from my morning flight and have about 45 minutes before time for lunch and then ground school. Flew 2 and one half hours this morning— dual transition— supposed to fly a tow target mission, but I missed flying my transition yesterday so I got it today. Had a wisdom tooth pulled Saturday afternoon and they wouldn't let me fly until today. Sorta glad to get rid of that tooth- upper left.It was coming thru out on the side of my gum and causing a little trouble. Everything is O.K. now, thank goodness. We get all our dental work free— think I'll have my teeth cleaned and checked before I leave here if I have time.

This morning we flew up to Boulder Dam and Las Vegas, Nevada just to see the place. Quite an immense piece of engineering and very pretty from the air. My first view of the Dam. We fly over into California every day, sometimes almost as far as Los Angeles. The other day we flew down Grand Canyon. It was just as beautiful and wonderful from the air as it was when we stopped by to see it on the way out here.

They are trying to finish us up here by the 7th in case our orders come thru ahead of time. I doubt if we will finish before the 12th tho. We are suppose to get 30 hours on this ship- I have 15 so far. This really is a wonderful course of training but I am a bit tired of ground school. Thank goodness we finish ground school this week.

Now that it's all over— I had trouble with the Doctor here when we reported— same old story, my heart. I still have that letter Doc Bertram wrote for me and that helped some. Of course the Doctor here still didn't understand my crazy heart actions and ran about a dozen tests. As a result he is letting me fly anyway and I am having to report to the hospital every night for a check-up. He says I'm O.K. 100% but he just wants to check me everyday. I have stopped drinking coffee- only one cup for breakfast- and have just about cut out smoking entirely. No more beer or any kind of alcoholic beverages but— that certainly doesn't bother me at all. I go to bed at eight o'clock every night. The things I won't do to keep on flying!...

In the fall of 1944, many of the male pilots were returning to the States to resume military and civilian duties. Hazel's tour of duty as a WASP was also coming to an end. The announcement of the deactivation of the WASP program was made in early November of 1944. In a letter of October 28, 1944, Hazel writes that she will be finishing her ground school by November 23rd, and will be going back to Kingman by December 20th, "the date this business is supposed to end." Her plans for the future are uncertain.

It seems that Macon is really getting ready for civilian flying after the war. I don't think I know the man in charge of the school out at the airport. I don't think I would like the idea of going back to Macon and perhaps instructing again. I believe I can find something more interesting and more concrete in a better part of the country; at least I'm going to try to see what I can find before I go back there. I would certainly like to have a place of my own. I wrote some of the people in Florida that I know around Fort Lauderdale and Miami to see what my chances down there would be. That would be much nicer, don't you think?

I do want to try and get something definite worked out between now and then before I go back to Macon for a visit with you and before I start out again. That's the reason I want to go into the aviation business for myself, that is, get into a branch of aviation that will not be taking me all over the country and where I can settle down for a while and we can be together. I think you understand me when I say I don't want to go back to Macon.

HEADQUARTERS OF THE ARMY AIR FORCES
WASHINGTON

TO ALL MEMBERS OF THE WASP:

3 November 1944

Since the announcement of the WASP deactivation a number of inquiries have been received from individual WASPs as to the opportunities for employment as pilots in various Allied countries.

I have no information at this time as to the need for women pilots by any foreign country. If sufficient number of girls are interested in foreign service, I shall be glad to get in touch with the various embassies and legations to determine whether any such need exists and if so, whether they would be interested in using WASPs. Before doing so, however, it will be necessary to know definitely how many WASPs are interested and under what conditions they would serve.

If a need exists in any of our Allied countries for women pilots and you wish to volunteer your service, will you please write me, giving the following information:

1. A statement that you will serve in any Allied country which might be willing to use your services.

2. For how long a period you would serve under contract conditions. It is probable that minimum contract might run from eighteen months to two years.

3. Would you be willing to enlist in the military service of an Allied country, under whatever conditions enlistments are accepted?

4. Would you be willing to travel by boat to your assignment?

5. Salary required. It is likely that salary will be much lower than that you now receive.

As you no doubt know, many personal hardships will be encountered in most foreign countries which you have not had to face in your service with the WASPs here. Before you make a decision, careful consideration should be given to all factors involved in foreign service. I want to be sure that you are prepared to face such conditions before I offer you any of the various Governments.

Because of the volume of administrative work involved in the deactivation of the WASP, it will not be possible to undertake this project until after 20 December 1944.

Jacqueline Cochran
Director of Women Pilots

The fact that this letter was found in Hazel's files, soon becomes clear. On November 7th, Hazel writes her mother of some possible plans for the future:

> Jackie Cochran was here the other day and explained to us why we were being inactivated— seems as tho they have a surplus of men pilots now in the Army that can do the jobs we have been doing. She has started a new plan, however, to try to get some overseas duty for some of us. This time in Australia or maybe China. That would be interesting but- the plans are not definite as yet. I would like to go to Australia.

Jacqueline Cochran in her autobiography had this to say about being the Director of Women Pilots:

> It wasn't easy being director of women pilots. Not because of the basic premise of the program so much as the hassle of breaking

such new ground for women in what had been a highly prized corner of a man's world: flying. My training program, my operations, the WASP - everything worked, and in fact, it worked extremely well. We were proving a point about women flyers, providing competent pilots to the ferry operation, towing targets was a nasty job-working on tracking and searchlight operations, simulated strafing, smoke laying, and performing other chemical missions, radio control flying, taking care of basic and instrument instructing, engineering test flying, as well as handling the administrative and utility flying. (Jacqueline Cochran and Maryann Bucknum Brinley, *Jackie Cochran, An Autobiography* 1987, p.207).

HEADQUARTERS
ARMY AIR FORCES TRAINING COMMAND
FORT WORTH 2, TEXAS

22 November 1944

Miss Hazel J. Raines
Women's Airforce Service Pilot,
Kingman Army Air Field,
Kingman, Arizona

Your services with the AAF Training Command, as a member of the Women's Airforce Service Pilots, have been of great aid to the accomplishment of our mission that I wish to extend to you our deep appreciation for a job well done.

During the past two years, under the stress of urgent wartime need, the WASPs have undertaken a variety of assignments requiring skill and courage, and you have fulfilled your share of them in a manner which has won the admiration and gratitude of us all. We have watched you perform your tasks, often under difficult and trying conditions, with an eager attention to duty and a degree of craftsmanship worthy of our most seasoned pilots. By ferrying aircraft and personnel, by towing targets and flying pursuit curves, by making engineering flights and radar calibration flights, and in many other important assignments, you and members of your organization have helped us meet a grave national emergency. At the same time you have proved the superior capabilities of women pilots, and we have shared your pride in the fact that members of the WASP have flown every type of airplane, from our lightest training planes to heavy bombers. We know that you have accomplished your duties without regard for possible danger or risk, placing the welfare of the nation above your own, thereby evidencing a degree of devotion which has not gone unheeded among the men of the Air Forces.

You have performed well as a volunteer in the service of your country, and in all the years to come you will carry with you our grateful appreciation. As a fellow pilot, let me wish you good luck and many happy landings.

B.K. Yount
Lieutenant General, U.S.A.
Commanding

Sunday Afternoon
November 26, 1944

Dearest Mother:

Well, here we are again— on our merry way back to Kingman. We finished up at Sweetwater Wednesday and drove up to Oklahoma City Wednesday night. Kay Van Doozer- one of the girls that was in England with me and who has been instructing Instruments at Avenger Field for the past three months- is with Sissy and me. Her home is in Los Angeles and she is driving as far as Kingman with us. She just finished up her last class at Avenger Field when we finished.

Had quite a nice Thanksgiving dinner with Sissy and her folks— turkey and all the trimmings. We left Oklahoma City Friday and got in here last night. Had quite an experience in a terrific snow storm Friday night. We were trying to make Alamogordo, New Mexico cause I wanted to stop by and see Peggy Parker the girl from Portland, Oregon, I was telling you about when I was home. She is getting married in January, and wanted me to go up to Portland with her for Christmas and the wedding. Of course I can't do that; so, I stopped by to see her on my way out here.

Now back to the snow storm. Just 50 miles before we got to Alamogordo Friday night, we ran into one of the worst snow storms I have ever been in— it took us four hours to drive 50 miles.

I left my car in Oklahoma City and we are driving out in Sissy's car. Thought I would let mine have a rest for a while. We are staying here today and tomorrow to rest up a bit before going back to the Kingman grind of up at 5 o'clock and in the air 'till noon. However, that won't be for long.

Really, I can hardly wait until December 20th. I feel that I do need a rest once again for about a month before starting out again. Of course, I don't know as yet what I will be doing but— something will be worked out I am sure. Sissy and I are still talking and planning our supply business which does seem to be a good idea. It will give me a chance to establish myself in something definite and concrete in Aviation and I do feel that the time has come when I should do just that. After all, I'm not getting any younger and I do want to get into something that will give me more of a secure feeling financially and something I can depend on other than making "just a living" flying. I know I won't be physically able to continue my flying for a living much longer. Seems as tho they are really serious about my heart and the funny little way it works. I know it's O.K. but I guess it is tired and needs a rest. The Army Doctor tells me I will be O.K. as long as I don't overwork myself. So— I have resigned myself to the fact that I must be sensible at last and take care of Hazel. Well, that's what I intend to do, that's why I think it's best to try to continue in the field of Aviation but not in a flying capacity entirely- just fly as a side line.

By the way, I'm not sure as yet that I will be able to get home for Christmas. We leave Kingman December 20th and will no doubt make Oklahoma City about the 23rd. It all depends on how this idea of ours works out as to when I will get back home. Of course, I am not too sure that I will be able to completely finance this idea of ours. I might need some help and maybe— if things are not complicated- I have been thinking maybe I could present my idea to Reginald and he could give me some good advice and maybe help me a little. But then we will wait and see. I might not need any help....

HEADQUARTERS, ARMY AIR FORCES
WASHINGTON

27 November 1944

Miss Hazel Raines
Kingman AAF
Kingman, Arizona

Dear Hazel,

Thank you so very much for the letter which was waiting for me upon my return to headquarters. I hated to discuss such an unpleasant subject with the girls as came up at the meeting at Avenger Field- but I have been so gratified at the marvelous expressions of loyalty which the girls have sent to me since that evening.

I am so glad that you have been able to obtain the training which the Army Air Forces has offered to women pilots. It is an unbelievable experience and I truly wish I might have had the

opportunity to obtain some of it myself. As you may know, I did get
a sort of bird's-eye view of the Bryan course and would have given
anything to complete it.

You can be sure that I will get in touch with you if any good
opportunities of foreign service or any type of flying arises, and I
have set down your Macon, Georgia address so I can contact you
immediately.

I hope you can avail yourself of a cross country so you can
attend the finale at Sweetwater. If not, I know our paths will cross
some time soon. Meantime, best of luck to you, and kindest personal regards.

Sincerely,
Jacqueline Cochran
Director of Women Pilots

In a short letter from Kingman Air Field, (December 5, 1944), Hazel
describes Las Vegas. After three years service to her country, Hazel is out of
a job with very few choices for the future. The deactivation of the WASPs
must have been devastating for her. Her reaction to Las Vegas and the "idle
rich" sounds somewhat bitter.

"Certainly enjoyed our drive out to Los Angeles and back. We
stopped in Las Vegas, Nevada Sunday and Sunday night. Met some
girls we knew stationed there and had fun seeing the famous resort
gambling Night Clubs where lots of movie stars and extra rich people go to throw their money away. That town is more or less one
Night Club after another. It was interesting but sorta hurts when you
think how foolish the idle rich American can be.

The drive did compensate for all that tho cause the mountains
were beautiful and covered with snow. All of the higher ones, about
10,000 feet high were snow capped and very magnificent."

Hazel's assignment at Kingman would end on December 20th, but the family
recommendation for an instructing job in Cochran, Georgia, does not appeal
to her. A letter of December 20, 1994:

Received a letter today from Mr. Walls about the job near
Cochran, Georgia, and am writing him a note in reply. I have
thought it over but don't think that would be my best chance in
Aviation at this time. If I am going to start out helping someone
build up a new business, I would rather that business be at least half
mine. Instructing is not the easiest job in the world, as I already
know, therefore; I am trying to establish myself in something that

will not require full time flying. I have even thought about aeronautical engineering and planning. There are quite a few openings in large aircraft factories at this time in that capacity which does involve a certain amount of flying. I feel that I would be going back instead of ahead if I started out once again in a little out of the way field as this "Red Dog" seems to be. I do hope you understand the way I feel about this and want you to know I am trying to do my best by shooting high as I always have.

Hazel's last letter in 1944 was written from Oklahoma City where she was visiting her friend and former WASP, Delrose (Sissy) Sieber. Hazel is still applying for jobs. The one in question is with Douglas Aircraft as a test pilot, testing C-47 Aircraft. December 26, 1944:

We (Sissy and I), left Pecos on the 21st, went to San Antonio where I investigated a job prospect with Sissy's brother-in-law who is in the Aviation Supply business. We arrived here Christmas Eve-had a quiet Christmas Day and today I have been trying another prospective job opportunity with Douglas Aircraft here in Oklahoma City. Have an appointment with the head man Friday to see about a job as test pilot testing C-47 Aircraft. They are the same as a DC-3, the type Eastern Airlines uses.

I do wish I could have been with you and the rest of the family but I did want to look around out here and if something doesn't turn up worth while I guess I will head back home.

The following address was made by General "Hap" Arnold to the WASP on December 7, 1944. It was found in Hazel's scrapbook along with the press release from Jacqueline Cochran:

WAR DEPARTMENT
Bureau of Public Relations
PRESS BRANCH

ADDRESS BY
GENERAL H. H. ARNOLD, COMMANDING GENERAL
ARMY AIR FORCES
BEFORE WASP CEREMONY,
SWEETWATER, TEXAS,
THURSDAY, DECEMBER 7, 1944

I am glad to be here today and talk with you young women who have been making Aviation history. You and all WASP have been pioneers in a new field of wartime service, and I sincerely appreciate the splendid job you have done for the AAF.

You, and more than nine hundred of your sisters, have shown that you can fly wingtip to wingtip with your brothers. If ever there was a doubt in anyone's mind that women can become skillful pilots, the WASP have dispelled that doubt.

The possibility of using women to pilot military aircraft was first considered in the summer of 1941. We anticipated then that global war would require all our qualified men and many of our women. We did not know how many of our young men could qualify to pilot the thousands of aircraft which the American industry could produce. There was also the problem of finding sufficient highly capable young men to satisfy the demands of the Navy, the Ground Forces, the Service Forces, and the Merchant Marine. England and Russia had been forced to use women to fly trainers and combat-type aircraft. Russian women were being used in combat.

In that emergency I called Jacqueline Cochran, who herself had flown almost everything with wings and several times had won air races from men who now are the general officers of the Air Forces. I asked her to draw a plan for the training and the use of American women pilots. She presented such a plan in late 1941 and it formed the basis for the Air Forces use of the WASP.

Frankly, I didn't know in 1941 whether a slip of a young girl could fight the controls of a B-17 in the heavy weather they could naturally encounter in operational flying. Those of us who had been flying for twenty or thirty years knew that flying an airplane was something you do not learn overnight.

But, Miss Cochran said that carefully selected young women could be trained to fly our combat-type planes. So, it was only right that we take advantage of every skill which we, as a nation possessed...

My objectives in forming the WASP were, as you know, three:

1. To see if women could serve as military pilots, and, if so, to form the nucleus of an organization which could be rapidly expanded.

2. To release male pilots for combat.

3. To decrease the Air Forces' total demands for the cream of the manpower pool.

Well, now in 1944, more than two years since WASP started flying with the Air Forces, we can come to only one conclusion— the entire operation has been a success. It is on the record that women can fly as well as men. In training, in safety, in operations, your showing is comparable to the over-all record of the AAF flying within the continental United States. That was what you were called upon to do—continental flying. If the need had developed for women to fly our aircraft overseas, I feel certain that the WASP would have performed that job equally well.

Certainly we haven't been able to build an airplane you can't handle. From AT-6s to B-29s, you have flown them around like veterans. One of the WASP has even test-flown our new jet plane.

You have worked hard at your jobs. Commendations from Generals to whose commands you have been assigned are constantly coming across my desk. These commendations record how you have buckled down to the monotonous, the routine jobs which are not much desired by our hot-shot young men headed toward combat or just back from an overseas tour. In some of your jobs I think they like you better than men.

I want to stress how valuable I believe this whole WASP program has been for the country. If another national emergency arises— let us hope it does not, but let us this time face the possibility if it does, we will not again look upon a women's flying organization as experimental. We will know that they can handle our fastest fighters, our heaviest bombers we will know they are capable of ferrying, target towing, flying training, test flying, and the countless other activities which you have proved you can do.

That is valuable knowledge for the air age into which we are entering.

But please understand that I do not look upon the WASP and the job they have done in this war as a project or an experiment. A pioneering venture, yes. Solely an experiment, no. The WASP are an accomplishment.

We are winning the war—we still have a long way to go— but we are winning it. Every WASP who has contributed to the training and operation of the Air Force has filled a vital and necessary place in the jigsaw pattern of victory. Some of you are discouraged sometimes, all of us are, but be assured you have filled a necessary place in the overall picture of the Air Forces.

The WASPs have completed their mission. The job has been successful. But, as usual in war, it has not been without cost. Thirty-seven WASP have died while helping their Country move toward the moment of final victory. The Air Forces will long remember their service and their final sacrifice.

So, on this last graduation day, I salute you and all WASP. We of the AAF are proud of you, we will never forget our debt to you.

Jacqueline Cochran's statement about the WASPs included her disappointment over the failure to militarize the program, thus providing the same benefits to female veterans who had died serving their country. In a final report on the Women's Pilot Program, she stated:

Failure to militarize was not the reason for demobilization of the WASP but rather successful completion of their double mission as above stated. The Director of Women Pilots did not make the original recommendation to deactivate the WASP but followed through wholeheartedly because of the logic of the pertinent facts and the timeliness of the action. Although the WASPs wanted to continue to fly with the Army Air Forces their disappointment over demobilization is overshadowed by the satisfaction that the war has progressed so favorably and our Air Forces are so strong that women pilots are no longer needed.

More than 25,000 women applied for women pilot training. Eighteen hundred and thirty (1,830) were accepted. 30.7% were eliminated during training for flying deficiency and another 2.2% for other reasons, with consequent lower elimination rate than among male cadet pilots. 8% of those accepted resigned and 1,074 graduated, or 58.7% of the total. Of the 1.074

who graduated, 900 remained at time of inactivation, or 83.6% of the graduates, to which should be added 16 of the original WAFS employed who were still with the program at time of inactivation.

The women pilots, subsequent to graduation from the training program, flew approximately 60 million miles for the Army Air Forces; the fatalities were 38, or one to about 16,000 hours of flying. Both the accident rate and the fatality rate compared favorably with the rates for male pilots in similar work.

For Hazel, the WASP program was another stepping stone. The jobs in Aviation were being filled by American pilots returning home and finding a job in aviation was difficult because an end of the war was in sight. Therefore, Hazel's next step was to volunteer to train pilots in another country.

WASP training

The WASPS were housed in
military barracks.

Hazel with instructor

Time Off

Hazel with a friend.

BOOK III.
BRAZIL... AS AN INSTRUCTOR

Chapter 1
PEACHES AND PORTUGUESE

Hazel's foreign tour would take place in Sao Paulo, Brazil. There is no record of why this country was chosen, but there may have been no other opportunities open to her at this time. Her correspondence resumes in July, 1945. Writing from Coral Gables, Florida, she is taking a three month course in Portuguese at the J.P. Riddle Company Instructors' School. It is assumed that Del and Harris teach at the School. Crum (Irene Crum) is a WASP whom Hazel met at Avenger Field and plans to instruct pilots in Brazil also.

Sunday Afternoon
July 1, 1945

Dearest Mother:

The peaches arrived yesterday and they are certainly good. Del and Harris came over last night and we cooked dinner together and had peaches and cream for dessert. They spent the night with us and we had some for breakfast. I have just finished making some peach ice cream for them and have it in the refrigerator freezing for supper. I have never seen anyone that liked peaches any better than Del cause she has been eating them constantly since they came. They took half of them over to their apartment and now we have about a dozen left. Believe me there will not be one peach that will not be eaten. I too have enjoyed them, and you know I don't really care too much for them, but they sure are good and I appreciate so much you sending them to us. The girls said to tell you thanks a million.

We have been studying, resting and eating peaches all weekend. I can't imagine why, but I have two new boils under my arm again. Same arm and I just don't understand why. Harris has been keeping hot packs on my arm and I don't think I will have to have my arm lanced this time. Looks like there is always something giving me trouble.

The weather down here is terrible now, I have never seen it so hot in all my life. I'm really glad we have only another month.

We received a letter from one of the girls that went down to Sao Paulo telling us how much she liked it down there. She found us a place to live when we get down there which is swell for us. I just hope I like it as much as everybody else seems to like the place.

By the way, we are doing much better with our new Portuguese Instructor. The past two weeks we have made 95 in Portuguese which isn't too bad. I am getting pretty good with my conversation now; you should hear me. A year in Brazil should really fix me up where I can speak that unknown tongue pretty good. Of course I will never forget English and the good old Southern way of talking. I have found out that we can study French while we are down there so, I think I will also take French. Who knows, some day I might need to know that language also.....

J.P. RIDDLE COMPANY
340 Alhambra Circle, Coral Gables
Miami 34, Florida

Mrs. F.G. Raines
Massee Apts. Macon, Ga.
July 12, 1945

Dear Mom Raines:

I am just about a month late acknowledging your sweet note. As for thanking you for the peaches I have waited until I devoured every one. They certainly were delicious. We ate them for breakfast, we ate them plain, we ate them with sugar and cream, we ate them for desert, in short I just couldn't stay away from them. With every bite I wished Mother could have enjoyed them with me.

My boss is back in the States, and consequently I have had practically no time to call my own. Even so we manage to see the girls several times a week although we have not done much studying together. They are doing well in school and their grades keep coming up all the time. It certainly is not do to any effort of mine but their ability to study and grasp and understand new things. Those two will make a success of anything they undertake....

Crum managed to find some chickens the other day and Hazel has promised to get her cooking arm working so Harris and I are prepared to consume great quantities of wonderful fried chicken tonight.

You had better get to feeling fit as a fiddle because there is no telling when you will want to prance off to Sao Paulo to see the kids and when you do, remember that my folks might not be able to give you peaches, but they most certainly will have the welcome mat out and our humble home will be yours to command.

Harris is busy at the hospital right now but I know she joins me in sending our very kindest regards and a big hug.

Sincerely,
Del

Wednesday Night
July 18,1945

Dearest Mother,

They truly have us in high gear now with speeches, exams and more speeches. Today I gave my speech for Del in Human Relations class. It was a ten minute speech in Portuguese and ten minutes in English on Getulio Vargas, President of Brazil. I am certainly glad that is out of the way. I only have one more to make and that one will be before the Board when I plan to talk on Instrument flying. I don't think that will be too bad cause I like the subject that I am going to talk on. Saturday we have more exams. Oh yes, that last speech will be next week, I think Wednesday or Thursday.

Monday we went to Miami to take our C.A.A. exam on engines. We finished about one o'clock, had lunch and I went shopping again. I found me a beautiful 100% wool suit. It is light blue with a small check. It is more or less a dress-up suit and I got two blouses to go with it. Of course, it had to be altered and I am going back to Miami Saturday to have it fitted. I now have three suits but think I will get one more; then I won't have to worry about my clothes for a while after I am down there. Del has suggested that we buy as much as we can here cause we may not be able to get good materials down there now.

I received a couple of cards from Martha and Jeaneane today from Daytona Beach. Guess they are having fun and are happy now with their car. Seems to me that this would be a very bad time to buy a car.

Don't worry about me not getting my things together. I have just about gotten all my clothes bought and am already packing my trunk and getting organized before the last minute.....

Tuesday Night
August 7, 1945

Dearest Mother,

I sat down last night and wrote you a two page letter, enclosed the insurance receipt, put the letter with some other letters I wanted to mail today and somewhere in the mad rush I guess I lost it. Maybe if it is found, someone will mail it to you, I hope. That's O.K. tho about the insurance cause I received a very nice letter from Ernest Redd along with the receipt and he knows it is paid until November 1945.

It was certainly nice talking with you Sunday. You sounded as tho you were feeling much better and I hope you are. Please promise to take extra care of yourself cause when they lift the ban on civilian travel, I certainly want you to come to Sao Paulo. Del said she would see that you got off from here O.K. That sure would be swell.

Well, we came over here to the Floridian Hotel this afternoon and checked in and went through the necessary red tape. We are not on the "alert" as yet but I sorta imagine it will be tomorrow. In that event, we will no doubt be leaving about Thursday morning when Del will send you the telegram. I will remind you again, don't worry if you don't hear from me for even a week cause sometimes they stop in Natal and we may be there for several days before going on to Rio. When we arrive in Rio, the Company will send you a wire saying we arrived O.K. If at all possible I will wire you from Natal, but I can't promise. Also, while I'm thinking about it, the mail situation between the States and Brazil is quite slow at times so don't worry when you don't hear from me as soon as you think you should. Remember, it was bad when I was in England and we are told it is not much better down there at times. By the way, I am sending you some stationary with my address on the envelopes. The postage fee for air mail is 20 cents.

I wish you could have seen us trying to get everything packed and the suit cases closed. We were allowed 65 lbs. of baggage and it was terrible trying to hold the weight down to that limit. Specially since I now have some sure enough clothes to pack. I bought some more shoes yesterday, two more pairs plus two hats. You know me and hats, I just don't like the things. I was lucky tho and found two very nice sport type hats that will be very pretty with my new suits. I sure was worried for fear I would not be able to find anything but something like those stove-pipe editions you see in all the shops.

I will drop you another note tomorrow if we are not on the alert and still allowed to mail letters. Take extra care of yourself, eat lots, rest and maybe soon you will be on your way to Sao Paulo. We can keep our fingers crossed.....

Rio de Janeiro
August 15, 1945

Dearest Mother:

Well, we finally made it. The trip down was very nice, quite interesting and pretty. We stopped in Natal for two days and are now in Rio. We will probably be here until Friday. This is truly a beautiful place but of course too big for me to enjoy very much. I just don't like such a rush and so many people.

While in Natal we had quite an interesting time. Last Sunday, Junior (Mr. Franchville, remember the man in our class), Crum and I went into the town of Natal to have a look around. We had lunch at the one and only Hotel after which we went for a walk down to the docks. Just as we walked up, three little native boys came scampering up to shine our shoes. They had just started the job when a man walked up and wanted to take us for a ride in a sailboat. We said yes, and away we went, shoe-shine boys and all. Those little kids sat there in the boat and worked on our shoes for two hours, the entire time we were sailing. One of the kids could speak some English and it was quite interesting talking to the people as best we could in Portuguese. That is certainly a grand way to learn the language. I am learning quite fast and can now ask for most anything I want, use the telephone and order my meals without too much trouble. Maybe after a year I really will be able to speak this unknown tongue!!

Yesterday was quite a day for us. We went to town and walked miles seeing the sights. The crystal came off my watch and we had one more time asking people where we could find a repair shop. We finally found a shop and I walked in and asked the man in my best Portuguese if he could fix the watch; he answered me in beautiful English and said that he could. Of course we both had a good laugh!! After walking our poor heels off, we decided to see what the shows were like down here. It was just like our movies with the only exception being they flash the Portuguese on the screen for the benefit of the people down here. That too is a good way for us to learn the language. Never in my life have I seen such beautiful buildings, their type of architecture is very modernistic and so very far ahead of anything we have in the States. Next time you see John Dennis, tell him he could come down here and study this type design in buildings and go back to the States and really start a new era in Architectural design and make a fortune. Last night we came back to the Hotel, changed our clothes and went to a night club. It was fun. We danced, watched the people gamble at the tables, and saw a floor show. Their shows are quite different from ours with a lots of fancy dressing and dancing.

Isn't it wonderful, the war is at last over. The American Consul has invited us over to the Embassy today to celebrate the victory. We are now going to dress and go over for a while. So long for now and I will write you another long letter tomorrow....

Sao Paulo, S.A.,
Brazil
August 20, 1945

Ministerio Da Aeronautica
Escola Tecnica De Aviacao
Rue Visconde de Parnaiba, 1316

Dearest Mother:

Now to catch up where I left off in Rio: we finally got away from Rio Sunday morning at six o'clock, arriving here just one hour and forty minutes later. Some of the girls that came down in the class ahead of us made reservations for us at the Grao Para Hotel and we now have quite a nice room, very large with twin beds, a big bath and a small reception room. The rent is just half what we paid in Miami. Yesterday we spent unpacking and getting settled but mostly resting.

Oh yes, let me go back and tell you about our little trip Saturday afternoon. After lunch Saturday, we went up the mountain where this huge statue of Christ stands, in a cog-wheeled train. It was a beautiful trip and we got a grand view of Rio from the peak of the mountain which stands 2300 feet above sea level. About the last five hundred feet we had to walk and I sure was tired when we got back to the Hotel that night. I am glad we made the trip, however, cause it was beautiful. After coming back to the Hotel Saturday night we took a bath, dressed and had dinner. Since we were leaving bright and early the next morning, we went back to our room and started packing again. I had just about unpacked everything I had cause we were there just about a week and we were wearing dresses the whole time.

This morning we were up at 6:30, had coffee here in the room, which is the custom down here and were out at school by eight o'clock. They run a school bus for us and the bus stops right here in front of the Hotel. About the coffee, it is strong but good: I always use about half milk. Oh yes, the breakfast they serve, good but quite different from ours. We have coffee, hard rolls, lots of butter and jam and fruit. I just take the coffee but Crum takes the works. She sure does like to eat and is getting fat as a pig. I don't think I will gain any cause I am taking my thyroid pills. We have our noon day meal out at school, which is only about twenty minutes from the Hotel. At night we eat at a place just a block away. The school is quite nice, very large and pretty. The flowers down here are beautiful and everywhere you look you see lots of them. This week we have to be there by seven. Don't know why, but I always seem to pick the job where I hafta get up bright and early. Tomorrow they are having a graduation at the school and I think we get a holiday.

The weather down here is quite good, although this is their winter. I find it very comfortable with a suit on and at night my coat does feel good. It sure feels good to be out of that heat in Miami cause that was bout to get me down.

We called Mr. and Mrs. del Junco this afternoon after we got home and they came right over to see us. They sure are nice people and were so happy to hear from Del or rather all about her. They told us they wanted to help us with anything they could and I am sure they will be lots of help to us.

You should hear me talk Portuguese now. Of course I am not so good as yet and no doubt won't be for some time to come, but it is coming to me by degrees. Some of the people speak English but most of them that do only know just a wee bit. Guess I had better stop and dress for dinner....

Saturday Afternoon
August 25, 1945

Dearest Mother;

This ends our first week in Sao Paulo and although we are not as yet settled we like it very much down here. The school is quite nice and much larger than I had imagined. Of course our biggest problem right now is the language, but then I don't think we will have too much trouble even tho we don't know too much Portuguese. After all, we only had three months to learn an entirely new language before coming down here. All the people seem so eager to help, and most of the people we have met speak a little English. However, I don't really see how one could come down here and get around without knowing some Portuguese.

This first week was spent in getting acquainted with the school and the people. They assigned us to our different departments today and, although I was assigned to Link and Instrument flying, I have been requested from that department to go to the Basic department and teach a few weeks of Theory of Flight. Not that I am proud of myself and my abilities, but they did say it was a shame that I could teach several different things. So, as a result I will probably find myself all over the school in many departments just cause I have had a few years experience in Aviation. It will be good for me tho, to teach Theory for a change and will give me a wonderful opportunity to learn the language. We still have Portuguese every day, one hour each day until we take what they call a proficiency exam. You cannot get a raise in salary until you take this exam and are able to write and speak the language quite well. They tell us it will be about four to six months before we will be able to pass such a test. I have hired a private tutor to teach me one hour every night in order to learn faster and if possible to take the exam sooner.

Honestly, I hardly can believe this is me, getting so eager to learn so many things. However, I do find the more one studies and tries to learn, the more they get out of life and know how to appreciate the better things. I must say tho, that this language is causing my spelling, which is already terrible as you well know, to get worse—-goodness, the way I say things in English——I find myself talking backwards.

We saw our first graduation the other day and it was quite interesting and very military. You know of course, that this is a military school and everything is very military. This is just fine for us since we have been associated with the Air Force so long.

I can't remember whether or not I told you about our living accommodations but we are still here in the Grao Para Hotel where the kids had us a very nice room fixed up when we got here last Sunday. They had a beautiful pot of orchids in our room. They are very cheap down here and very beautiful. We have a large bedroom with twin beds, a small reception room and a very nice bath which is quite large too. Although we like it here, it is very noisy and we are thinking of trying to get an apartment. Our meals we eat like this; breakfast is furnished along with our room here at the hotel, it is not an American breakfast at all but coffee, hard rolls, butter and jelly and fruit, lunch we have at the school which is very clean and not too bad, at night we have to go out to dinner which is the thing I don't like cause when we get in I am tired and would much rather just undress and fix something for myself. Maybe we can have a place soon where we can fix our own food at night when we want to. Speaking of food, the food down here is wonderful, specially the steaks. I tried some fried chicken today and it just wasn't the same— but then it never will be the same no matter where I go. There is no chicken in the whole world to compare with your fried chicken. I guess you will hafta come on down and cook chicken for us.

Next week we start on the regular schedule, up at six and at school by seven. The school bus stops right here in front of our Hotel. We finish at four and usually get home by 4:30....

Sao Paulo, Brazil
September 2, 1945

Dearest Mother,

Friday I received my first letter from you since I have been down here and it sure was good to hear from home. Gee, that is just fine about you gaining some weight. Keep up the good work.

I certainly am sorry there was such a delay in the telegram to you from down here. We were under the impression that they would notify you when we reached Rio but found out when we arrived here that the telegram was not sent until we did get to Sao Paulo. I sure am sorry I did not know this or I would have wired you from Rio.

Well, I am liking it down here just fine. It is a very interesting place, some spots are very beautiful, and never in my life have I seen such pretty flowers and they are so very reasonable. We keep flowers of some kind in our room all the time. Right now we have a dozen red roses and two big bowls of sweet peas. When we arrived the kids had a big pot of orchids in our room, but they have just about seen their best day now. Yes, the food is good, I like it cause I can get all the steak I want, and it is truly good. I have had a steak for dinner every night since I have been here except once and that was the time I told you about having fried chicken that wasn't good at all.

This is the end of our second week in the school and as yet I have not started teaching. The past week I spent observing and getting my material ready. I was assigned to Instrument flying and Link, but due to the shortage of instructors right now, they have asked that I teach some theory of flight. Never in my life have I taught ground school and this is certainly going to be funny when I start standing before a class of about twenty boys and try to explain why an airplane flies and all such stuff in Portuguese. I did a little last week. I helped out one of the girls and explained some things about a wind tunnel to the boys.

We are still trying to find another place to live cause I am getting tired of living in just one room. I do like to have my own room where I can be alone when I want to. We have been looking for an apartment or a house, but so far no luck. Places down here are very hard to find, just like it is back home. However, I imagine things will begin to get better along that line with the war over. I can hardly believe that the war is over, but I certainly am glad. I hear that they have taken gasoline off the rationed list. That should make Reginald's business boom again.

The one morning we could sleep, is Sunday morning but, of all things—at 7:30 this morning they really did start whooping things up. I don't know exactly who or what they were but they started a Parade right out in front of our hotel window, with drum and bugle corps included, and I want you to know they marched past this hotel in a steady stream until 11:30. The Brazilian Army was on parade too, and they came by going one direction and these young boys, who looked like high school kids in white uniforms, marched past going in the other direction. It was a sight to behold, but of all the noise, they had at least thirty different drum and bugle corps cause just time one group would get around the corner, here would come another group just tooting and beating their drums with all their strength. It seemed to me that their main objective was to see how much noise they could make. Of course the boys were kids of every color, which is only typical of the people down here.

We had another graduation at school Friday. They graduate a class from school about every week. We are told that we will be having a holiday this Friday and maybe Saturday. That sure will be swell if we do, I think I will just sleep all I can. You know they run sight-seeing trips for us from the school every weekend with all expenses paid but as yet I haven't taken advantage of any of the trips. I will have plenty of time to be going so therefore, I have been resting on the weekends.

Well, Crum is having a fit for me to stop and dress and go with her to eat. You should see her, she is getting as big as a house. I'm just holding my own, haven't gained any weight or lost any. I don't much think I will gain or loose. She said to give you her love, take care of yourself and hurry down here....

Saturday Night
September 9, 1945

Dearest Mother,

Friday and Saturday were holidays for us and some of the folks out at the school had planned a trip to a place northeast of Sao Paulo some 133 miles, they talked me into going along on the trip, and I am very glad I did cause it certainly was beautiful. The name of the place where we went was called "Campos do Jordao". We left here by bus Thursday afternoon at 3:30, and after six hours arrived at the Grande Hotel at the Campos do Jordao. Never in my life have I had such a ride. The roads down here are just about all dirt and the trip was around curve after another. After the first hour I just sat back and said I might as well relax. We made it there and back O.K. Now to get back to the story. We arrived at the Hotel Thursday night about ten o'clock, very tired, dirty and cold. It was truly cold up there, but they had a wonderful big fireplace in one end of the reception room that sure did feel wonderful. After getting settled in our rooms and getting the first two layers of dirt off, we went to dinner. Never in my life have I seen people eat so much. All the meals we had while we were there were seven course jobs.

The next morning we were up about 8:30, had breakfast and seven of us took a ride through the mountains on horseback. It was beautiful and we saw many flowers and birds that were quite beautiful and not like anything I have ever seen in the States. We finally made it back to the Hotel about one o'clock, cleaned up, and had lunch. That afternoon we spent sitting out on the terrace, soaking up the warm sunshine and playing cards. Friday night we had dinner, and after dinner they had an orchestra to play for dancing. Saturday we spent the same way, with the exception that I did not go riding this time, cause I was so sore I could hardly sit down. A couple of us stayed behind and just rested.

The weather down here is still quite cold, specially every morning when we get out about six thirty. The middle of the day warms up a bit and then it is quite cold at night. I think it is for that reason that I have had a cold for the past few days. I bought some nose drops and they are doing the trick.

Tomorrow I start teaching more than I have been. One of the Instructors at the school in the Theory of Flight department has gone to Rio and I am taking his classes for a couple of days. This is interesting work and very educational but I am getting tired of being inside a building all day long. I sure hope they get the flight school set up soon and we can start some flying.

We are still looking for a place to live. The hotel is O.K, but just a little too noisy for me. Then too, I want a room by myself. I yet so tired of Crum and people in general being around all the time. If we can get us a nice little apartment, that will be better I think. However, places to live are certainly hard to find....

Chapter 2
TALK OF REVOLUTION

Once again Hazel's health problems begin to surface. She has lost ten pounds and is taking cold shots and vitamin shots. There is a hint of discontent with Brazil. In her next letter (September 23, 1945), Hazel is missing England and I would venture to say flying most of all.

Things down her continue to go along in the same old routine. This is certainly not at all like those months I spent in England. Although this place is interesting we just go through the same old routine every day. Maybe when I take another trip or something I will have more to tell you....

Got in from school yesterday around noon, went out and had lunch, came back and washed my hair. Last night I had a date with a fellow that has been down here for six years with Firestone. We went out for dinner and dancing and had a very nice time.

Friday Afternoon
September 14, 1945

Dearest Mother:

Your letters are coming thru much better now; it only takes about six days. I think mine take longer due to the fact that they might not get them off as quickly as they should out at school. Sure enjoyed the nice long letter I received from you the first of the week. Glad the children liked the books so much. Wish I could send them something from down here but— that is impossible as you already know. It would cost too much when you received the package customs fee. I will hafta bring them something when I come back.

They certainly have lovely materials in the shops down here for suits. They are quite reasonable too, and I think perhaps I will have a couple of light weight suits made. I was walking down the street the other day after we came in from school and saw the cutest little shop where they make dolls. I thought of the children right away. All you have to do is go in and tell them the kind of doll and the size you want, and they make them right there. They sure are nice. It made me sorta wish I liked dolls, but then I never did, did I? The leather goods and jewelry are just out of this world and very reasonable. I saw some of the most beautiful pocketbooks I have ever dreamed about the other day. I know if they were for sale back home they would cost a young fortune and down here —- it is amazing: you can get one of the most beautiful pocketbooks you have ever seen for not more than $10.00. They make them in all colors of pigskin, calf, and alligator. I am going to have some alligator shoes made.

Just about all of our gang have been sick with colds this week. I have had a slight cold, the first I can remember having in months. Stayed home a couple of days this week and plastered on the Vicks and nose drops. Yes, they sell Vicks down here. I think they must sell it all over the world. Did I tell you about my experience the other day when I was trying to get a mouth wash? I decided I would try to get some Sodium Perborate to use a couple of time a week when I brush my teeth. It keeps them white and it is also a good

mouth wash to use when one eats out as much as I do. Well, I
chased all over town asking for it and finally at the last pharmacy
they told me it was impossible to sell it to me cause it was con-
trolled by the Minister of War due to the fact that it was highly
explosive. Wow! I don't think they really understood what I wanted.
I tried to get it out at school, went in and explained what I wanted to
the Doctor- in Portuguese- and he nodded his head and said he knew
exactly what I wanted. Well, I sure was happy when he gave me a
bottle all wrapped up and said he knew exactly what I had asked for.
When I got home I unwrapped the package to find cough syrup
instead of mouth wash. Maybe I should blame it all on my
Portuguese and study more, I don't know....

Monday Night
October 1, 1945

Dearest Mother:

Gee, I'm tired tonight. Monday is always a long hard day cause
it is the first of the week and seems so long until the week-end. I
sure look forward to week-ends when we can sleep and rest and just
laze around. I was really lazy this week-end and didn't do the first
thing I had planned to do. In fact, I usually try to catch up on my letter writing on Sunday and didn't even do that.

This business of teaching Theory of Flight is fun and interesting cause the boys are swell. My Portuguese is getting better too
since I hafta talk about four hours each day. If someone tied my
arms I am sure I couldn't say a word. Poor Crum tho, I think she
gets worse instead of better. Maybe I shouldn't say that, but it is
true. If she would only study some, she could do better, I am sure. I
just can't understand that girl at times, she must have had someone
pushing her all her life.

By the way, I'm feeling O.K. now. I just had a slight cold and
that week-end trip we made several weeks ago didn't help any cause
there was so much dust. Very few of the roads down here are paved
and the dust is awful. My ear is still giving me a little trouble but I
am going to the Doctor out at school and he is treating it every day.
He seems to think he can cure it for me. That is certainly odd how it
continues to give me trouble. I think when the infection is cured it
will be O.K.

We haven't seen the del Juncos in about two weeks but tonight
they sent us some fruit. They are always sending flowers, fruit or a
note. I was sorry I couldn't go out for lunch that Sunday with Crum,
but my cold was bad and it was raining.

Please don't worry about trying to send me something Christmas. Even if you could, I just don't want you to. I can't say that I like Christmas very much now either and doubt it will seem like Christmas down here. At least things won't be like they were in England. Over there it was grand getting your packages and specially your Christmas packages but it is different now.

Crum and I went out and looked at an apartment the other day, but I'm not too sure we will be able to get it. It sure would be nice if we could get a better place to live but rents down here are worse than they were in Coral Gables. I sure would like to have my own room and a place where we could cook some food the way we like it. Then too, one bad feature, I know I would hafta look after everything and I just hate to think of the time and trouble it would take. We would just have to have a maid to take care of it and a good maid is hard to find. Very few of them speak English at all and it would be tough trying to tell her how and what to do.

Well, there just doesn't seem to be any news to write about. It seems that all the news of interest is happening back home. We get *Time Magazine* each week and things sure look bad back there as far as jobs are concerned. I guess this was the best thing for me to do right now....

In Hazel's next letter, she states that "the talk of a revolution is quite common." In 1930, the President of Brazil was overthrown and Getulio Vargas became the Dictator. Although he did help to modernize Brazil, he ruled without a congress and set up a totalitarian state. On October 29, 1945, Vargas was forced to resign by the Army, and a new constitution gave the people back their individual rights with an elected legislature. Hazel, true to form, reassures her mother that "the American Consul is just behind our Hotel and after all they look after us, don't think they don't."

Sunday Morning
October 7, 1945

Dearest Mother;

Sure was nice getting your letter yesterday. I always get your letters on Saturday. Thanks for sending me the mail that I get there at home. Yes, I have received one of the letters you sent me but the other has not come yet. It will probably be out at school when I go tomorrow. The first letter was from a boy I knew in England. Nothing interesting, just dropped me a note to say he was back in the states.

Glad you told me about the dolls and pocketbooks. I will get these things and hope I can pick out something you will like. All of the pocketbooks are beautiful and all lined in leather. It would be impossible for me to get any shoes for Martha cause they measure your foot and make them specially for the person. Also, if she was wanting grey alligator, I am very much afraid there is no such thing. If they have such, I have not seen it. All of the pocketbooks are in various shades of brown, however, I do believe they have grey pocketbooks made out of snake skin which is beautiful. The price of snake skin is beautiful too, lots of difference in those and alligator. Don't understand why cause they certainly have enough snakes down here.

Last week we thought we were going to have a little excitement—but we didn't. You see they are having an election down here December 2nd for a new President of Brazil. Although they have a President down here, the government is not quite the same as ours— not as democratic nor is it a government by the people as a whole: that is to say, the government set-up is not representative of the people as a nation. Well, anyway, true to the past history of Brazil, they are having political campaigns and rallies all over Brazil and the talk of a revolution is quite common. Last week they told us out at school to prepare for it by getting at least three days supply of food on hand cause if anything happened, we would not be able to leave the hotel. You see they were having a big meeting here in Sao Paulo and thought there might be trouble but—-not one thing happened. They said the meeting went off in fine style and there was no feuding. This is really some place down here! We are not worried about ourselves and our safety cause the American Consul is just behind our Hotel and after all they look after us, don't think they don't.

No, I have given up the apartment and house idea cause it is too much to worry about. If Crum would only help out on such things it wouldn't be so bad but she just doesn't have one bit common sense or judgment on things like that. Then too, she is so lazy until I know I would hafta do all the work and I just don't want to be bothered cause I am lazy too. I'm not so lazy tho that I would let things go to pot like she would. We had another chance on an apartment last week but the prices are so unreasonable. It's expensive to eat out all the time and I do get tired of it but I can't see where we would gain anything by renting something that cost so much. I'm just forgetting the whole thing for a while— in the meantime, I'm going to get me a room by myself here in the hotel.

Well, guess that is just about all the news for this time. Did you get my letter with the picture in it. I have made hardly any pictures since we have been down here but when I do I will send them to you.…

In a letter of October 14th, Hazel remarks that one year in Brazil will probably be enough.

Sao Paulo, Brazil
October 14, 1945

Dearest Mother:

We have certainly had a nice Sunday. But first, yesterday when we got out of school, we came back to the hotel, changed our clothes, and went out and had lunch. After lunch, we went to a movie, came home and opened some sardines and onions, and had a stinking time eating these things. This morning, we slept until 10 o'clock, got up, had a bath and dressed, and Mr. del Juncos came by for us. We met Mrs. del Juncos and went out to their house for the day. It sure was nice cause they live out from the City about seven miles and have a lovely place. Lots of chickens, ducks, a horse, a vegetable and flower garden, and lots of fruit trees.

We went out on a "bonde", (street car), arrived about 12:15, had a very nice lunch, and then went for a walk around the place. We had been invited over to a friend's house, a friend of Mrs. del Juncos, for tea, but we didn't go cause we had to get back to the hotel. Crum and I do a little school work and wash out a few things and write letters. It was a lovely day today, and we did enjoy our outing.

School is still the same, up at six every morning, out at school by seven, and we finish up at four o'clock. I think I am soon going to start flying, thank goodness. Right now, I am teaching Theory of Flight, but they are trying to work it where I can get in some flying along with the course.

There is still lots of talk about trouble down her between now and December second, due to the coming election. We have no fear tho, since we are next to the American Consulate, and they give us ample warnings about things. I will be glad when they finish this election tho.

Crum and I are still looking for a place to live. It will not be a house, but if we can find an apartment, we think we would like that much better than this hotel business. I sure am tired of living in one room. If we can't find a nice apartment, I am going to move by myself.

My ear has been giving me more trouble and I have been going to the Doctor every day. It is better now, and I will be glad when it is finally O.K.

It is nothing to worry about cause it is something that would have happened even if I had stayed in the United States.

The time down here seems to be going extra fast. Here it is the middle of October and the first thing we know it will be Christmas. I like it O.K. down here, but doubt very much if I stay longer than my year, which will be over next August 4th. There is so much sickness and disease down here, and the weather is so bad until I can't see why anyone would want to stay longer than a year. Health conditions down here are horrible and things are too dirty to be healthy. We have to be so careful about what we eat and where we eat until it isn't a pleasure to eat at all. Then too, prices are much higher than at home for everything. I think the reason for that is cause they have some Americans down here and they think they can charge any price and get it....

> Sao Paulo, Brazil
> Monday Night
> October 22, 1945

Dearest Mother,
Received a nice long letter from you today and felt awful cause I didn't get to write you yesterday as planned. We slept until ten o'clock, got up and had a shower and by that time Mrs. del Junco came by to have lunch with us and then we took her to a movie. Mr. del Junco has gone out of town, left Saturday and she was sorta lonesome. She is quite a big talker and sat around last night and talked until way past our bedtime before going home. Yes, they are nice people and have been lovely to us.
I certainly hope you have not been worrying too much about that ear of mine. It is much better now and I'm going to a new Doctor the del Juncos have told me about. I think maybe he will be able to help me lots. Of course the worse thing that could happen would be to lose my hearing completely in that ear but I think perhaps this Doctor can save it for me. I guess it is a good thing that I am not flying right now cause even if I was supposed to be flying I would hafta stay on the ground until this thing cleared up.
We are having a holiday tomorrow and do not have to go to school. They are celebrating something like "Wings Day" or something crazy. These people have a holiday on the least little excuse. Of course we don't mind, that much the better for us. Next week we have Friday and Saturday off too. Most everyone is planning to take a trip but I think we will stay in Sao Paulo.
These trips are so awful cause the transportation down here is so awful and slow. Most all the roads are dirt and the dust just is too much for me. Of course things are interesting and different but I have seen places I liked much better. I certainly hope conditions

improve at at home by next August, cause I don't think I could take two years of this down here. Of course the job is a good one but after all I had rather be happy and not make quite so much money. Of course I am already thinking about what I will do when I get back and one of my crazy ideas includes China. Don't worry tho, we will wait until the time comes and see what happens. I know my yen for travel and new places won't let me stay anywhere too long at a time. I must be part Gypsy. How about that, am I?

That was nice of Dr. Johnson to ask about me. Next time you see him give both him and his wife my best regards. I have thought of them several times and just wondered how she was getting along. Do you ever see Quinn or Mrs. Eubanks? I think perhaps one of these days soon, when I have more time off, I will write Mrs. Murray a note. She has certainly been one teacher that has seemed to be interested in me and what I was doing. I'll never know why cause I sure didn't care for that Home Economics stuff I had to take. I doubt very much if she ever knew I really didn't like her course. It was the sewing that got me, and I still don't like to sew. I had almost rather throw away something rather than have to mend it.

Time for a shower and bed. Gee, I'm getting lazy, I'm looking forward to sleeping late tomorrow. No doubt I will wake up at six per usual. Don't forget,

I love you,
Hazel

In October of 1946, the President of Brazil, Getulio Vargas, was forced to resign by the military leaders. Eurico Gaspar Dutra, an army officer, was elected President.

Sao Paulo, Brazil
Novenber 1, 1945

This has been quite a week for us. Friday and Saturday of this week are holidays and of course we don't mind that at all. Tuesday morning of this week, we came out to the school as per usual but only stayed five minutes. They made us get right back on our bus and took us back to the Hotel. The reason being, as you know doubt have heard, the sudden resignation of their President and a shake up in the government in general. I think perhaps they expected trouble as a result of all that but— we went back to to our Hotel, stayed there all day and not the first thing happened. Don't worry about me tho, if anything should happen, we will be safe. I'll be careful. This certainly isn't anything compared with England.

Sao Paulo, Brazil
Sunday Afternoon
November 4, 1945

Dearest Mother:

The past three days have certainly been lazy ones for us, we have done not one thing but sleep and rest. I got a smart spell and did some sewing, took a hem in one of my slips that was too long. I told Crum, I sure wished her camera would make pictures inside—I would have gotten her to take a picture of me sewing. One of the girls here in the hotel has a little electric sewing machine, and I took my slip up to her apartment and fixed it all by myself. Found out today that I have got to do the job all over again tho, cause it is still too long. I also got out several pairs of stockings, mended them, and washed them out. I sure am rough on hose, and they are very expensive down here. You can hardly get a pair that you would think of wearing under $3.00. I bought me some socks the other day, and have started wearing socks with my suits at school. All of the girls wear them, and it sure will be less expensive and much cooler this summer. Doesn't that sound funny, this summer, and here it is winter at home. All of the seasons down here are just backwards from the way they run at home. When you will be having spring, it will be fall here. So far, the weather hasn't been too hot, but believe me, we have more than our share of rain.

Today is such a beautiful day, until I feel that we should get out a little this afternoon and maybe go for a walk. We didn't get up this morning until 9:30, then we took a shower, dressed, and went out for breakfast. During the week, all we ever have for breakfast is coffee, so on Sunday morning, we always treat ourselves to ham and eggs at one of the restaurants near by. It is the only place in town where we can get food sorta cooked semi-American style. I have given up trying to find fried chicken; they just don't know what it is or how to cook it. They cook about everything in olive oil, and all the food is so greasy, until I can hardly eat it.

While we were eating breakfast, we saw some of the new girls that have just come down from Coral Gables. They were feeling just about like we felt when we first arrived. They wanted to order something to eat, but couldn't read the menu, so we helped them order. They are coming by the hotel tonight, and we are going to take them out to eat with us. It is sorta tough at first, trying to get around and ask for things when you don't know the language too well...

Honestly, the time sure seems to be going fast, here it is almost Christmas again and once again I find myself a long way from home. I just wonder where I will spend next Christmas. I wouldn't be too surprised if it turned out to be China. Don't worry tho, I'm not going anywhere until I get back to the States again and spend some time at home....

Sao Paulo, Brazil
Saturday Afternoon
November 17, 1945

Dearest Mother:

The time certainly seems to be going fast; here it is another week-end. I really look forward to these Sundays when we can sleep and not have to get up at 5:30 in the morning.

We got in from school about 11:30, had lunch at the big department store near the hotel, Mappins, and then I went to see the tailor. He did such a good job on the grey tropical he just finished for me, until I am having him make me another suit. This time it is a blue green material, tropical, and should make up quite pretty. He can really make suits to fit and you know how I love suits, since I can't be wearing slacks. They tell us now tho, that we are going to have to wear uniforms. Isn't that the limit. I sure am tired of wearing a uniform. Just as long as they furnish it, I won't mind too much cause it will save my clothes. They will be a tan color, something like khaki but better material. They measured me for mine last week. So, I guess by December 1st, I will be wearing my third kind of uniform. What next?

Wish you could see our room; it is very spring-like today. We have a big vase of red and white roses and another big container of some of the funniest flowers you have ever seen. They are red and look very much like the beak of a parrot. They call them, "Beco de Papagaio", which when translated does mean beak of a parrot. We couldn't find anything to put them in since they were so big and heavy so, Mr. Franchville, (we call him Junior, he was in our class in Miami and his wife will be down here any day now), well any, he went out and got us a big water bucket. We took some green wrapping paper and fixed it up so it wouldn't look too bad and now we have Christmas colors—-red and green. Guess that will be just about as near as anything that we have down here that will look like Christmas. These people don't seem to go in for Christmas and don't decorate or celebrate like we do. I really am glad since I am so far away from home, I had just rather forget about it being that time of year...

Tomorrow, the American women instructors are having a luncheon at the Jockey Club. They tell us it is a beautiful spot and one everyone should see and visit while here. They are having horse racing and it should be lots of fun for a change. I just hope it is a pretty day and we can get some pictures. I will wear my new suit and hope I can get Crum to take a good picture of me. The enclosed picture isn't so good. Crum made it the other day out at school.

We certainly have been having lots of time off lately. Next week we have another holiday with Thursday off. I rather imagine we will be getting off a few more days than this before the month is over cause the election is coming up December 2nd and I imagine things will pick up before that is over. I'm not worried tho and certainly don't want you to give it a thought cause we are plenty safe right here in this hotel.

I have thought many times about trying to arrange for you to come down, but I honestly don't think it would be worth you taking the chance on it just now. The weather down here is awful and the food and water worse. Maybe if I decide to stay longer than a year, we can work out something and I could get an apartment where we could fix our own food. They tell me that is more of a problem since it is hard to get vegetables....

Election day, December 2, turns out to be an uneventful day, but the American instructors are ordered to stay at the hotel all day.

> Sao Paulo, Brazil
> Sunday Afternoon
> December 2, 1945

Dearest Mother:

This is one of the prettiest days we have had since we have been down here and we hafta stay here at the hotel. The reason being, today is election day, and they instructed us out at school to stay in our homes and not go out just in case anything happened. So far it has been an unusually quiet day, but we haven't been out and won't, since we were told to stay in. We just made some hamburgers, with lots of onions, and now our room smells something fierce.

Well, I finally moved yesterday into another room here at the hotel. I have a room higher up, on the seventh floor, and think I will like it much better having a room of my own. It was just a little too much trying to live in one small room with another person even tho Crum is really a grand person to live with. She always went to bed by eight o'clock and I always like to read a bit before I go to bed so, all in all I think I have done the best thing by moving.

Incidentally, the enclosed picture is a snap that Crum made one afternoon about two weeks ago just after we had gotten out of school. We saw this contraption of a hearse sitting in the street and of course I climbed right in and she made a picture. This is the best hearse down here, believe it or not, and they tell us that only the so called "high class" of people can afford to use it. Isn't it the craziest looking thing you have ever seen?....

In a letter on December 16, Hazel seems to be struggling with her feelings about remaining in Brazil. She associates her dislike of the job with the fact that she is not flying.

Well, here it is just about that time and I can hardly realize another year has passed. It is so warm down here, and not at all like Christmas weather. Yesterday, I went shopping, or rather window shopping, cause I didn't buy a thing. More of the stores here have put up a few things that look like Christmas, but somehow, I can't feel that it is. As I have said before, most of the instructors here are planning to go to Argentina for the holidays, but we will stay in Sao Paulo until the 29th, when Crum and I plan to fly up to Rio. I guess Sissy will arrive about the 30th, and I will stay in Rio about three days with her, and then we will fly back here. That will be my Christmas. After all, I guess I should feel lucky to be able to do that, and to have a nice friend like Sissy that can come down and be with me for awhile. I just dislike this place so much until I am afraid if I didn't have something to cheer me up, I would be heading back for the good old U.S.A. soon. I just don't want to break my contract tho, and will try to finish my year down here. I am sure the reason for all my unhappiness is cause I'm not doing what I like to do most and you know that is flying.

I sure enjoyed the account of the air show you sent me and wish I could have been there to enjoy it with you. Better still, I wish I could have one of those to participate in the show. It must have seemed like old times to go out to Herbert Smart and see some of my old flying friends.

The flowers down here are certainly beautiful. They have so many and they are so cheap at all the flower shops. For about fifty cents, one can buy an arm full of American Beauty roses that would cost about six or eight dollars at home. I sometimes wish that I loved flowers more than I do. You know it's funny, since I have been down here and have been around lots of flowers, they make me sneeze again. We used to buy lots of them and keep them in our room, until we discovered they were giving me asthma. They have such a loud smell, until I think maybe that was it. After all tho, they are not as pretty as they were in Ireland and England, that place has all the rest of the world beat for beautiful country-side and deep colors in flower gardens.

Well, Mother, the news down here just isn't interesting at all because there is so little to write about. Life is always the same with me: to work by seven, home at 4:30 every day of the week.

Sure wish I could be with you this Christmas, but since it is impossible, I do wish for you and all the family the happiest holiday possible and remember, I will be thinking of you and loving you...

Excerpts from Hazel's letters in early 1946 reveal that life for her in Brazil is not only filled with inconveniences, but very confining because of the routine of classroom instruction. She does write with great enthusiasm about the Carnival in Rio which took place in March.

Saturday Afternoon
February 2, 1946

Right now while I'm writing this letter I'm also running a bottling business. I have my coffee pot on my alcohol burner and have another pot full on the stove. We haven't been too careful about our drinking water lately and we were told yesterday to be on our guard again and boil water. They have had 200 new cases of typhoid in the city this week. Of course, I don't think we have a thing to worry about cause we had shots for typhoid, tetanus, and a dozen other tropical diseases before we came down here. We had all those shots while I was in England and again in the WASPs, then just to on the safe side, they gave us booster shots in Miami....

Friday Night
February 15, 1946

You know this indoor life down here is just about to get me down. I miss being in the wide open spaces— you know me. Then too— the food one eats just doesn't seem to supply me with any too much energy. I think half of it is the climate too— no pep— no life— no nothing. I have been going to an English Doctor the past few weeks taking shots of calcium and iron. He said I was O.K. in every way but really needed more fresh air and sunshine so— thru his suggestion I am going to take 10 days off from school and rest up....

Friday Morning
March 8, 1946

Now to go back a bit. I told you about us going to Serra Negra the last of February. It was very nice up there and I got a lot of good rest. We came back to Sao Paulo February 27th and took off again

March 1st for Rio. It was Carnival time in Rio, and quite an interesting celebration. The people dressed in the craziest costumes, some of them very beautiful, and danced in the streets night and day for three days. We left Rio on Tuesday, March 5th to return to Sao Paulo but, when we arrived here, we were unable to land because the weather was too bad. So, they flew us on to the city of Bauru which is fifty miles west of Sao Paulo in the interior. It was really a treat for us to get to go there, and we really had a wonderful time. We were there overnight, and it was the last day of Carnival. Pan American put on a party for us at one of the Clubs where they were celebrating Carnival, and we had a grand time dancing Brazilian style and making merry. All of our overnight expenses were paid by Pan American. We left the next morning at 7 o'clock and arrived here at 8:15. We were all glad that we couldn't land in Sao Paulo the day before...."

Friday Afternoon
March 22, 1946

Winter is just about here now and it has been quite cold lately. To make things worse, we have been without hot water here at the hotel for two weeks. I have a little alcohol burner that I can heat a certain amount of water on but not enough to take a good bath. I am also trying to find a little heater for my room since we do not have any kind of heating in the building. Isn't that odd; hardly any of the hotels or larger buildings have central heating in Brazil. No wonder these people are half sick all the time....

Chapter 3
ON TURNING THIRTY

Wednesday Morning
April 3, 1946

Dearest Mother:

While my boys are having an English lesson, I'll get a note off to you to let you know I'm O.K. Still here plugging away and counting the days until August. The time is going right fast now but not fast enough for me.

Last weekend we went out to the Lake I was telling you about where we plan to spend the week before Easter. We went out Saturday afternoon after school and came back late Sunday afternoon. The cottage really is nice and we had great fun. Crum and I took some chickens out with us to have some fried chicken. I know you won't believe me but- there were three of us and we took six chickens and all we had left were the bones. They have a wood stove out there and it took me a total of three hours Saturday afternoon to get that thing fired up. Crum and I stood around that stove blowing and stuffing paper and sticks in it and wishing every other puff that you were with us. I know you would have started that fire without any trouble. The chicken didn't turn out good at all — I had to use olive oil to cook it in and somehow it just didn't cook it right. Hope I can have better luck when we go back out there.

I didn't get to do any fishing cause I didn't have any hooks with me but now I have bought me some rig and plan to try my luck. The open fireplace was nice and it was just cool enough to enjoy it and still be comfortable....

Thursday Afternoon
April 11, 1946

Received a nice long letter from you today and I'm certainly glad it came before Sunday, cause tomorrow is our last day at school until April 23rd. We are certainly lucky to get such a nice long vacation and believe me I am ready for it. Crum, Dotty and I plan to go out to the lake, where we have rented the cottage I have been telling you about, and we are sorta excited over the idea. No kidding, I'm looking forward to that week out there just like it was going to be a trip to China or something like that. It will be so much fun just lazing around— wearing slacks for a change—cooking up a few things we like to eat like fried chicken—and staying outdoors fishing. Don't worry about me and the boat—you know I'm not too fond of the water but I can swim pretty good—much better than I used to.

Wish you could hear all the noise outside now—drums and bugles all over the place. The boys are out practicing for the exercises they are going to have tomorrow afternoon after school. They are having a big parade and ceremony in commemoration of Roosevelt. We finish instruction at one o'clock, have lunch, then go stand for a couple of hours for all that useless noise. I think the idea is fine but—if we just didn't have to stand so long.

Significant dates in Hazel's life would only be remembered by her family through her letters. A long way from home, Hazel celebrates her 30th birthday with her friends, Crum and Dotty. Perhaps it was a time of contemplation.

Monday Night
April 22, 1946

Dearest Mother:

Well, vacation days and birthdays are over and tomorrow, bright and early, we start to the old routine again.

Our week out at the lake was wonderful and I had much better luck with the wood stove this time. We ate fried chicken until it ran out of our ears, but it just couldn't compare with your fried chicken. I also made corn bread, egg bread really, and everyone seemed to enjoy it too. I got lots of rest, fresh air and sunshine cause I spent most of the time on the lake fishing. Didn't have too bad luck catching fish. I caught five with a pole, about the size of your hand, and put out a trap overnight and got forty. I was the only one that did any fishing but was glad cause I liked getting out in the open by myself.

The cottage was just across the lake from a little Swiss Inn and Saturday night Crum and a few others that came out for the weekend had a little party over there for me. They were having a dance to celebrate the end of Lent and most of the people that came to the dance were dressed in their native costumes. Most of the people who live around the lake are Swiss so therefore, most of the dancing was Swiss style. Two of the men did some exhibition dances which were very interesting and entertaining. The owner of the Inn came over and wished me a happy birthday and presented me with a small plaque that he himself had made and painted of a typical Swiss mountain scene with a rustic background and frame. He is going to paint me another so I will have a pair.

You know what we did yesterday? Crum and Dotty got up early and took all the eggs we had for breakfast and boiled them and we hid them all over the cottage. We had to find them and eat them for breakfast. It was fun even if we did act like kids, running all over the house looking for eggs.

Take care of yourself. It won't be much longer before I'll be heading home....

Shortly after Hazel's thirtieth birthday, she writes about being eager to return to the States and start a business. Included in these plans would be a car rental service from the airport—a novelty in 1946. Unfortunately, cars were all but impossible to secure.

Sunday Afternoon
April 28, 1946

Mother, I guess you know that Sissy and I have been planning to go into some kind of business in Oklahoma City together when I

get back. They have opened up the big municipal field in Oklahoma
City to private aviation, and she can get a hanger and office space
for us on the airport, where we plan to have a couple of planes to
rent, plus a rental car service for pilots and airline passengers that
come to Oklahoma City for business and need a car for a couple of
days. Personally, I think it is a good sound idea and it is an idea that
is being tried at many of the larger airports all over the country right
now. Transportation to and from an airport, which is always a few
miles from the city, has always been a major problem for people that
travel by air in commercial planes and for those that fly their own
planes. It is a business that we can try without making a large
investment, and one we can get out of without losing any money—
just selling the equipment. Our big problem at present is getting the
equipment or rather getting automobiles. We think it would be wise
to start out with new equipment if we can get it. I have been thinking of writing Reginald and asking him if he could help us buy at
least two new Fords. I know cars are very hard to buy back home
now but I was wondering if maybe we started trying to get them
now they would be available when I get home. I know Reginald
does a lot of business with several of the automobile places there in
Macon, and with his influence, I am wondering if he could get us
two new cars by August. I know the idea will work cause one of our
W.A.S.P. friends in California has started the same deal on an airport out there and she is going to town with it....

Sunday Afternoon
May 5, 1946

Dearest Mother;
    While I'm thinking about it I want to tell you about a friend of
mine down here that is returning to the States in about two weeks.
She is Helen Adams, from Armington, Illinois, and a swell person
that has been awfully nice to me since I have been in Brazil. She
lives in the hotel just above us and we both work in the same department at school. Well, Helen is leaving in a couple of weeks to go
home, and it might so happen that she will have a stop-over in
Macon on her way home. I told her Frankie or Martha would be
glad to pick her up wherever she was, and she would be welcome to
stay either place. She has been down here almost two years and is
going back to get married. She does not plan to marry until late
August and has insisted that Sissy and I be there for her wedding,
which is something we are going to try our best to do. I'm not too
sure Helen will be calling you, but in case she does, I know you will

find her a charming girl; really she is a most refined person. She is exactly the same age as I.

Well, Crum and I are counting the days now- only 106 more out of which we have about 84 working days. The others are either Sundays or holidays. Have you said anything to Frankie about you all meeting me in Miami? I think that would be lots of fun, I could send you a wire from here when I start to leave and you could be there when I get in. It will take about three days to fly up cause it is about 6,000 miles from here to Miami and we wouldn't be able to fly at night. The company is operating five DC-3 aeroplanes of their own to fly personnel back and forth. I will probably be in Miami two or three days getting my baggage cleared thru customs and winding things up with the Company. If you can't drive down I'll get a plane out of Miami soon as I can.

Another holiday this week, Wednesday, which is the 8th and the one year anniversary of the end of the war in Europe. It is nice to get holidays in the middle of the week; it breaks up the week for us and makes the time seem shorter between now and August 19th.

Hope you got my letter that I wrote last week telling you all about the plans Sissy and I have. I also hope Reginald can help us on the car situation. I believe that is going to be a good deal for us and can hardly wait to get back and started on it. I definitely want to settle down in the states when I get back cause I have had enough of traveling for a while. We have had a couple of offers since we have been down here to go to China after we finish our time here but I said NO, I want to get back to the good old U.S.A. Besides, I would have to start studying Chinese and I am tired of going to school, I want to rest for a while....

Chapter 4
IN GOD WE TRUST

In a letter dated June 5, 1946, Hazel makes the decision to return home before her contract expires. She has been in Brazil for eleven months.

I thought it all over carefully and decided it would be to my advantage in the long run to get back just as soon as possible. They are having a big aviation convention in Oklahoma City the first of October, and we definitely want to be started in our business by that time, so we can rent what cars we can get to the aviation people that fly in. It will also give us a good chance to meet and contact important people in aviation. You see, I will have to work extra hard at first and try to meet people, cause I am not known in Oklahoma City and have lost contact with people in the aviation industry since I have been away from civilian flying for the past five years. With all these things in mind, I have decided to not wait until my contract expires in August but resigned today effective as of July 1st. I should be back in Macon by July 5th. Isn't that good news? I can hardly wait to get back and see you and the rest of the family. Of course I am also anxious to get back in the air again. I really have been more than unhappy since I have been down here sitting on the ground teaching ground school. Since I do have something in the way of a job to go back to that I am almost sure will result in a good sound business for me now and for the future, I think I should get back and look after my interest and try to work toward making my life secure financially in the years to come, or in the event I should get where I can't work too hard. I have thought this all out and worried about it a lot in the past few weeks but believe I am doing the right thing. I am sure if I could have talked it over with you, you would agree with me. So, I'll be seeing you soon.

P.S.

How is the chicken situation in Macon? I can taste that fried chicken now. Wow!!!!!

Apparently Hazel visited with the family for a few weeks in July, and then took off for Oklahoma City to begin the new business. However, this new venture was not getting off the ground as planned. Her next letter arrived from Oklahoma City.

Friday Afternoon
July 26, 1946

Dearest Mother:

I certainly hope it isn't as hot in Macon as it is here. Of course I don't mind the heat but I do get tired of being wet and sticky all the time.

Did I tell you Mr. Sieber took us fishing Tuesday but I didn't get a thing. Sissy doesn't care about fishing so she sat and read a book.

Mr. Sieber got one and that was the catch of the day. We took Spinner (my dog) and she just had the time of her life. She loves the water and would jump in and swim way out in the lake and back. She really is a beautiful dog and the Siebers are crazy about her. Do you know she remembered me when we came in Sunday and almost had a fit jumping all over me. She follows me everywhere I go now and won't pay much attention to the Siebers anymore.

Well, our deal with the City has been postponed another two weeks due to City, County and State elections. One of the members of the City Council told us yesterday we were going to get space out at the field and not to worry about it. We are also seriously considering the Aircraft parts business again and Mr. Sieber says if we do take on the parts business, he will fix us up a nice store and warehouse and an office in one of his buildings nest to the Hotel. He wants to fix it up and give us the building just to help us off on a good start. I think he is certainly nice to want to do that for us. He said he wanted to see me set up in a business where I would not have to work so hard. They certainly have a lot of confidence in me. Whatever we do I'm really going to do my best to make it a success. I'm not worried cause I know you will be pulling for me as you always have. I'm sure that's why I have been so lucky and have gone as far as I have. By the way—do you know I think you are the most wonderful Mother in the world? Well, I do....

The next letter which was found was written almost two months later.

Saturday Morning
September 21, 1946

Dearest Mother:

Have been busy as a beaver this past week working on a "deal". Finally got it all worked out and am going to try something new and different from anything I have ever done before. Here is an outline of my new job.

Several weeks ago I heard about a new type coin-operated radio that was on the market so I investigated. They are made in Houston, Texas, and are radios made for hotels and tourist courts, and operate for two hours when a quarter is put in the slot. The man from the Company came up Monday, and we finally made a deal whereby I have the franchise for distributing these radios in western Oklahoma; in fact, about two thirds of the State. It sounds like a good deal to me. I have been appointed distributor and it will be up to me to find operators in different sections of my territory. These radios sell for $63.15 to hotels and courts, and I pay $50.00 for them, or I will rent them out on a percentage basis: giving hotels and courts 32% or 8¢ out of each quarter put in the radio. After deducting taxes, I will make 14¢ out of each quarter. We figure we will take in at least one quarter per day per radio. Mr. and Mrs. Seiber have agreed to let me install 50 radios here in the Hotel. I believe I can either sell or rent at least 1500 radios within the next year. It is going to be lots of work, but I think that after a year I should have a nice income. You know how people are, they love to put money in a slot and I see no reason why this should not work out to be a good deal for me. I will have to travel lots, but will like that. I have gotten to a good start with an order for 500 radios to be installed in three different towns in southern Oklahoma just as soon as I can deliver them. My chief problem now is getting an automobile and I have run my legs off trying to promote a new car but can't get anyone to promise me a car before the first of the year. I sure wish I could get one....

Unfortunately, Hazel's correspondence with her mother after October, 1946 does not resume until late November, 1950. These letters were apparently lost after her mother's death in 1972. Hazel came home from Brazil, and found she had limited abilities as a female in the civilian world outside of aviation. The "radio business" was short lived, and these years must have been difficult for her, although there are some references to being a flight instructor in Oklahoma. However, during this time, Hazel was active in the women's organizations associated with aviation during this time. A brochure from the Women's Aviation Convention sponsored by the Texas Ninety Nines, (February 8-9, 1947), featured Hazel as a speaker along with Nancy Love, the former director of the Women's Auxiliary Ferrying Squadron (WAFS). Hazel's topic was "Flying in Three Countries".

The WASP newspaper in December 1948 listed Hazel as a Flying Day Winner at the National Convention:

"Girl with the most flying hours was Hazel Raines and her award was a handsome ladies' wrist watch, donated by Davison's Jewelry Store in Los Angeles."
She also took part as a WASP honor representative in the memorial service for the 38 WASPs who lost their lives in World War II. This service was held at the third Annual Convention Order of Fifinella (September 15-18, 1948) in Glendale, California. The Order of Fifinella was the peacetime organization composed of former members of the WASPs. Hazel was the national president of this elite group in 1950. She explains the organization in an article by Mary Holtzclaw in the *Atlanta Journal and Constitution* Magazine, December 17, 1950:

When the Wasps were deactivated about five years ago, they started the peace-time organization call 'The Order of Fifinella.' Hazel's pretty dimples show when she tells about it. 'You know,' she says, 'all of us in the Air Force believe in gremlins. Some of then are bad gremlins that hop up and down on the wings, or pour water in your fuel, or shriek like banshees. But Fifinella is a good gremlin. She was designed for us by Walt Disney.' The girl gremlin is pictured on the emblem Hazel wears— a pretty little elf seated atop a plane, with her hair blowing in the wind.

She's good luck too— but not as good as that silver dollar that has gone with Hazel on every flight since her first one 13 years ago. 'Each time I take to the air,' she says, 'I get that silver dollar from my pocket and finger the words, In God We Trust. Those are great words, and flyers have to believe them.

Hazel in Rio
August, 1945

Hazel in Brazilian hearse. 1945

Brazil–1946

BOOK IV.
UNITED STATES AIR FORCE.....AS A DESK PILOT

Chapter 1
"MODUS OPERENDI"

In September of 1949, Hazel received a Reserve Commission of 2nd Lt., USAFR. She then participated in the Organized Reserve Program at Lackland Air Force Base in San Antonio, Texas, in May of 1950. This was about the time that the guerrilla attacks along the 38th parallel between North and South Korea began. On June 25, 1950, North Korean Communist troops invaded South Korea, and war was declared. Since the United Nations Charter which was signed in 1945 had outlawed aggressive attacks, the U.N. asked member countries to aid South Korea. Apparently, Hazel realized that this conflict offered another opportunity to serve her country. Eager to be called to active duty, she wrote directly to the Director of the Women in the Air Force:

Yukon, Oklahoma
May 17, 1950

Colonel Geraldine P. May Director,
Women in the Air Force
Pentagon Building Washington, D.C.

Dear Colonel May:

This letter may be an unpardonable course of action as well as a breach of "Channel" procedure but, I have exhausted every other known effort in an attempt to secure satisfactory disposition on my application for Extended Active Duty.

For your information, will you be kind enough to give consideration to the following facts relative to my situation.

As of 15 September 49, I received a Reserve Commission of 2nd Lt., USAFR, Authority of appointment—AFL 35-103 B dated 17 November 48. As of 21 February 50, I was attached to Hg & Hg Sq., 3700th WAF Training Group, Lackland Air Force Base and given a DySSN 2520. In March I reported to this Base for 15 days Active Duty Training as well as twelve periods of "On-the-Job" training as Assistant Group Training Officer.

The training I received while at Lackland has definitely led me to believe that there must be a place for me in your WAF Program. My experiences in the past have been broad due to affiliated service with the RAF in England, 1942-43, 14 months as a member of the WASPs, (Women's Air Force Service Pilots) and one year as a Ground School Instructor for the Brazilian Air Ministry in Sao Paulo, Brazil. As an over-all picture, for the past fourteen years I have been working with men and women in a training and supervisory capacity.

While at Lackland, I learned that they do have a need for additional Training Officers. I am confident that I do have the interest, desire, and ability to work with the WAF Program in this capacity. By virtue of the above facts, I made application for Extended Active Duty through the 12th Air Force, Brooks Field. The date of my application was 11 April 50. At the same time, I wrote Major Marjorie Hunt, Continental Air Command, and asked her for any help she might give me. Major Hunt has advised me that my request for active duty has not as yet arrived at her headquarters. She surmised they were holding my application on file at the 12th Air Force due to the fact that I do not have a critical MOS.

Due to the fact that I have never before been service connected, my MOS was just "assigned" to me without any consideration of my qualifications or past working experience. Therefore, it seems reasonable enough for me to assume, I am qualified somewhere along the line for a critical MOS that would afford justification for my recall. Recall, that is, to some type of duty that would be of value to the WAF Program or in our Air Forces.

I can well appreciate the fact that you are quite a busy person, however, I would like to ask you if you would be kind enough to give me a bit of help in regards to recall request.

Sincerely, I shall greatly appreciate anything you might be able to do for me at this time.

It is my understanding that you plan to be in San Antonio in June. If you could possibly spare me a few minutes of your time, I would be more than glad to drive down for an interview.

Sincerely,
Hazel J. Raines
2nd LT USAFR AL-1855750
Yukon, Oklahoma

This letter is significant for several reasons. In the first place, one is shocked by the phrase: "Due to the fact that I have never before been service connected, my MOS was just "assigned" to me without any consideration of my qualifications or past working experience." Since the WASPs were not militarized until November 4, 1977, there were no military records or precedence of Hazel having served her country. Not until 1977 did Congress grant the WASPs honorable discharges— thirty three years after they had been deactivated. Hazel had to scramble around for a *"modus operendi"* so that she could be called to active duty. However, the letter must have been effective, for an article in the *Atlanta Journal* (December 17, 1950) stated:

> "Georgia's Flying Lady is the first WAF Reservist in the nation to be returned to active duty on a mobilization assignment..."

The next letter describes Hazel's reaction to being inducted as an Officer in the United States Air Force. It made quite an impression on her.

28 November 1950
Maxwell AFB, Ala.

Dearest Mother:

Just finished up my paper work and have everything in order whereby I plan to leave here first thing in the morning. Never in my life have I seen so many forms to fill out and sign.

After my papers were declared in order and they told me I was ready to ship out to my new assignment in San Antonio, they instructed me to report to a certain Officer to take the Oath of Office of appointment in the United States Air Force as a Commissioned Officer. I was the only female to stand with a group of 19 men to pledge allegiance to my Country and to our Government. It really gave me goose bumps all up and down my spine as I stood there with my right hand raised, repeated the oath of office, and for the first time really realized and felt that I had been accepted to duty with our United States Air Forces.

With great difficulty, I swallowed a big lump in my throat, and breathed a silent prayer that God would give me the strength and courage to perform all duties assigned. Since I fear not, not even Fear, I have complete faith in my ability to serve honorably.

I am enclosing the $20.00 you let me have when I left. Since they paid me my uniform allowance, I do not need this money. Thanks lots.

Just as soon as I arrive at Lackland, I shall drop you a note and give you my correct address. Bet my uniforms arrived the day I left....

From a letter the next day on her way to Lackland:

Baton Rouge, La.
29 November 1950

Left Montgomery this morning about 8 o'clock. Arrived Baton Rouge this afternoon 5:30 after a very nice easy drive. Only drove 415 miles today and feel not the least bit tired. Driving my Pontiac is just like relaxing in a big comfortable chair while I watch the scenery change from a town to a city then on to another state. One thing never changes— the people. No matter where I stop I meet good American people. With a cheerful smile and good wishes for a safe and pleasant journey, they send me on my way rejoicing in the true fact that I too, am an American....

The war news looks anything but good. It comes not as a surprise, the sudden turn of events, but is exactly as I had expected. Although I am far from being a military strategist, I still contend we shall be forced to withdraw from Korea and such action shall be the advent of World War III.

Soon as I get myself settled at Lackland, I'm going to get another Cocker Spaniel— I need someone to talk with, someone that understands....

Lt. Hazel J. Raines
OMS Box 355
Lowry AFB
Denver, Colorado

Sunday Night
24 December 1950

Dearest Mother:

Can't think of a better way to spend Xmas Eve away from home than to sit down and write you a letter. Well, I am just about settled here and my room is straight at last.

Now I can tell you about my assignment. The primary mission of Lowry AFB is to train men and women in a certain speciality job in the Air Force. That is to say, after the women have finished their basic training at Lackland, some of them are sent here to take more advance training in certain fields of endeavor. Well, those women are grouped here in what is called a WAF Training Squadron while they attend school. Naturally there is a certain amount of attention, paper work, recreation and so on that they must have while they are here. Therefore, we have a WAF Squadron. We are not responsible for their classroom training but are responsible for them otherwise. So, we have a Squadron Commander, she is Captain Watt, then we have what is called the Adjutant of the squadron, that is ME. So, I am now Adjutant of the 3429th WAF Student Squadron here at Lowry. We also have another Officer who is a Captain as well as about twelve enlisted women who work in our office.

I haven't had too much to do as yet, but imagine I will be quite busy after the first of the year. After all, we are responsible for the welfare of several hundred women, and that is no small job. As a matter of fact, something came up night before last and I had to go to Cheyenne, Wyoming. Was up most of the night and didn't get back until late yesterday afternoon. You see, some of these kids are just 18 or 19, first time away from home, and they just go wild.

Have been invited to have Christmas dinner with our Squadron C.O., Captain Watt and her mother. They have a home just ten minutes from the base....

Only three letters survive from 1951, one from Major Watt to Hazel's mother, a reply to Major Watt, and a letter Hazel wrote at the end of the year. New to the military life in the United States Air Force, Hazel was making her way as a "desk pilot". Had she been given the opportunity, one is convinced she would have taken to the air.

3429th Student Squadron
3415th Technical Training Group
Lowry Air Force Base
Denver, Colorado

Mrs. Bessie P. Raines
Massee Apartments
College Street
Macon, Georgia

5 March 1951

Dear Mrs. Raines:

Hazel has been here at Lowry with the WAF Squadron since 20 December 1951, and it occurred to me that you might like to hear a little bit about the fine job she has been doing.

When Hazel reported in and was assigned as adjutant, I am sure that you, as well as she, wondered how she would like "flying a desk". She has probably told you that during my absence on leave in January the acting commanding officer received her orders for transfer and as a result, Hazel was catapulted into being commanding officer, adjutant and supply officer, all at one time. Her handling of a difficult situation certainly reflected her fine previous training. Upon my return I found everything in calm good order.

In other words, Mrs. Raines, Hazel is successfully qualifying as a competent "desk pilot" with far less "flying time" than that which made her skilled in her former field. Her adjustment has been remarkable both as to attitude and approach to the tasks to be done. She has gained the admiration and respect of the "old timers" among our enlisted personnel, quite an accomplishment in itself.

As her mother you must always have been extremely proud of her. This is being written to add to that pride.

We are all looking forward to the time when you will visit us here.

Sincerely yours,
Marion L. Watt Major,
USAF Commanding

In her mother's handwriting is a draft of her reply:

Dear Major Watt:

Naturally I am proud of Hazel but getting a letter from you concerning her has made me more so. Hazel has written me about her "commanding officer". She appreciates the fact that you have been understanding and patient in helping her learn the Air Force way of life.

Denver seems such a long way from Georgia so I am indeed glad she is happy there. Doing the thing you like to do in life makes all the difference and Hazel seems to be completely happy in her work.

Thanks so much for writing the nice letter to me.

My best regards to you.

Sincerely,
(Bessie Raines)

Chapter 2
FLYING A DESK

The *Lowry Airmen.* (9 March, 1951) featured this article:

"Although she is flying a desk in the Air Force now, you can tell the way she glances out the window at the sound of a plane that flying a desk isn't her idea of the best way to spend your time and you'd be willing to bet that at the first opportunity, she will be back in the air adding to those 6,000 flying hours she has already logged."

Saturday Night
29 December 1951

Dearest Mother:

Just want to thank you for the wonderful Christmas present. You really should not have sent me six spoons. How proud I am to have them and also the knife and fork Frankie and her family sent me. Gee, I sure am proud of my wonderful start on my favorite pattern. I just love Chantilly silver. As I have said, if I never have a chance to use it, and I hope I shall, I can always give it to someone in my family.

This has been such a busy week for me. As you know, Major Horn went to Tucson to be with her husband, and the other officer flew home. I have been working night and day, but think it has been the best thing for me to keep busy. Had a wonderful Christmas dinner with friends. Turkey and all the trimmings. Hope you had a nice day too. It has been cold here, lots of snow.

As it stands now, I shall be going to Maxwell to school in March. That is Montgomery, and shall be there until the last of May. So, I think it will be best that I wait and take leave either before I start school in March or when I finish in May. In any event I shall see you in March, and shall be able to drive home on week-ends while I am at Maxwell. I plan to drive down from here. I will be in school almost three months. After I finish school I probably shall be sent overseas. Thought it best to tell you at this time....

Correspondence in 1952 is limited to several articles and four letters. When the letters resume, Hazel is a First Lt. stationed at the United States Army and Air Force Recruiting main Station in Tampa, Florida. An article in the *Tampa Daily Times* (Monday July 28, 1952), tells of an up-coming radio interview:

First Lt. Hazel J. Raines, USAF, WAC/WAF Procurement Officer for the Tampa Bay Area, and the first women Reserve Pilot recalled to active duty, will be interviewed tomorrow by Van Wilson on "Greeting Time" (WDAE, 9:30 A.M.).

Lieutenant Raines was national president in 1950 of the Order of Fifinella, made up of 1500 ex-Wasps who were pilots during World War II. During her 13 years of flying, Hazel has made each flight with a silver dollar bearing the slogan, 'In God We Trust.'

Friday Night
16 May 1952

Dearest Mother:

Well— just call me Recruiter Raines. Reported in yesterday morning. The Station Commander is Major Fritz, Air Force. I am Assistant Station Commander in charge of 17 counties. We have 21 enlisted people and 5 civilians working in the Tampa Office. Major

Fritz plans to retire next month and if he does I will assume command of the Tampa District.

Of course I still don't know what this is all about but believe I am going to like my job. Actually, I am the direct Supervisor of female recruiting and although I will not have go out and recruit women, I will have to spend better than half my time away from Tampa making my rounds checking and helping Recruiters in the 17 counties. They have given me a staff car for my own use—a 4-door Chevrolet—the olive green Army type. I plan to leave Tampa Tuesday and won't be back here until Friday. Will be in Orlando, Tuesday & Wednesday - Lakeland, Thursday - and St. Petersburg and Sarasota, Friday. Normally, we work 5 days a week with Saturday and Sunday off. However, Since I am new at this job I probably will work for the next 2 or 3 Saturdays.

Well—guess what— I rented an apartment today. Gee, I sure am happy about that. Plan to move tomorrow afternoon. Have to go to St. Pete tomorrow to a luncheon as a guest of the Business and Professional Women's Club. Hope to get back here about three o'clock. You know I wrote you about meeting Mr. and Mrs. Williams. Well, I am taking the apartment across the hall from them. It is a 4-unit building only built 2 years ago. It really is beautiful and everything is so new and clean. Have a nice big living room, bedroom, tile bath and shower, kitchenette with electric stove and refrigerator. Everything is built-in and very modern.

Went to town this afternoon and bought 4 sheets, 2 pillow cases, and a yellow spread. Mrs. Williams bought plastic drapes for the entire apartment, and helped me hang them this afternoon. Now I am all set whereby you can come visit with me anytime you please. The sofa in the living room folds down into a very comfortable double bed. That will be my bed when you come down. Think maybe this fall, when it isn't so hot, we might plan on a trip for you, O.K.? O.K. I will now have plenty of room for two people— three in a pinch.

Have to stop now and pin up my hair and get ready for tomorrow....

Friday Night
June 10, 1952

Dearest Mother:

Have had a busy but interesting week. As you know, I drove to Jacksonville Tuesday Morning to attend a WAC/WAF Recruiters Conference. Got back last night at 11:30. Would have gotten back sooner but had to stop by Orlando on business.

Yes, the drive up was hot but I was lucky. Took my Recruiting Sergeant with me and she did most of the driving. Coming back was nice and cool with some rain and I didn't mind the drive at all.

Now I am busy getting ready for next week. Plan to leave here Monday and will be in Orlando until Saturday—maybe Sunday. That will be a full week since we are staging a WAC/WAF Rally and "Get Acquainted" week in that area. The main purpose of our week of activities is to acquaint the public, and especially the parents of young girls that might sooner or later join the Service, with just what our young women in the Army and Air Force are doing today. I am scheduled to make several speeches and radio broadcasts. The final and grand finale of the week will be held in the Auditorium in Orlando Friday night, June 27th. That night we plan to have two guest speakers—the Commanding Officer from the Air Force Basic Training Center at Lackland, and the C.O. from the Basic Training Center for the Army at Fort Lee, Virginia. The newly activated WAF Band will be on hand for a concert. We also plan to have a style show. That is, we will have young girls to model the WAC and WAF uniforms. Then, as a climax to the entire program, we plan to perform the actual ceremony of giving the Oath of Enlistment to four young women who are joining the Air Force. If everything works out as planned, we should have quite an interesting program to present to the public.

Seems as tho the girls have been having a gay time, with Reg going to Cuba, Fabia on a House Party, and Jeaneane off to camp. Think that is all mighty fine and I am glad they can do the things they choose as their main interest and pleasure. They truly are three wonderful young girls, and I burst with pride and joy to know they are my nieces. Guess they sorta fill a vacancy in my heart and life that fate took away.

By the way, when I was in Jacksonville, I checked on my accrued leave. I now have coming to me almost forty days but—they say I cannot take any leave before September. I am in an essential spot again. However, I am pretty sure I will be able to take some time off Thanksgiving and Xmas. How about that! I am almost sure that I will be able to be home for both occasions. In the meantime, soon as this awful hot weather is over, perhaps in September or October, maybe you can come down and stay just as long as you choose. I just wouldn't want you to come down now, cause the heat is almost too much for me. Besides, I am going to be on the road most of the time for the next sixty days.

Gee, this has turned out to be quite a long letter for me to write. But then I had to tell you about what I have been doing and plan to do. Quite different from what I could say and write about when I was in Squadron work. My work and activities are now "public information" contrary to my former assignment. Think I like this better. At least I can keep you posted on what I am doing from day to day.

Well Mother, I had better stop now. Have things to do, or as you say— "I have to do around". Although I don't usually work on Saturday, I plan to drive down to a little town about thirty miles from here tomorrow afternoon to call on a family. They have a very fine young daughter who is interested in joining the Air Force. She is only 18 but with one year of college at Wesleyan—this past year. She wants to enlist in the Air Force and when she is of age- 21-; she plans to make an application for Officer's Candidate School. Her Mom and Dad are against it. She can't afford to go back to Wesleyan, and is now working in a Department store here in Tampa. So, I am going down and talk with her parents. They just do not realize that their daughter can continue her college education while on duty in the Air Force, and eventually become an Officer and a leader in Military and civilian life that will make them justly proud. It sure does my heart good to know that only the "cream of the crop" and best qualified young women are now being accepted for duty in the various branched of the services.

Goodnight. Will try to find time next week to drop you a note. If I don't, at least you will know where I am and what I am doing. Give my love to all the family and take care of yourself....

Hazel's loyalty to her country is expressed in the following letter of 18 October, 1952:

Wish you could have been here today. They had a big parade here in Montgomery, Red Feather Kick-Off parade. Three of my enlisted women and I marched behind the color guard and led the parade from the State Capitol building down through town for about a mile. Even tho it was a bit warm and I was tired when it was all over, I enjoyed every step of the way. With Old Glory in front of me and the Maxwell Air Force Band directly behind playing familiar march music, I stepped out with pride and a prayer of thanks to God that I am an American and I have the unique privilege and pleasure of wearing the uniform of the United States Air Force. Too bad we have living in our great country so many people who are so called "good people" who go to bed at night with a prayer in their hearts that their sons and daughters, grandsons and granddaughters, will never have to serve the Country that has given them the freedom and abundance of happiness they enjoy every day.

Chapter 3
SQUADRON COMMANDER

1/Lt. Hazel J. Raines
Company A, TAG School
RMO, Class 60
Fort Benjamin Harrison,
Indiana

Thursday Afternoon
8 January 1953

Dearest Mother:

Arrived here yesterday and don't mind telling you it was one heck of a drive. The ice and snow was rough but my Colorado experience in driving in this sort of stuff helped me make the trip without incident. I really am glad I drove up cause a car is most essential since my quarters are so far from where I shall be eating.

Well, I am not only the only Air Force Officer in my class, but the only female among 200 men. So, you can see I am going to have quite a time. Of course this suits me just fine, cause I always did get along better with a group of men than women.

Have very comfortable quarters, steam heated. There are only three officers in this building; two Army and myself. Oh, I forgot to say that this is strictly an Army Post and 99% of the people that come up here to school are Army. The reason I am here is cause I am on loan to the Army. Sounds crazy I know but that is the way it is.

The other two officers are going to the Adjutant General School. One is a Captain, (Negro), and the other a 1/Lt., white girl. The colored Captain is quite nice and has a room across the hall from me. Yes, I know, this is the first time I have had to live with a colored person but believe me after talking with her ten minutes, I forgot all about the fact that she is black and I am white.

Well, I want to go to the PX and get a few things so will say so long for now. Take care of yourself and write soon....

Saturday Afternoon
17 January 1953

Dearest Mother:

Sure was glad to get your letter the other day. It seems like ages since I was home and I was anxious to hear from you.

Well, my first week of school is over. We go to school six days a week but only until noon on Saturday. This is an interesting course and is just beginning to get rough. We have our first exam Monday and start our practical work in Public Speaking Tuesday. That is to say we actually start making talks. I have a talk to make Tuesday, Wednesday and Friday. That's what takes so much time, preparing for these talks.

By the way, they have divided up our class and I am now in a class of 36 people. There are five other Officers, 29 Enlisted men and one Enlisted woman. We will continue to have classes with the enlisted people for two more weeks, then they will separate the six Officers because we take more advanced subjects than the enlisted people.

Guess I don't have to tell you what I will be doing this weekend. That's right, studying and washing out a few things. I really don't mind cause the weather is awful—cold, raining and they predict snow.

Guess this is just about all the news for now. Give my love to all the family and write soon....

Monday Night
9 February 1953

Dearest Mother:

Well, here I am back in Alabama. Left Indianapolis Saturday and got in here Sunday night. Had a nice trip back and did not run into snow and bad weather like I had on my trip up.

Glad that school session is over. I did enjoy my school and am glad I had the opportunity to attend, even if it did work me like crazy. Now I have another diploma to add to my varied collection. Maybe some day this child will get educated one way or the other. Now I hope to settle down and take up a course or two toward a college degree. I'll get it if it takes the rest of my life.

Was good walking in the office this morning. Of course I have had a cut in my personnel, lost three women while I was away. Now only have four left. Have three in my Southern half of the State and only one in Birmingham. This will mean that I will be on the road quite a bit, but I don't mind.

We had quite an impressive graduation from The Adjutant General School—TAG School. The Chaplain opened the exercises with a prayer and closed the event with a prayer. A full Colonel, C.O. of the School, gave an address then we marched up, saluted and were presented with our diplomas. Thought it was quite nice and felt right good inside.

Sure seems swell to be back down South and find good weather for a change. It was cold and wet while at Fort Ben, and I don't mind the cold—just the dampness. Glad to see some sunshine for a change.

My apartment is anything but clean, so guess I will spend some time cleaning tonight. Just wanted to drop you a note to let you know I am back in Montgomery.

Hope everything is O.K. with you. Give my love to all the family and write soon....

After a visit to Macon in April, Hazel writes:

> Walter Bragg Smith Apts.
> Montgomery, Alabama
> Monday Night
> 20 April 1953

My trip back was fine with the exception of my long and tiresome drive through Columbus. Honest, I have never seen such wholesale destruction. It just made me sick to see the demolished homes, up-rooted trees, power and telephone lines all over the roads, cars in ditches and all sorts of twisted and torn household items hanging from trees. From the time I entered the city limits of Columbus, until I crossed the bridge, and actually passed thru Phoenix City, it took me one hour and thirty-five minutes. Traffic was awful, and they had City and State police on duty directing the curious Sunday sightseers. To my way of thinking, they should have given a ticket to every motorist on the road who did not have a good reason for being out in a car. In a way, I guess it is a good thing that I did not have to go by and see Gene's folks, cause it would have taken me at least another hour to get back to the highway after I left Phoenix City. However, this I would not have minded and would have done gladly for Gene.

Sure did enjoy my visit with you and all the family. Sure appreciate the silver you gave me, as well as the other gifts from the rest of the family. The chicken and steaks were mighty fine and I must report that I weighed today and found that I had gained two pounds over the weekend. And speaking of chicken, I ate both pieces you fixed for me before I got back to Montgomery. I don't know but there is just something about the way you fry chicken that makes it extra good. Although I was full as I could be when I left Macon, I started thinking about the chicken you had fixed for me by the time I got to Roberta. Ate one piece before I hit Columbus then the other before I got to Montgomery.

In late September, Hazel has been transferred to Offutt Air Force Base in Omaha, Nebraska, but this assignment is short lived.

Offutt Air force Base
Omaha, Nebraska
Monday Afternoon
28 September 1953

Dearest Mother:

Well, here I go again. Will leave here Wednesday for Travis Air Force Base, California, which is located at Fairfield, California just a few miles from San Francisco.

Went to Headquarters this morning and had quite a long talk with Colonel Tenges—who is the WAF Staff Director for this command—SAC. She was quite anxious to see me take that assignment which will once again be Squadron duty, only this time I am being assigned as Squadron Commander—that I like.

I'm feeling fine—knew you would want to know— and am all rested up for my trip. I will have seven days travel time— it is 1700 miles from Omaha, so I will have plenty of time and can take it easy....

1/Lt. Hazel J. Raines
28th WAF Squadron
Travis A.F. Base, California

Sunday Afternoon
11 October 1953

Dearest Mother:

Have spent all day yesterday and most of today unpacking and getting settled. I have a nice big room right next to the bathroom. I told you we live in a long building, very modern, that is divided into apartments and there are three to each apartment. In my apartment there is only one Flight Nurse. There was a WAF, but she is away at school. Anyway, we have a nice big living room and a big kitchen. Everyone is so friendly here and always running in and out. I think all the nurses do on their time off is cook and eat. Every time I turn around someone is trying to get me to eat with them. So, you see I won't get lonesome or hungry.

Yes, I am sure I am going to like it very much here at Travis. The Captain who is C.O. of the Squadron now, will be leaving the last of the month, then I will take over. We have a nice Squadron, rather small with only 100 girls— the average age being about 20. This is about 1/4 the size of the Squadron at Lowry....

In her next letter Hazel writes about the soldiers returning from Korea:

28th WAF Squadron
Travis Air Force Base
Travis AFB, California
21 October 1953

Told you I live in a building with eighteen flight nurses and they are just wonderful. I came in tonight and before I could get my uniform off I was invited down to dinner in an apartment just below me where two nurses live. They had a wonderful roast beef dinner and asked five others in to eat. That is the way it has been every night since I have been here. Since they all like fried chicken, I plan to cook a chicken dinner for them this weekend. Wish I could cook like you and really give them a feed. I never saw people eat like they do. Of course, they do work hard on their trips all over the United States and Alaska. They have been carrying P.O.W.s and the things they tell are most interesting and heartbreaking about the boys returning from Korea.

Now that the 'sweat' is over, I might tell you I was tagged for another change the first of the week——overseas shipment, but I got out of it. You see all Officers are classified in a specialty field; mine is personnel and administrative work. Because of that, I do head the list for those most wanted for an overseas assignment. Since they do need me here, it has been requested that I be retained for Squadron Commander; I doubt if I shall be shipped out any time soon. I didn't want to go because I would like to make my promotion to Captain first. My paper work on my promotion will go forward next week. However, I will not know the results probably until February. If they should ship me out, it might mean another year before I would get my promotion.

At the beginning of 1954, Hazel is thirty-eight years old, but is beginning to assume the role of "mother" by some of the younger Air Force personnel. This ability to function in an advisory capacity is reinforced by her overseas assignment in September as Adjutant of the 11th Commanding Squadron at South Ruislip in England. By December of the same year, Hazel is the WAF Staff Advisor of all enlisted personnel "on matters such as marriage, mal-assignment, health, and personal matters."

Travis Air Force Base
Wednesday Night
10 February 1954

Dearest Mother:

Have been so busy I haven't had time to take care of my personal chores the past ten days. Tonight is the first time I have had free from duty. Of course I like the idea of staying busy.

Received a letter from Lt. Webster and her husband, Lt. Bristow, saying they had stopped by Macon and paid you a visit. Sure was glad they did, cause they are two favorite people of mine. I met Webster when I came out here to Travis. She is a wonderful young lady and a very fine WAF Officer. She was married to Lt. Bristow in December and they invited me to their wedding at Uplands, California, December 19th. Needless to say, I could not make their wedding. I sorta adopted them as my "son" and "daughter". In turn they call me "Mother". I had no idea they had planned to stop by Macon to see you. They were on their way to French Morraco, North Africa. He received orders shortly after their wedding transferring him over there. She came to me and wanted to know what to do in order to go with him. Of course I got busy and contacted the WAF Staff Director at our Headquarters at SAC in Offutt and she approved her transfer immediately. Webster did not know that; she thought her transfer was due to a letter I helped her write to Colonel Tinges at HQ., SAC. Anyway, they are happy and on their way to a new assignment and will be together....

Travis Air Force Base
Friday Night
23 April 1954

Dearest Mother:

Sometime I just can't imagine what happens to the time, days, weeks—-even months roll around faster than they did when I was a young sprout. You know, I can hardly realize that I have just passed the 38 mile post. Oh well, I am still your "Baby Daughter". My roommate and I drove up to Travis Lodge last weekend and had a very nice trip. The Lodge is 135 miles from Travis; is owned by the Base. I spent part of my time planning the Scout encampment program. We left Travis in my car Saturday morning at nine. Arrived at the Lodge at noon to find it snowed in. We had to park the car about a mile from the Lodge and walk down. It wasn't easy going since we had boots, jackets, a weekend kit and had to carry these things in our arms through all the snow. The snow was soft, and we would sink in half way up to our knees while walking. I was so tired when we finally arrived and could do nothing more than just sit by the big fireplace for about an hour and drink coffee. After we rested and had lunch, we hiked over to the ski Lodge about a mile from Travis Lodge; sat out in the sun and watched many people ski down a slope some 2800 feet high. We were too tired to walk back, so we took a cable car back to the highway that was about 1/4 mile from Travis Lodge. Even then, we had to walk down a steep hill, over a train shed and down a 30 foot ladder, then down another hill before we were home again. We got back just in time for supper. After we ate, we just sat around the open fire, talked with twelve other people that had driven up for the weekend, toasted marshmallows, drank orange juice, and had a very relaxing evening.

Sunday morning I was up bright and early. I wanted to take care of my survey work on the Scouting program. At eight, we had a very nice breakfast, and by nine Poole and I were off again for the Ski Lodge we had visited the afternoon before. This time we walked back up the highway and took the cable car to the Lodge. The only way we could get there was by walking thru the snow, as we did the day before, ski in or take a cable car. When we reached the Ski Lodge, which is some 7,000 feet above sea level, we decided to ride the chair lift up to the top of the summit, 2800 feet, where the ski run begins. That was where I made a big mistake. Although the ride was beautiful and something I had never done before, I failed to take into consideration that the sun reflected from the snow could burn one much worse than the sun at sea level. We stayed on top, 9500 feet, about two hours before we rode the chair lift down again. When we finally got back to Travis Lodge for Sunday dinner, my face felt like it was on fire. I plastered it about an inch thick with sunburn lotion. After we finished eating and resting a bit, we hiked back up the hill to my car and took off for Travis about two o'clock. By the time we arrived here, just a little before six, my forehead had begun to swell and puff out so that I looked like an "egg-head". Since this had never happened to me before, I decided I had best go to the Hospital and have a Doctor look at me. This I did Sunday night, and he said I had second degree burns, gave me some pills, and told me to keep cold compresses on my head Monday. Well, Monday I did just that, and the fluid in my forehead moved down to my eyes and they were closed all day Monday. Tuesday, I continued to put the cold compresses on my eyes, and Wednesday it all went away. Now my face is red as a beet and is in the process of peeling. Never again shall I do that! The odd thing about it all is, I never had one bit of pain. I sure did get a lot of kidding from the people up at Headquarters about how I looked. I was only away from the office two hours Monday afternoon and half a day Tuesday. I just sat at my desk with a bowl of ice and a wad of cold gauze over one eye and then the other while I took care of my work.

I am enclosing some pictures we took while at the Lodge. The one of me with the snow up to my right knee was taken when we made our first trip to the Ski Lodge on Saturday afternoon. The one in the car was made on Sunday afternoon on our way back to Travis.

Thanks again for the lovely birthday card and the silver. When I get home again I will get it all together and see just what I have of what. I believe I left some of my silver in the footlocker that Gene stored in his attic....

Chapter 4
MY SECOND HOME

The correspondence begins again in September with Hazel starting her journey back to England. She has been assigned as Adjutant to the 11th Communications Squadron of the Third Air Force.

Camp Kilmer, N.J.
Wednesday Noon
1 September 1954

Dearest Mother:

My flight to Kilmer was uneventful—just another plane ride. Arrived here at five o'clock. Landed at Newark to Kilmer (15 miles) and the fare was $12.00. I took a bus for 65¢. Had more help than I needed with my baggage, since there were 21 enlisted men on the same bus; and I was the only female and the only Officer.

When I checked in at the WAF Squadron, where I was given a private room in the female B.O.Q., I met Lt. Johnson, a WAF Officer I knew quite well at Lackland back in '50. She is stationed here. I had dinner here in the Quarters with her last night—she has a kitchen. We sat and talked until midnight.

Started out on my processing at 0800 this morning, and since Lt. Johnson has a car, she took me everywhere I had to go, and as a result, I have finished processing. Have a briefing at one o'clock, then one more tomorrow.

Don't know my A.P.O. number yet or exactly where I am going in England. Will probably know tomorrow. Anyway, I am trying to pull a few strings and get them to delay my shipment until next Tuesday. If they do this—and I think I can work it— I will be off from 5 o'clock Friday afternoon until 0800 A.M. Tuesday morning. I am keeping my fingers crossed cause Lt. Johnson and I have plans to spend the weekend in New York.

Sure did enjoy my visit home a well as the trip to Raliegh with you and Frankie. It was lots of fun.

Going to the Officers Club for lunch so must go now. Will drop you another note before I leave Kilmer....

Camp Kilmer, N. J.
Friday Morning
3 September 1954

Dearest Mother:

Well, luck is with me. I won't be shipping out until next Tuesday. I will be off duty as of 5 o'clock this afternoon and don't have to report back here until Tuesday morning. How about that! So, I am taking off for New York tomorrow morning bright and early and plan to return Monday night.

Last night I was sitting in the lounge here at the B.O.Q. looking at T.V. when a Lt. came in and asked me if I knew where she could find Hazel Raines. I looked at the girl, thought she looked familiar, but asked why she was looking for Raines. She said she was in training at Sweetwater, Texas with her when she was a Wasp, and at this point she recognized me. She pointed to the scar on my head and laughed and said, "Up to your old tricks again, you can't fool me, you are Hazel." Sure enough, she was Virginia Sweat, whom I had known in Texas in '44. She has the same assignment as I have for England. We will be shipping together. She has a '51 Chevrolet she is taking to England. Also, Virginia is from up-state New York and knows New York City quite well. So, she is going to New York with me. Lt. Johnson is going with us too. We have decided to go by bus. It is only a one hour ride from Kilmer and the round trip fare is just a dollar and a half.

This afternoon I am going to the Special Services office to pick up some tickets for some radio and T.V. Shows. Won't know what plays they have tickets for until 3 o'clock. However, they told me I wouldn't have any trouble in New York getting tickets if I wear my uniform. That's easy, cause that's all I have to wear.

Besides Virginia and me, there are three nurses processing for England, but are shipping out tomorrow. There is another WAF going out tomorrow to Germany.

They tell me my A.P.O. number might change after I arrive in England, but any mail you send to the address I have given you will reach me in about a week.

Well, That is about all the news for now. Will write again before
I leave Kilmer. Anxious to hear about my car—hope I didn't lose
too much on it.

Give my love to all the family and tell Frankie I sure did enjoy
my trip to Raleigh. Wish she and you too could go to New York with
me this weekend....

11th COMMRON SQ.
APO 125
Postmaster New York, N.Y,
Saturday Afternoon
11 September 1954

Dearest Mother:

This trip over was quite different from my trip over twelve years
ago. We left Camp Kilmer Wednesday afternoon at 5:30 and arrived
at Westover Air Force Base (by bus) Wednesday night at one A.M.
Westover is near Springfield, Mass. We took off in a 4 engine C-54
at 9 o'clock Thursday Morning. We flew the Southern route and
landed in the Azores at Lajes Air Force Base at 7 P.M. Here we had a
two hour delay for dinner at the Officer's Club. They gave us a very
nice lunch in flight plus all the milk, fruit juice, and coffee we
wanted to drink. It was also here that we ran our watches ahead five
hours which made our take-off time 2 A.M. We landed at Preswick,
Scotland Friday morning at 8 A.M. Total flying time was 16 hours.

We certainly did have a comfortable flight—smooth all the way
and excellent weather. The ship was just as plush as any commercial
airplane. We flew at 17,000 feet all the way and I did get some sleep
between the Azores and Scotland.

After going through the usual routine of clearing thru at the
Airport; we had breakfast, then were taken by bus to the Heads of
Ayr Hotel, Ayr, Scotland which is only 8 miles from where we
landed. The hotel is very beautiful and semi-modern. The country-
side is fresh and green with millions of all sorts of beautiful flowers
growing everywhere. It is cold and damp, but that was to be
expected. The greatest change I have noticed thus far has been in the
food. Of course they are no longer rationed, and while the food is
slightly different from ours, it is well prepared, good, and served
beautifully. Actually, I do not feel as tho I am in a strange or new
place this time but rather feel as tho I have returned to my second
home.

This morning we were taken by bus back to Preswick for a
briefing and re-assignment. As I told you in my cable, I have been
assigned to 3rd Air Force, which is in South Ruislip just outside of
London. I will be here tomorrow morning at 9 o'clock and will

arrive in London (via train) Sunday evening at 7:30. Will report for duty Monday, at which time I will find out what my new assignment will be. I will be living in London—not on a base—so I imagine I will spend most of the next week getting settled and finding a place to live.

We had 58 passengers coming over which included three nurses, two WAF officers, and myself. The nurses and two WAF were assigned to bases in various places in England. Frankly, I got the choice assignment and they all envy me. I realize I am lucky to get such a nice assignment.

That is just about all the important news for now. Will write again after I am settled in London....

Ruislip, England
16 September, 1954

Dearest Mother:

Arrived in London last night after a twelve hour train ride from Scotland. Reported for duty this morning and was assigned as adjutant to the 11th Communication Squadron. The Squadron is 90% male—10% WAF enlisted personnel. My first crack at serving as an Officer in a male Squadron. Should be quite interesting.....

With the job I have, I shall be going to Europe often. Tomorrow I am flying to Norway, will be back Monday. Next week I go to Germany for two days. The first week in October I shall be in Paris, France. Needless to say I like my assignment. Oh yes, I almost forgot, I am going to Sweden the middle of October.

At this point I have not had time to contact the Littlehales in Maidenhead, but hope to do so next weekend. I am only 20 miles from Maidenhead now....

Ruislip, England
Saturday Afternoon
2 October 1954

Dearest Mother:

Well, I have been busy and on the go. Last weekend I went to Maidenhead and spent Saturday afternoon and Sunday with the Littlehales. Naturally they were quite surprised to see me but we truly had a nice visit. I had planned to go back this weekend but had to work today.

Things have indeed changed over here but I am glad to be here again. The weather hasn't been too bad as yet.

My trip I wrote you about was interesting, and I really feel lucky to know I will be able to see quite a bit of Europe. Next weekend I am flying to Portugal. Will leave Friday and be back Sunday night. Maybe I will get to practice up on my Portuguese. I know one thing; I am going to study French while I am here cause I can sure use it when in France.

Decided not to buy a car for a while as yet. I haven't really needed one since I do know how to get around here in the U.K.

I am enclosing a folder that will tell you all about where I live. Since I am only 15 minutes by bus from the base, I have decided to stay here a while.

Must go for now. Time to eat. Give my love to all the family....

Chapter 5
WAF ADVISOR

Hotel Metropole
Lisboa, Portugal
Friday Evening
8 October 1954

Dearest Mother:

We had quite a wonderful flight today from London to Lisbon, Portugal. We left London, or rather Ruislip, which is where I am stationed, at 0900 hours and landed here just five hours and fifty minutes later. Since we made the trip in the General's plane, it was quite a plush jaunt. Ten minutes after we took off this morning, I was stretched out in my compartment sound asleep. The pilot awakened me at noon for a sandwich and from then on out, until we landed here, I sat up and took notice of things. Yes, I was tired, because even though my travels are interesting, I honestly haven't had a chance to rest since I have been over here.

Tonight I am in Lisbon, Portugal, and as I write this, I am sitting on the balcony of my hotel room that overlooks Avenida de Republica, the heart of Lisbon. If I knew not otherwise, I would say right off that I was in Brazil. My scant knowledge of Portuguese is more than helpful. Have about a half day's work to accomplish tomorrow, then hope to "sight see" for a while. If things go right, we take off from here Sunday for Greece. Will be in Athens one day, then to Rome, Italy for a day and plan to be back in England about Wednesday. Wish I could write you all about what I am doing but I can't. I think perhaps some day I shall write a book. Of course you would probably be the only person that would read it; but then you are my best supporter.

Travel is a wonderful medium of education—perhaps a supplement for many things. I am still wondering if maybe what has happened to me isn't just that supplement for what could have been.

People in the square below are dashing about, going where for what and why, they don't know, nor do I. But, perhaps in our Democratic World of today, they are in haste to find an answer to a simple and peaceful way of life. Is it possible!

Well—anyhow—before I go off on the deep end— I had best say—so long for now— Give my love to all—....

Just what Hazel was doing at this time in her life as Adjutant to the 11th Communications Squadron of the Third Air Force remains a mystery, for she could not write this in her letters.

Tuesday Night
12 October 1954

Gee, I sure am tired. We landed here just an hour ago after a wonderful trip to Portugal, Italy, and Greece. Even tho it was part business and part pleasure, it was tiresome...

If I continue to travel as I have been doing since I arrived here, I shall soon be an authority on travel in Europe. Believe me, my ability to speak Portuguese and Spanish was a godsend for me on this trip. I do not know Italian, but my Portuguese came in handy in Rome. I have hired a tutor for French and German and start my lessons tomorrow. I am afraid I am going to have trouble with German, it is quite difficult.

Wish I could tell you more about my job but I can't. All I can say is it is interesting and I love my work....

A letter of 31 October 1954:

Well, I have decided to move from the hotel. First of all, even tho it is quite nice here, warm and all that; it is too expensive. With meals, it is costing me better than $130.00 a month and that does not include the cost of my noon meal at the base. I have decided I can do much better. In fact, I decided this several days ago, and as a result got out and started looking for a place to live. Yesterday I found it. I found a large clean bedroom with a small kitchen in a home. A young couple about my age, no children, own a typical English house and they decided to fix up this semi-apartment and rent it to an American. It isn't anything extra, but it is in a nice section, just ten minutes by bus from the Base and as I said, very clean. The people are Mr. and Mrs. Allen and they both work in London for Greek Air Lines. He is an ex-RAF pilot; she is from Greece and has been in England only six years. I don't know, but from the way she talked, I believe they own an interest in the Air Lines. Anyhow, she will furnish everything; linens, dishes, utilities—all but heat and I have a nice gas heater in the bedroom that operates on coins— all for $10.00 per week. I believe I can live for about half what it is costing me at the hotel. I also think I will be able to relax more. I can come home in the evening, get out of my uniform, and kick around the house. They have a T.V. set and a radio, a cat and dog, a garden, a garage for my car when I get it, and all in all it will be more like having a home rather than a room. I am sure I will be better satisfied living in a home with a family and these people are highly recommended out at the Base.

Had a nice letter from the Littlehales last week. They want me to come down for Thanksgiving, but I think I shall go to Bournmouth instead and visit Phil and her husband. I think I told you she was Met Officer at Hamble when I was stationed down there....

Friday Night
5 November 1954

Dearest Mother:

Wednesday I moved to my new home, and I must say I like it much better here with Mr. and Mrs. Allen than I did the hotel. This is more like being at home, living in a house and having my own room and a little kitchen where I can fix what I want when I want it. The Allens are certainly lovely people and treat me just as tho I was one of the family. I went down last night after I fixed my supper and sat and watched T.V. with them until eleven o'clock.

Tomorrow morning I am not working, so I plan to drive to London with them- they both work in London- and get my British driver's license. You see, I am only about thirty minutes by tube or car from London. And speaking of cars, I get mine next week.

The manner in which cars are sold over here is something. I placed my order for my Consul a month ago, at which time the dealer called the factory near London and they started building my car at that time. They are all made to order, custom built; they do not carry stock on the floor. I had to specify how I wanted it built, and what I wanted in the way of accessories. They have only a basic plan for the auto and the buyer specifies the interior and exterior design. I must say I have gotten quite a bang out of "planning" my auto. It will be light blue with blue leather seats. The only "extra" I ordered was a heater——no radio. If I had ordered a radio, I would have to obtain a radio licence. It should be most economical to operate since it will do about 35 miles on a gallon of petrol. After I get it, I will take a picture of it and send it to you.

I was scheduled for a trip to Denmark today, but passed it over since I must go to London tomorrow for my driver's license. Next weekend I plan to drive down to Bournemouth to see Phil and her husband. The following week I am going to Germany for five days. I hope to be able to pick up a few Xmas presents for the family while I am there.

Monday week I start to school four nights a week. I am taking Business Law and French. The classes are conducted out at the Base, and I will receive four college credits for my Law course and three for my French for the next semester, which is three months. One of these days maybe I shall be educated one way or another. I still think travel is the best education one can receive. Believe me, after this tour over here, I should be a well traveled individual. When I go to Germany, I will miss two classes, but they give me an opportunity to make that up during the day.

That is just about all the news for now. Give my love to all the family and take care of yourself. Write soon....

Along with Hazel's quick trips to numerous foreign countries, public relations seem to be a part of her duties:

Sunday Afternoon
21 November 1954

I have quite a big job between now and Christmas. I am in charge of planning a Christmas party for 53 orphans out at a Catholic home. There will be much work and planning to buy presents for 53 children between the age of five and seventeen. Also, we will decorate a tree for them, and I plan to have a movie for them. I can get a projector and hope I can find a nice film for them. The First sergeant in the Squadron, a man of about 240 pounds, is going to play Santa Clause. I think it will be fun.

Sunday Night
28 November 1954

Dearest Mother:
Just got back about two hours ago from Bournmouth and a very nice visit with Phil and her husband. Phil was the RAF Met Officer

on duty at Hamble when I was stationed there in 1943. Since then, she got out of the service in 1946 and taught school until three years ago, when she got married. They have a seven month old baby boy, and he really is adorable.

I left here yesterday morning at 8:30 and arrived in Bournmouth about noon. It is only 100 miles from here, but I had to drive slow since I only had 300 miles on my car. These English cars are quite different from our American automobiles. I can't drive over 40 miles per hour until I reach 1000 miles. My car is only a four cylinder, 45 h.p. English Ford. Over here that is considered a big auto. I checked my miles per gallon on the trip and find I am getting 33 miles per gallon of petrol- almost twice what I got on my Pontiac. But then, this car is less than half the size of the Pontiac. It is a right-hand drive, and I have had to get used to that, plus the fact I have to shift gears with a clutch. Oh well, it is good enough for me and my needs.

Back to my trip, I did enjoy it very much. Phil and I sat up until two A.M. last night talking over old times. She brought out pictures, many of which you have seen, and we just sat there and said, "remember this—remember that". Her husband is a gem, quite a typical English gentleman. He just sat there and listened while we talked, and fed us coffee until we went to bed. This morning when I awakened about eight, Phil brought a hot cup of coffee to my room and Denis, her husband, prepared a typical American breakfast for me. After breakfast, he disappeared, while Phil and I fed the baby and did the dishes. The next thing I knew he came in wet and dirty—he had gone out and washed my car, polished the chrome and put a protective coat of wax on it. Due to extreme dampness, the chrome on my car had begun to rust. He noticed that and cleaned it up for me. We fussed around in the house until noon, and Phil cooked a wonderful roast beef dinner so that I might eat before I started back home. They have invited me down for Christmas so I plan to buy a turkey at the Base and go down about December 23rd.

This week will be a busy time for me. I plan to shop for the 53 orphans we have adopted for Christmas. I also must plan a Christmas party and all the details. Thursday, I am going to Germany and will not get back until next Monday. On this trip I hope to have time to do a bit of Christmas shopping. My German, incidentally, is improving and I can now speak enough to get along quite good in Germany. You should hear me speaking German with a Southern accent. The same is true with my French, but I manage to make people understand.

Oh, I must tell you what I did Thanksgiving Day. I took a tube to London Thursday Morning and met three American friends of mine from the Base. We spent most of the day looking and wishing

—the clothes they have in London are beautiful but expensive. Late Thursday afternoon, we went to the American Embassy and had our Thanksgiving dinner. I am sending you the menu. When I got home Thursday night I was so full of turkey and all the trimmings until it was all I could do to crawl in bed. One nice thing about being over here in the American Forces, you can always go to the American Embassy and get almost anything you desire. On American holidays they always have a special dinner for all Americans on duty in England. You don't feel quite so far away from home when your own Embassy provides for you in such a manner as that.

Well, I believe I have given you all the news up to now. Will write again the first of the week when I get back from Germany....

A letter of 5 December, 1954:

Just got back from Wiesbaden, Germany—Never in my life have I eaten so much as I have on this trip. German cooking is out of this world, and even if half the time I didn't know what I was ordering; it was always delicious. Frankie would go mad over there, also in Paris, or anywhere in France. I don't care what anyone says, you just can't get along in any foreign country unless you know the language or have someone along that does. My German and French are getting better, even if I do struggle along with both with a Southern accent. I am finding the German language rather difficult to speak, but can understand it rather well when it is spoken to me or when I read it. The people in West Germany are very friendly and most courteous and seem to be taking to our American ideas and ideals without resentment. Their pace of recovery from the war is unbelievable both socially and economically. From the standpoint of new government, they are making remarkable strides in what we hope is the right direction. I won't go any further on that subject because it might get involved.

As I have said before, this is a small world. I saw seven people in Wiesbaden and Paris that I knew back in the States three or four years ago. Yet, to top that, I ran into a WAF Officer in Wiesbaden who had been at Sweetwater when I was down there in 1943, then —-a Major (male pilot) that I had taught to fly when I was teaching flying at Fort Lauderdale. He took me out for dinner then to a German night club Friday night and we really did have a nice time....

Wednesday Night
8 December 1954

Dearest Mother:

Received a letter from you today and my fruit cake. I haven't opened the package yet, and think I shall wait until Christmas.

Well, things have been happening and I now have a new job. As of today, I have been assigned direct to Headquarters 3rd Air Force for duty as WAF Advisor. I am what is known as ACS Personnel which is, Assistant Chief of Staff Personnel. It is a much better assignment for me than the one I had as Adjutant at Squadron level. It is a job very much the same as Commanding Officer of the WAF Squadron, but since we don't have a separate WAF Squadron, I am known as the WAF Staff Advisor. My principal duty is to supervise and guide as well as advise all WAF enlisted personnel on matters such as marriage, mal-assignment, health and personal matters. I also supervise their athletic and recreational activities and will accompany them on all trips they will be making to France and Germany when they go as an athletic team such as softball, basketball and etc. The Basketball team is going to Wiesbaden, Germany Friday, and I am supposed to take them over; but since we are having a big inspection of the barracks Saturday, I am sending another WAF Officer in my place. After all, I was just over there last week.

Also, I hope I can get down to Maidenhead Sunday and spend the day with the Littlehales. I promised them I would drive down. It is only forty miles from here. So, with my new job I think I am going to be much better satisfied over here.

Oh, I liked my work with 11th Communications, but I much prefer working with the WAF. Now I have to plan a Christmas party for over 100 WAF. I still plan to help with the 53 orphans, but the Lt. that replaced me in the 11th Com. will be in charge.

Did I tell you I was planning to move again? I sure hate to leave the Allens because they are wonderful to me, but I want more room and privacy. I have only one room as it is plus a small kitchen, and I also share the bath with them. The heating isn't adequate, and as a rule we have hot water about twice a week for a bath. You know me, I must have a bath every night. So, I have found a flat just a mile from the base. It is small with one bedroom, a living room that has a couch that can be used as a bed, a kitchen and my own bath. The living room has a gas heater, and I plan to buy an Alladin oil burner for the bedroom. Also, I plan to buy a small electric heater for the bath. I can heat the kitchen from the stove oven. Heat is the biggest problem over here. There is almost no such thing as central heating. I plan to move next weekend, the 18th. I really think I will be better satisfied having my own private flat where I won't have to worry about disturbing anyone, and will have a place where I can invite friends to come for a meal or a game of cards or just a visit.

I finally found my trunk. They shipped it to Bremerhaven, Germany. They say they are shipping it to me on the next boat to Southampton and from there, it will be shipped to me here. How about that! I doubt very much if I shall get it until after the first of the year. At least it isn't lost....

Wednesday Morning
28 December 1954

Dearest Mother:

Well despite the fact that I worked Christmas, it was a nice one and quite different from what I had planned. I had to cancel my trip to Bournemouth because I wanted to be with the girls in the Squadron Christmas morning — thought it my duty. So, instead of going to Bournemouth, I went to London for the weekend. Stayed with another WAF, Major Bacchus, who is stationed at Ruislip too.

Anyway, Christmas Eve they called me from the Base and said one of my girls had been in an accident. Of course I went right out, and she had been in a car accident, and had received a rather bad head injury. She is much better now and will be O.K. Of course I have been out everyday to see her, so I couldn't have gone anywhere after all.

Christmas morning, Bobbie (my WAF friend), and I drove out to the Base and cooked breakfast for 50 WAF, then we all sat around and sang Christmas carols till noon. We did enjoy ourselves.

I bought an eight pound turkey and my first sergeant cooked it here in the Squadron for me. We have had turkey every day since Christmas. Sure was good. Having turkey tonight and that will finish it up.

Know you had a nice Christmas. Thought about all of you and wished I could have been with you.

Must go— have lots to do since I haven't done much work since last week. Write soon....

Hazel's duties as Staff Advisor are described in a letter of January 18, 1955.

Tuesday Morning
18 January 1955

Dearest Mother:

What happens to the time is beyond me. It just seems to fly by and I never seem to be able to sit down and write as many letters as I should. However, I must say I like staying busy and believe me, my job as Staff Advisor is keeping me on the fly.

Now, more about my job. From now thru June, I will spend most of my time working on the WAF athletic program. Last weekend the basketball team team from Wiesbaden, Germany came over and played my WAF team. We lost one game and won one. My team is now second place in the Western Conference and I am taking them to Bremerhaven, Germany next weekend. Then, on 3 February, I am taking the team to Wiesbaden for the USAFR championship game. If they win, there is a very good chance that I will have to take them to the States for about two weeks to play for the Air Force wide championship. Of course that is a big if, but we are working hard and keeping our fingers crossed. This would mean that I would be able to get home for a few days. Let's hope we win!

I have also organized a bowling team. Have everything all set to take them to Bremerhaven for four days 24 February. As a rule, they supply us with a plane for this travel; however, on our trips to Bremerhaven, we go by boat to Belgium, then take a train to Bremerhaven. I have done this once and found it most interesting. Supposed to go to Paris again this weekend, but just don't see how I can since I will be gone about half the time next month. I just must take some time out to get my clothes cleaned and also take care of other personal matters. Yes, I will be traveling over half my time in this job but I certainly don't mind since it will give me a wonderful chance to really see France, Holland, Belgium, Denmark, Norway, Sweden, Germany, Switzerland and I hope, Italy. Actually, this assignment has turned out to be much better than I ever dreamed. Honestly, I am a lucky gal..."

Hazel's letters in February and March are filled with enthusiastic accounts of the WAF athletic events, most of which are held in Germany. On leave in April and part of May, she travels through Europe leaving a trail of postcards from France, Belgium, Germany, Austria, Switzerland and Italy. By June, Hazel is back at work at Ruislip.

16 June 1955

Dearest Mother:

Thought I might as well finish the day with a note to you before heading home. Just can't understand how the hours in a day pass so fast—-never have time for anything—-work—-eat (when time will permit)—-sleep—-then, I start this routine all over again the next day. Sounds rather dull, but it isn't too bad.

With luck, I do plan to take time out the weekend of July 4th. Since this is a holiday for Americans only, we might take a trip Westward toward Bath and Bristol thru the Cheddar gorge, (that's where they make that tasty cheddar cheese). Also, on July 5th, we have tickets to see Danny Kaye. He has been playing in London for the past month. We were just down right lucky to get tickets.

June 30th will be a big day at S. Ruislip for WAF Officers and enlisted personnel. We will celebrate our eight birthday as women in the Air Force. There will be open house for everyone at the Service Club from 2 to 4 o'clock at which time the C. G. of the Third Air Force and Alfred Drake, British stage and film star, will cut our birthday cake. After that all the "Big Wheels" and little "cogs" like me, will inspect the WAF billets. A buffet dinner will be served between six and seven, then there will be a dance at the club. This sort of thing sure takes a lot of planning and hard work but then— what worth- while project doesn't take a lot of effort! I really think, and hope, this will be a super fine affair.

We have another big "do" coming up July 10th. Colonel Gray, WAF Director from Washington, will be here for four days. With these few extra activities added to my daily routine, I rather imagine the next few weeks will fly by before I know it.

Gee, it's almost ten o'clock. Guess I had best call a halt and head for London. Take care and write soon.…

Monday Afternoon
1 August 1955

You must think I have broken my arm but I haven't. Big doings again— Getting ready to take 15 girls to Germany is no small chore. As I say— we take off this weekend for a week at Ramstein. Who knows, we just might win, which means we will be going to the good old U.S.A. the last of the month. Of course, all we can do is keep our fingers crossed....

A letter of August 28, 1955:

You will never guess what I had given to me last week. A friend of mine has one of the most beautiful Miniature Poodles and she had a litter of seven pups two months ago. Yep, she gave me a male pup and he is the cutest little thing you have ever seen. He is white and probably won't weigh much over eight or ten pounds when he is grown. I brought him home with me, but had trouble trying to make him use paper rather than a rug so took him out to WAF barracks. My First Sergeant has one too and she is keeping "Andy" for me until he is house broken. During the day he stays with me in my office and sleeps under my desk. He will be lots of company for me this winter....

Fried some chicken today but it just didn't taste like your fried chicken. The chickens that they sell out at the Base in the Commissary are frozen and are flown in from Denmark. I wouldn't think of buying a chicken on the English market. When they kill them they leave the insides in them then just hang them up in the market until they are sold. Sometimes they hang for days just the same as the beef and other meat they sell—no refrigeration. Can't see it myself!....

Monday Night
10 October 1955

Dearest Mother:

For the past ten days I have been standing by in hopes that I might find out something definite in regards to my trip home Xmas. Just today I did learn that I am scheduled to go to Washington on business around 15 December. I was also told that my business in Washington would require some twelve to fifteen days, but I could plan on taking leave from there around 22 December for the purpose of going home for Xmas. In other words, it is definite that I will be flying out of Washington to Macon on 22 December, but expected to return to Washington around the first of the year. My opinion on this trip in regards to being to take care of my business in Washington is, if I don't get there until after 15 December, I doubt if I will be able to do too much "business wise", until after the Xmas holidays are over, which will be around the first part of the new year. At least I do know that I will be home for Xmas and at no expense on my own, other than my ticket from Washington to Macon and return. For the sake of being able to come home for Xmas, that will be cheap traveling since I will get Military rates which will be some 40% less than the normal charge. I am most happy about this....

By the way, you might just see a change in your "baby daughter". My hair is turning quite grey. Due to the color of my hair it doesn't show too bad, but the beauty operator here on the Base has a rinse solution that covers this mark of distinctive approaching middle-age symptoms that I have been using. Don't get me wrong, I am not adverse toward recognizing the fact that I am getting along in years BUT, I never dreamed I would show such definite signs. My grey hair appearance should make you feel younger.

Time to sign off. Just wanted to let you know the latest on my plans about Xmas....

A letter of 4 November 1955 is the last one on record for that year.

Hazel writes from Paris which "is one place I just do not like. Those people try to take an American for every penny they can. Prices are sky high on everything. Germany is different, the people are nice to you and they do not try to rob you when you go shopping on the Germany economy."

Chapter 6
LOTS OF LOVE ALWAYS

Hazel obviously returns home for Christmas in December of 1955. In a letter of 8 January 1956, she states that "At long last I am on my way back to Jolly Ole England. Right now I am half way across the North Atlantic— flying at 19,000 feet in a Boering Aircraft. Due to bad weather conditions, plus the London fog that was so terrible last Thursday and Friday—- my return flight was delayed and I had to take a commercial plane—- Pan American—- out of New York today."

By June, Hazel's assignment as WAF Advisor seems to be taking a toll on her and she has asked to be reassigned.

Well, since I have been here as WAF Advisor for 18 months, and since the job is beginning to get me down from a health standpoint, I have asked for a new assignment. Don't know what it will be as yet but I will let you know.

Monday Afternoon
18 June 1956

Dearest Mother:

Enjoyed talking with you— just wanted to call to let you know I am O.K. and wish you a happy birthday even if my wishes and birthday thoughts were ahead of time.

I do hope you will not worry, but I have been having trouble with my back again— guess I will always be bothered with it. The Doctor told me today he thought it might be wise for me to see a Doctor in Weisbaden, Germany. So, chances are, I will fly over there maybe next week and see what the score really is. If they should decide that I will need some special type treatment that cannot be given over here, I am going to insist that they send me back to the States. Oh well, I am not going to worry about that now.

Well, I guess Frankie and family are having a gay time in Paris now. Have thought about them lots since they started out on their trip. I know they will have a wonderful time.

Must stop— want to get this in the afternoon mail. Don't worry— I am feeling fine and will write often....

A letter of reassurance from the Hospital in South Ruislip:

Thursday
21 June 1956

Dearest Mother:

So glad to receive your letter yesterday— Also enjoyed talking with you— Just felt like I wanted to call home since I had not been feeling too good. I am feeling much better now, even though I am back in the Hospital again. They have been making all sorts of tests and X-rays—- just giving me a complete checkup which is routine in the Air Force for everyone once a year when a person reaches, or rather hits, the 40 year mark. Then too, the rest is good for me— I have gained six pounds. I really needed this rest as well as the increase in weight, cause I now weigh 123. The Doctor told me he would probably let me out tomorrow.

Remember how much trouble I used to have passing a physical due to the extra beat in my heart? Well, that has had them stumped here, but the Doctors finally decided my heart was in excellent condition. Same old story but as I say— I am quite O.K.

Oh well, when they release me from the hospital tomorrow, I just hope we will have a pretty weekend as far as the weather is concerned. I think I will take a drive over to the East Coast—perhaps Dover, and relax in the sun on the Beach.

Did I tell you that I requested to be relieved as WAF Staff Advisor? I think I have had that job and responsibility long enough. After 18 months of being on call for duty on a 24 hour basis and working on an average of 18 hours a day, I think I not only need a change but also the rest I am getting now. They are going to assign me as Special Assistant to the Assistant Chief of Staff of Personnel. At least I will still be at the Staff level and will have a good job that will be from 8:30 to 5 o'clock only five days a week....

Sunday
22 July 1956

Dearest Mother:

What a beautiful day today— have been sitting out in the sun but had to come in— got too hot. Maybe I had best bring you up to date on me before I continue. I flew over here to Weisbaden last Tuesday and have been doing absolutely nothing but resting, eating, and sleeping. I am in the 7100th USAF Hospital and they truly have been giving me the best attention possible. I am feeling fine, but do not know how long I will be here as yet. The only thing they can find wrong is my old back and leg but even so— I am much better since they have been giving me underwater treatments.

Well, guess who walked in yesterday afternoon? Frankie, Reginald, Fabia and Reg. Gee, it sure was good seeing them. Last night they visited with me about two hours— brought some magazines as well as many other nice presents. It sure was good seeing them and hearing about their trip. The only thing I am disappointed about is: I rather doubt if I will be out of here and back in London while they are there. Sure do hate it, but it can't be helped. They all looked good and have been having a wonderful time. Sorry they could not stay longer, but they had to leave on their tour this morning. A friend of mine took them out last night after they left the hospital.

I would suggest you write me over here, but I expect to go back to England soon so—- guess you might as well continue to send your letters to APO 125. They forward all my mail to reach me over here anyway, which only takes one more day for Stateside mail to reach me.

Well, guess that is just about all the news for now. Don't worry about me, as I said, I am getting along just fine. Will write again in a few days. Take care of yourself. Give my love to all.

Love always,
Hazel

Excerpts from a letter written to "Frankie and family" after a visit with Hazel in the United States Air Force Hospital in Weisbaden:

Hello 'You-All',

Sure was good seeing all of you last Saturday. Thanks again for the books, magazines and all the gifts. You really did boost my morale 100%.

Well, here is the latest medical report on me. The Doctor checked my back and leg today, it is much better but he wants to do another mylogram. This they will do Friday which means they will tap my spine, inject a fluid which acts as a dye substance in the spine, then take x-rays. If there is any damage or trouble within the spine, it as a rule, will show up when they do this type of examination. After they do this I will hafta stay on my back for 24 hours. So, by next Monday, I should know something definite....

To her mother on August 3, 1956:

Received a letter from Frankie yesterday— said they were having a fine time in London. They left London for a tour of Scotland. I sure hate it, not being able to be there and show them around England and Scotland....

Fabia told me all about her wedding plans when she was here. I know that will be quite an event— wish I could be there for the wedding. Who knows— I might be able to make it— Oh well— At least I can dream....

A letter of August 11, 1956:

Well, I am still here in the hospital but feeling fine. Thought sure I would be out by now, but they just won't release me until they are sure I am 100% fit for duty. I am still taking Physical Therapy treatments and they seem to be helping my back and leg quite a bit. I get around much better than I have in a long time; however, the Doctor told me yesterday that I might need a brace for a while. If they do decide to make a back brace for me, I will be here another two weeks. It will take that long to have the thing made and fitted properly. Won't know for sure about this tho until the first of next week. Oh well, I shouldn't worry as long as I am feeling good and know I am getting better every day....

I am afraid this hospital life is making me lazy— all I do is eat— rest and sleep. The hospital movie is down on the first floor and now that I can get around so well, I have been going down every night for the past week. It gives me something to do and I can get away from sick people for a couple of hours. Some of these people seem to enjoy being sick and complain all the time. I think some of them wonder why I am here cause I never talk about feeling bad but laugh and joke all the time….

A note to Hazel's mother from the Third Air Force:

Hazel had been hospitalized here at South Ruislip on 5 June 1956 for a recurrence of an old back injury. On July 10th, 1956 she was transferred to the 7100th USAF Hospital in Germany for further neurological examinations and treatment. Subsequently she was transferred back here on August 26th and discharged from the hospital on August 31st.

Wednesday
27 August 1956

Dearest Mother:

Just a quick note to let you know I am finally back safe and sound. True, I am still in the hospital; but they told me today they might discharge me Friday, then give me about 15 days leave to get back on my feet again before I hafta return to full time duty. Won't mind that in the least since my legs are sorta rubber—- like from staying in bed too long.

Well, it has been a long haul, tiresome at times, but I am feeling just grand and know all this rest I have had will make me feel like a new person. Sure tired of hospitals. Be glad when I am strong enough and can go back to full time duty.

How's all the family? Tell Frankie I found some mail for them when I went by my flat yesterday before returning to the hospital. Will send it to them soon as possible.

That's all the news for now. Will write again soon. Take care and give my love to all the family.

Lots of love always,
Hazel

WESTERN UNION

1956 Sep 20
Mrs. Bessie P Raines
Massee Apts
College Street
REMAINS OF YOUR DAUGHTER, THE LATE 1ST LT HAZEL
J. RAINES ARE BEING CONSIGNED TO HART MORTUARY,
CHERRY STREET, MACON, GEORGIA DEPARTING VIA RAIL
DOVER, DELAWARE 6:26 P.M. 20 SEPT 56. ESCORTED BY
CAPTAIN ANNE M. GREGG. REMAINS DUE TO ARRIVE
MACON 8:05 PM 21 SEPT 56 ON C OF GEORGIA TRAIN NR
108. MY DEEPEST SYMPATHIES ARE EXTENDED TO YOU
AND MEMBERS OF THE DECEDENTS FAMILY.

COMMANDER DOVER AFB DELAWARE

I never heard my grandmother speak of Hazel after her death in 1956.
One wonders if she did not want to share Hazel with anyone, or possibly her
death was too painful to mention. Hazel died of medical complications at the
age of forty, shortly after being released from the hospital in London.

Hazel had come a long way since her barnstorming days in the 1930s,
and had proved herself in ways few women would have dared or even wanted
to try in the 1940s. Her legacy to women in aviation, and her role as
"Georgia's Pioneer Lady of Flight," merited a recent posthumous award.
Hazel was one of three women honored by the Georgia Women of
Achievement in 1995.

A more revealing source of Hazel's life, however, are the personal memories gathered from her friends and family. Hazel's visits to Macon, Georgia,
were obviously limited, but the entire family gathered when she returned.
There was always music, for Hazel played the piano by ear and "could get
music out of anything" including the bugle, saxophone, cornet, drums, and
harmonica. In fact, Hazel claimed "she could hear music from the wind
whistling through the struts of the wings of an airplane."

Memories gathered from her friends portray a modest, yet determined
young woman, who was considered to be "a sport." In 1939, "she was seen
racing against experienced pilots, accepting defeat with a smile and extend-
ing congratulations to the winners."

In 1940 and 1941, Hazel was training pilots in Cochran, Georgia. Lucian
Whipple, who was a student of hers, learned to solo in eight hours. He recalls
that Hazel always carried an empty coke bottle on their flights. The student
would climb into the front of the Taylorcraft and Hazel would sit in the rear.
Inevitably, the question would be asked:

"Why do you have that empty coke bottle?" Hazel would answer: "If you
freeze and refuse to relinquish the controls, I might have to knock you out."

Lucian became a liaison pilot in Texas and Louisiana, and also had a brief stint in combat duty. Although Hazel maintained a serious demeanor while teaching, she sometimes took her student pilots for a ride at the nearby Herbert Smart Airport in a World War I airplane to spark their interest in flying.

Mattie Baxley also knew Hazel during the years she was training pilots in Cochran. She and Hazel frequently went to the local "road house" to dine on a "50 cent steak". According to Mattie, Hazel was the reason Mattie was able to attend Wesleyan College in Macon. Mattie was a few years younger than Hazel and was a student at Middle Georgia Junior College in Cochran. She needed two credits to complete her curriculum, and Hazel was able to convince Margaret Roper, the psychology professor, that Mattie was qualified to graduate. Hazel's willingness to "go to bat" for her friends endeared her to them.

Nancy Miller Stratford was "just down the road from Mrs. Porter (while Hazel was at Hamble), but saw Hazel, Kay Van Doozer, Grace Stevenson, and Bobby Leveaux a few times out of 'work'. Each of the girls seemed to have different experiences, personal and flying. The American women were perhaps in four or five different pools and one didn't see each other often. It wasn't until 1978 that we had our first re-union in New Mexico and eight or nine came."

Diana Barnato Walker, author of *Spreading my Wings,* is an English ferry pilot who trained at White Waltham. She remembers Hazel, but was not in the same ferry pools during 1942 and 1943. Her autobiographical book elaborates on certain aspects of ferrying planes in World War II which Hazel leaves out in her letters to her mother. Dodging balloon barrages, and desperately looking for an airfield through the mist and fog, were everyday occurrences. She also states that being fired upon by "our own side" was not unusual. "I suppose it was very difficult, in poor visibility, to decide, with a finger on the trigger, so to speak, whether it was one of theirs or one of ours."

When Hazel arrived at Avenger Field to join the WASPs, she seldom discussed her experiences as a ferry pilot. According to Peggy Parker Eccles, a fellow WASP, Hazel did not brag. She, however, was exempted from cross-country flying, and her reputation as a pilot followed her there. Peggy remembers that Hazel was "never at a loss as to what to do, had a good sense of humor, liked people, was good company, and had a deep Southern accent."

One aspect of Hazel's personal life revealed in her correspondence to her mother was her self-doubts. She may have felt that certain options were taken away at an early age, for she had an ovary removed at the age of 22. Dr. Charlotte Newbury immigrated from Germany in 1939 to join the staff of the Middle Georgia Hospital in Macon. She remembers Hazel, and felt that the surgery was totally unnecessary. While the medical practices of the 1930s and 1940s would be highly questioned in the 1990s, they worked to Hazel's advantage in some incidences. Hazel's irregular heartbeat and obvious bouts with asthma would not be tolerated in the world of aviation today. Only her determination to fly and her persistent conversations with doctors kept her in the air.

Hazel made a lasting impression on those who knew her. She was a true pioneer and a woman who persevered in difficult situations. Her dedication to her country was very simply stated in a letter to her mother after finally being inducted into the Air Force in 1950. She stated: "One thing never changes— the people. No matter where I stop I meet good American people. With a cheerful smile and good wishes for a safe and pleasant journey, they send me on my way, rejoicing in the true fact that I too am an American..."

Carefully recorded in one of Hazel's log books was a list of forty-four types of aircraft which she had flown.

1. Taylorcraft
2. Rearwin-Trainer
3. Aeronca -k
4. Tailorcraft Trainer
5. Aeronca Trainer
6. Culver
7. Interstate Cadet
8. Stinson-SM8-A
9. Stinson-105
10. Kinner Bird
11. Davis
12. Ercoupe
13. Rearwin-coupe
14. Cub Cruiser
15. Great Lakes
16. Howard
17. Fairchild-M62
18. Fairchild-24
19. Stearman
20. Waco Trainer
21. Waco Cabin
22. Beachcraft
23. Cessna-single
24. Cessna-twin
25. Harvard
26. Miles Magister
27. Miles Master
28. Hart
29. Tutor
30. Tiger Moth
31. Lysander
32. Hurricane
33. Spitfire
34. Seafire
35. Anson
36. Oxford
37. Martinet
38. PT-17
39. PT-19
40. A-T-6
41. UC-78
42. BT-13
43. TB-26
44. AT-11

Maxwell Air Force Band
Oct. 18, 1952

Hazel "Flying a Desk"

Hazel as a WAF recruiter.

BIBLIOGRAPHY

Douglas Bader, *Fight for the Sky,* W.S. Cowell Ltd., Buttermarket Ipwich, 1973.

Ralph Barker, *The RAF at War,* Time Life Books Inc., 1981.

Jacqueline Cochran & Maryann Brinkley, *Jackie Cochran,* Rufus Publishing Inc. (Bantam Books), 66 Fifth Ave., New York, N.Y., 1987.

Winston S. Churchill, *The Second World War,* Houghton Mifflin Co., 2 Park Street, Boston, Mass. 02108, 1949.

Chronicle of Aviation J. L. International Publishing Inc., 244 West Mill Street, Liberty, Missouri, 1992.

Deborah G. Douglas, *United States Women in Aviation 1940-1985,* Smithsonian Institution Press, Washington and London, 1991.

Elizabeth Simpson Smith, *Coming Out Right,* Walker & Co, New York, N.Y., 720 Fifth Ave., New York 10019, 1991.

Diana Barnato Walker, *Spreading my Wings,* Patrick Stephens Ltd., Haynes Publishing, Sparkford, Nr. Yeovil, Somerset BA 22 7 JJ, 1994.

Vera Williams, *WASPs,* Motorbooks International, 729 Prospect Ave., Oceola, W.I. 54020, 1994.

Derek Wilson, *The Astors,* St. Martins Press, 176 Fifth Ave., New York, N.Y.10010, 1993.

The Atlanta Journal